A HISTORY OF
SPANISH CIVILIZATION

VISIGOTHIC TRADITION

Miniature from Beatus' Commentary on the Apocalypse

(*Torre do Tumbo, Lisbon*)

" Incipit explanatio suprascriptae historiae "

A HISTORY OF
SPANISH CIVILIZATION

By
RAFAEL ALTAMIRA

Translated from the Spanish by
P. VOLKOV

With a Preface by
J. B. TREND

LONDON
CONSTABLE & CO LTD
1930

PUBLISHED BY

Constable & Company Limited
London W.C. 2

.

BOMBAY
CALCUTTA   MADRAS

Oxford University
Press

.

TORONTO

The Macmillan Company
of Canada, Limited

.

NEW YORK

Richard R. Smith Inc

PRINTED IN GREAT BRITAIN.
CHISWICK PRESS: CHARLES WHITTINGHAM AND GRIGGS (PRINTERS), LTD.
TOOKS COURT, CHANCERY LANE, LONDON.

CONTENTS

HISTORY OF SPANISH CIVILIZATION

LIST OF ILLUSTRATIONS

FACING
PAGE

PREFACE

THE author of this book needs no introduction to English readers. His *History of Spain and of Spanish Civilization* is known to all serious students of history—in those four little volumes not a few of them must have learnt to read the Spanish language —while his *Psychology of the Spanish People* is familiar to all serious students of Spain.

A history of Spain which should also be a history of Spanish civilization, from the time of the earliest men "who have left no testimony of their existence other than their bones," might almost be said to be an invention of Professor Altamira himself. The last chapter, it is true, mentions one earlier book with a similar title; and there is the brilliant essay by the Portuguese historian, Oliveira Martins (translated into English as *A History of Iberian Civilization*), which is based, however, on a view of civilization more restricted and less objective than that held by Professor Altamira.

The book now presented to the English-speaking public does not presuppose more than a general knowledge of the outlines of Spanish history, such as can be obtained anywhere, even from a guide-book. It describes enough of the political background and the international relationships of each period for any reader to know where he stands; it explains not only what Spanish institutions were in existence at various times and what functions they performed, but also what was being built and painted, thought and written. Travellers are apt to look for the traces of a civilization entirely in art or ancient monuments, scholars in its literature or philosophy. For Professor Altamira there are other monuments no less important: institutions, customs, laws, which have come down from ancient times and can still be observed in operation to-day. His book is, in fact, an answer to the question why Spanish things are as they are—both in Europe and America.

It need hardly be said that Professor Altamira is not one of those writers who come to their conclusions first and then try to justify them, who start with a definite bias and endeavour to make out a case for a particular point of view. To take an example which will occur to the mind of every reader: What was the effect upon Spanish civilization of the " Moors " in Spain? A brilliant Spanish historian of the younger generation, Prof. Sánchez Albornoz, has suggested that all the misfortunes of Spanish history have been due to the presence on Spanish soil for more than 800 years of men whose faith and institutions were those of Islam. Their only contributions of any value to the civilization of Spain were their Greek science and their Persian and Syrian art. On the other hand Oliveira Martins, whose manner was somewhat hasty and whose mind somewhat too " Latin," regarded the Muslims as amateurs: an army following a prophet, more curious than scientific, and incapable of giving serious consideration to the deepest things of the spirit. It may be so; but such sweeping generalizations do not fall within the province of this book. Nor does it come within its province to suggest—as a careful study of Professor Altamira might lead one to suggest—that one of the main reasons for the ultimate failure of Muslim civilization in Spain (the most brilliant perhaps that the Muslim world has ever known, and, in its time, the most brilliant of any in Europe), lay in the deficiency of its municipal organization; while the more backward Christian Spanish States possessed, in the *fueros* and charters of their *municipios* the possibilities of a free economic and cultural development of which Muslim institutions have so far proved incapable.

Professor Altamira describes the causes which were active in Spanish cultural history at various times, and how they worked to produce such and such an effect. The effects were often new and surprising. We are accustomed to recognize the Spanish people for a race of pioneers in the discovery and colonization of America, but we do not generally admit that there were other fields also in which they have been pioneers and explorers—international law (for instance), certain branches of applied science, navigation, metallurgy, to name only a few of those subjects in which Spanish researchers were among the first in the field or the most advanced of their time. There is also the public theatre and the fact of the Stage becoming a great force in national life, as it was in Elizabethan and Jacobean England. The darker side of the picture, too, is squarely and honestly faced. If modern historical research has made Philip II seem less terrible than before, it has made him appear as a slightly pathetic figure, devoted to preserving the inviolable purity of dogma and to unfortunate policies which he sincerely believed to be for the good of his country. As to the activity of the

Spanish Inquisition, readers will find it analysed here with the coldness and clarity of a legal historian who shows that what seem to us now the most inhuman features of the procedure were common to all judicial procedure of the age, although the Holy Office made no attempt to reform abuses which it alone might have had the power to reform. The modern historian, also, attaches great importance to the economic mistakes made by Spain with regard to her oversea dominions, mistakes from which all other colonizing nations have received both instruction and profit.

There are some things in which the early experiences of the Spanish people are so valuable that we might well learn from them more than we do. Professor S. de Madariaga, speaking not long ago at a Rhodes dinner at Oxford, described himself as " an empire-builder retired from business." Yet the results of Spanish empire-building still go on; Spanish institutions, Spanish culture, the Spanish attitude to life and the Spanish language are spread over a considerable portion of the globe. Spanish, like English and perhaps alone with English, may justly be described as a "world-language," and it is certainly one of the finest and most perfect instruments for the expression of human thought. Owing to its very nature—the purity of its vowels and the distinct articulation of its consonants—it rings with a clearness and precision especially noticeable when heard alongside of French and colloquial Arabic, as it is to-day in Morocco. A common opinion—one of those which Professor Altamira would probably include under that state of mind which he rather suggests than describes as " Hispanophobia "—is

that the Spanish language and many of its most characteristic expressions are mere " rhetoric," sound and
fury and signifying nothing.   It can certainly move
us by "rhetoric "; but it is also capable of a con-
cision and directness which on occasion can exceed
that of English itself.   There is a line from a living
Castilian poet, a line which might almost have been
taken as a motto for a book on Spanish civilization:

lleva quien deja y vive el que ha vivido.

—nine words which would need almost twice as
many to translate them adequately into any other
modern language.   The people, the peoples, who
have this language as their birthright, are the subject
of this book.

The author attaches great importance to the
Appendix, which is a list of the more important and
useful books connected with the subject, with short
notes on their contents.   The value of the bibliography printed in vol. iv of the *Historia de España y
de la Civilización Española*, published in 1914, is
universally admitted.   For this occasion the bibliographical appendix to the author's more recent
Epítome de Historia de España has been used; it has
been thoroughly revised by Professor Altamira himself, and brought up to date.

J. B. TREND.

HISTORY OF SPANISH CIVILIZATION

INTRODUCTION

1. *Civilization*

THE word *civilization* is of frequent occurrence in daily life. We call certain peoples civilized, and others barbarians or savages. Amongst the former we meet with certain conditions of social life and knowledge which we consider to be relatively high in development. When these conditions are lacking, the word civilization is not used.

But what are these conditions? In general terms we all believe ourselves to be in agreement about them, though in a negative rather than a positive sense. Thus, we do not call those people civilized who are ignorant, superstitious, lazy, cruel, gross, dishonest, un-humane in their international and internal social relationships, lacking in industry, commerce, and the amenities of life. And though, in considering these things, and trying to reduce them to scientific terms, men disagree as to the number and extent to which they must be combined in order to deserve the name of civilization, yet we all agree that the criterion lies in our actual conception of human life, though this varies in every individual within certain limits common to all. We also notice that this criterion has changed in our own time, passing through various stages to the highest and most complete conception of which we are capable to-day, and that the nations which are called civilized have adapted themselves to it in very different degrees.

It is also certain (as we have already implied) that

B

this criterion sometimes refers to the combination of a number of different circumstances, including many which we consider necessary and desirable to a high level of human life, and which we therefore demand of a given people if it is to be deemed civilized. But at other times, especially in contemporary thought, the ideal is fixed in one single circumstance, or in a small group of circumstances, either in the material or spiritual order; and compared with these all the others seem secondary or insignificant. Within this variety of opinions it is not difficult to note the general agreement as to the indispensability of certain of the circumstances indicated, and consequently we find a common basis of doctrine to which both specialists and public opinion of all countries now subscribe.

Finally, experience shows us that it is very rare to find any people, ancient or modern (if any such exist), in which all these conditions are fulfilled. Among even the most civilized nations that we know it is easy to discern, alongside of a great development of certain of these conditions, the absence or imperfect development of others, even of such as are most commonly recognized as of supreme importance. We are therefore led to the conclusion that no fully civilized people yet exists, but that there are examples of peoples which have brought to perfection in a special manner certain of the conditions demanded by the qualification " civilized."

2. *History of Civilization.* The series of efforts by means of which Humanity has approached this ideal type of life which we have imagined, and the succession of forms under which it has been conceived or more or less completely realized, constitutes the *History of Civilization.* And since to this end man has left a primitive state of *uncivilization,* and has of necessity committed many errors and transgressions against the ideal, or has achieved it unevenly (as has already been suggested) in its various constituent conditions, these things too, while not being civilization, acted either for or against it, and must be included in its history.

Thus in a certain sense, *everything* realized by humanity

or by a given people (for the moment we are concerned with Spain), falls within the limits of our study, since everything is significant of the state of civilization and of the ideal of life of the men of each different period. But writers generally leave on one side what is known as *external history* (political events, wars, territorial conquests, succession of kings, changes of dynasty and of political parties, etc.), and understand under the title of History of Civilization only *internal history* (a designation as erroneous as the other), that is to say the history of *social and political institutions* (social classes, organs of government and administration, agriculture, industry, commerce, religion), *intellectual development* (science and art), and *customs*.

3. *Elements and Factors of Civilization.* These elements are usually distributed in two groups: the one refers to the bodily needs of man, forming what is called *material civilization*, and the other to his spiritual needs. The first comprises the development of industry and commerce, and of science applied to the needs of physical life; the second, the development of social ideas and feelings, of institutions, of communal life, of conduct in general (morality), of scientific research; and the fine arts.

The two factors of civilization are man and nature. Nature influences man within certain limits. Thus we see that peoples living in mountainous districts differ greatly in character and mode of life from those living in the plains; those living by the sea, from those living inland; those living in cold countries from those living in hot; the inhabitants of fertile lands from those of arid wastes. On the other hand we may say that a great part of the history of civilization lies in the struggle of man against nature, and that the greater part of modern progress corresponds to the successive victories of humanity over physical matter, either modifying it, or using its qualities and powers for his own benefit.

Yet we should keep in mind the *geographical* and *climatic* conditions of each country, both to explain certain characteristics of its inhabitants and to deduce the necessities with which its civilization will be chiefly concerned, and the direction or forms which at times it has taken.

4. *Geographical Conditions of Spain.* Since our special subject is the history of Spain, we ought first of all to take into account these conditions, that is to say, the natural setting in which the Spanish people has moved.

Spain forms a Peninsula, situated to the South-West of Europe, joined to the rest of the continent by an isthmus some 300 miles in length (the French frontier) and otherwise surrounded by two seas, the Mediterranean on the East and South (as far as the Straits of Gibraltar), and the Atlantic Ocean to the South, West, and the North; this latter, in the part that bathes the northern coasts of the Peninsula, is usually called the Mar Cantábrico or Bay of Biscay. The whole Peninsula is in the form of a great promontory, whose summit, broad and of great height, covers more or less the centre (the central plateau, Castille, Estremadura) and whose two main slopes, towards the Mediterranean and the Atlantic, are unequal both in development and steepness. The former, inclined to the East, is short and abrupt; the latter, looking West, is extended and gradual in its descent towards the ocean. But this general configuration is modified in the interior by the mountain ranges which cross the Peninsula and divide it into broad bands. The *Pyrenees*, after defining the French frontier, continue westwards, under the name of the Cantabrian Mountains, and for the most part abruptly separate the coastal provinces (Biscay, Santander, Asturias, Galicia) from the rest of Spain. On its Southern slope the range rises little above the central plateau, which is very high, whilst on the North the difference in altitude between the passes and the valleys is enormous, making communication difficult. The *Iberian* or *Celtiberian* chain makes a similar division (though not so accentuated at most points) between the plateau and the valley of the Ebro, the regions of Valencia and Murcia, and part of the Andalusian provinces. The central plateau, in its turn, is cut up by a series of mountains which form the so-called *Carpetana* or

Carpeto-Vetónica range, which separates old Castille and León from New Castille and Estremadura. Less important are the *Oretana*, which crosses the provinces of Cuenca, Toledo, Ciudad Real, Cáceres and Badajoz, running into Portugal, and the *Mariánica* (Southern slope of the plateau) which forms the boundary between New Castille and Estremadura, and Andalucía; but each forms great independent watersheds, those of the Guadiana and the Guadalquivir. Finally, the southernmost range which some geographers consider to be derived from the Iberian Range, and others, as an independent range which they call *Bética* or *Penibética*, divides the Andalusian region from N.E. to S.W. into two unequal parts. That of the South is narrow, near to the sea, and very varied in altitude; it contains the highest peaks of the Peninsula, the Sierra Nevada, and, in its varied extension, it formed, in past centuries, the wild scene of some of the most important incidents in the political history of Spain.

5. *Historical Consequences.* (i) The Division of the Peninsula into sections, separated by mountain ranges, which encouraged isolation and the formation of distinct groups of inhabitants. (ii) Difficulties of communication between the centre and the periphery, *i.e.*, between the central plateau and the coastal regions. (iii) The limited extent of the latter in comparison with the former. (iv) Great inequalities of the soil and of the distribution of water, which, on account of the steep declivities, produce swift rivers, unsuitable for irrigation and navigation, or only adaptable to these uses with great difficulty. (v) Excessive altitude of the greater part of the country, lowering its agricultural value. (vi) The dryness of the climate and, particularly, the irregular alternations of rain and drought, which produces a mean rainfall in the Central, Eastern, and Southern regions less than the minimum rainfall recorded in the plains of the Continent. (vii) Frequent floods, due to this irregularity and to the steepness of the ground. (viii) A great variety of temperature, according to the locality: ranging from extreme cold which in certain years has reached 13° Centi-

grade below zero (8.6° Fahrenheit) to such high tempera-
tures as 40° and 48° C. (104° and 118.4° F.). In general,
however, the temperature is equable compared with that of
other regions of Europe.

All these conditions—unfavourable for the most part to
the easy and prosperous development of the inhabitants—
were largely counterbalanced by the following: 1. Extraordinary fertility of the coastal plains, and of the banks of
certain rivers, inland, where there flourish important crops,
unique in Europe, or of better quality than those found in
other countries, such as the vine, olive, orange, rice, early
fruits, and garden produce. 2. Special facilities for stock-
breeding in the Cantabrian zone, through the extensive
natural grazing grounds, chiefly furthered by a constant
and abundant humidity and a general mildness of climate,
except at high altitudes. 3. The wealth of mineral de-
posits, from the precious metals (gold, and, in greater
quantities, silver) to those of more common industrial use
(iron, coal). 4. The abundance of subterranean springs,
most of them medicinal. 5. Great extent and regularity
of the sea coast (2,562 miles) which offer excellent opportunities for navigation and commerce.

Since times more ancient than we know of there have
come to this land peoples of very diverse origin, who have
formed by their association, the Spanish People, and by
their deeds, Spanish History. The former is characterized
by the mixture of its elements, the originality of spirit that
resulted from the internal riches of its being; the latter,
by the variation, movement, and complexity of its events,
as we shall see.

I

THE PRIMITIVE AGE

6. *The Earliest Settlers in Spain*

LITTLE is known of the original inhabitants of Spain, or of their achievements, for their civilization was very rudimentary and they did not know how to write. They could, therefore, leave no testimony of their existence other than their bones (preserved in tombs, or, in remote ages, simply in the earth) and certain objects of their arts and industries. We do not know who they were; we have no account of their life, nor examples of their language. This is true, of course, of the aborigines of all countries.

The only thing that can be stated with certainty is that the oldest inhabitants of Spain were semi-savages—perhaps related to others, of whom traces have been found in Europe and other parts. They lived at first on the shores of rivers, where they found abundant hunting and fishing. As the temperature changed and the great Ice Age set in, they began to occupy caves and natural caverns, situated in high places, so as to escape from floods and to guard themselves from the inclemency of the elements and their most pressing dangers. Their food consisted of flesh and fish, and perhaps also of fruit and herbs. It is not certain that they knew the use of fire, and they wore no sort of clothing except for adornment. But the most characteristic point of the civilization of these people was that all the objects which they used for their various needs were made of stone, which they shaped. Thus the period in which they lived is called the Early Stone Age (Palaeolithic). Remains of this civilization have been found in the Pradera de San Isidro, near the Manzanares; in the cave of Perneras

(Murcia), and in other places. It is thought that not one but two races then inhabited the Peninsula.

7. *Cromagnon Man.* At a later date (not exactly determinable) a new race came into Spain. It is called Cromagnon from the place in which traces of it were first found. We do not know whence these people came, nor what route they followed on their invasion. However, it is certain that they dominated the whole Peninsula, for remains of them and of their industry have appeared in regions so diverse as Catalonia, Valencia, Alicante, Murcia, Andalucía, Castille, Cantabria, and Portugal. The men of Cromagnon belonged to a tall robust race, with a large irregular cranium, long and narrow (dolichocephalic) and flattened at the base, a broad straight brow, a face of greater breadth than length, a thin prominent nose and a strongly protruding jaw-bone. Their civilization was noticeably superior to that of the former peoples. They lived in caves and perhaps occasionally in huts; they used both shaped stone (flint and other minerals), and bone and stag's horn. We note a difference in the forms of the objects which they made and a considerable increase in the kinds of objects used. Engraving and a primitive type of sculpture now appear. We infer the rude beginnings of tailoring from the bone needles that have been found, and we find a profusion of ornaments (bracelets, pendants, necklaces). They used amulets, which lead one to infer certain religious ideas, and these objects may also have served as insignia of authority, which would seem to show differences of social class and a hierarchy. These people were probably grouped in tribes and they buried their dead in caves with arms, utensils, and objects of adornment, denoting either that they paid homage to their dead or that they believed in their resurrection and in a second life for which, by reason of its similarity to this on earth, all such things were necessary.

The principal objects which they made (and which are found in distinct types) are: axes and lances in the form of a laurel leaf (such as those found in the cave of Cueto de la

Mina) with narrow pieces which were inserted in the handle; arrow- and dart-heads; chisels and awls; pointed splinters and knife-blades; daggers with a handle and a species of short sword; engraving tools; harpoons and needles; ornaments of shells and stones and other things of unknown uses.

8. *Neolithic Civilization.* Paleolithic civilization suffered a considerable change, whether by the natural development of the Cromagnon race or by the incoming of other extraneous peoples is not known. Since a new method of working stone—polishing instead of merely shaping it—was the first thing noted about this culture, the period that coincided with this method is called the Neolithic, or New Stone Age. Man reached this period by means of transitions and gradual improvements, and during its course further improvements in human life were brought about. Pottery appeared and developed first in vases of clay, made by hand and hardened probably in the open air, by means of fire from within; other objects followed later, large earthen jars, lamps, vases, etc. In stone and in bone were made axes with bevelled edges, little spades, hammers, mill-stones, mortars, bracelets, combs, pins, round buttons, etc. Men began to weave vegetable fibre, probably for clothing. They knew and employed gold, amber, jet, and other materials. As well as hunting and fishing, man already tilled the fields and sowed cereals. He understood navigation in *piraguas* or canoes and had learned to domesticate various animals such as the dog, the goat, the bull, and the horse. Life was no longer led principally in caves but also in huts, in the open air, on artificial islands, in habitations built on wooden piles on large lakes, and in constructions in stone and earth, which had probably a defensive object, camps, entrenched mounds, etc. In certain of these inhabited sites (in Asturias, Galicia, and Portugal) have been found large piles of cooking utensils (*Kioken-modingos* or *paraderos*) and also stores of materials, especially stone, for making other objects. These stores lead one to believe in the existence of workshops, such as

have been found in Argecilla (Guadalajara) and therefore of an industry which developed perhaps for the exportation of these products.

To this time also belong the megalithic monuments, so called because they were built of large stones. These seem to have been a conception original to Spanish civilization, for the monuments of this type found in Southern Europe are of a later date. They were meant for sepulchres and are known in several forms: dolmens, formed by one or several slabs, reposing horizontally on others, standing upright; *mamoas* or *mamblas*, where the dolmen is covered with earth; tumuli, made of small stones and earth; menhirs, stones of great size set upright, indicating the place of a sepulchre; cromlechs, or circles of stones, set up at a regular distance one from the other. The bodies were buried in a sitting position, surrounded by objects of common use, or placed in a large earthenware jar. It also appears that cremation existed in certain places. As time went on megalithic monuments were used for other purposes than burial.

In them, in caves and sometimes on the face of a rock, there have been found pictures, painted in black (vegetable carbon), yellow, red, green, and blue. In tombs and caves there have also been discovered small, roughly made statues of alabaster, aragonite, and ivory, and pottery, with remarkable ornamentation, perhaps symbolic, sometimes geometrical, sometimes with palm trees or rustic scenes.

Of these arts the most perfect and even, one might say, the most inspired, were the paintings—sometimes combined with engraving—which take advantage of the natural contours of the rocks. We know of two different kinds of these paintings which belong to two different parts of Spain, and which, no doubt, represent two types of civilization, and perhaps the ideas of two different peoples. Those of the North (Cantabric region) reach their perfection in the admirable paintings of animals (bulls or bisons, horses and stags) in the cave of Altamira (Santillana), which, according to the calculations of archaeologists, date back from 15 to 20,000 years. The Southern group is characterized by the predominance of human figures (which do not appear in the North), both of men (huntsmen, warriors, dancers) and of women. The movement of the figures is remarkable. The latter group covered the geographical region in the East of Spain, between Lérida and Albacete. The paintings of both regions, especially those of the North, surpass any corresponding work found elsewhere in Europe, both in observation of reality and in technique. In the same way the pottery of the Neolithic period found in Spain (funeral vases and ornamented vases of common use) is superior both in shape and decoration to the contemporary pottery found in France. To this phase of ceramic art belong the examples from the caves and places situated in the regions now called Almería, Alicante, Murcia, Málaga, Granada, Guadalajara, etc.

All these industries and arts were greatly improved as time went on. The greatest progress was made in architecture. Houses were built of more than one storey, the walls being of stone cemented with earth, and the roofs of reeds and branches. A number of buildings of this type have been found, grouped together in a village, surrounded by a defensive ditch, in the province of Almería, near the river Andarax. In the caves in different parts of Spain linear and semicircular signs have also been found, which seem to represent a form of ancient script. Similar specimens, which also belong to the Neolithic Period, have been found in different parts of Europe.

9. *The Age of Metals.* A new step of great importance in the civilization of these primitive times was the employment of metals for making weapons of war and implements of labour, and also for ornaments. It is believed that the first metal to be employed was copper, worked by hammer, not by foundering. Objects of this class, of the same forms as those made in stone, have been found in Carmona. The pottery contemporaneous with this first employment of copper was already much developed. Its characteristic

form is the bell-shaped vase (Ciempozuelos, Millares, Palmellar). Bronze followed copper, and was used more extensively; it characterized a whole period, and, whether brought in by foreign peoples, or invented here, seems to have developed in Spain on lines of its own. The objects made from this metal belong to various types: axes, scythes, knives, daggers, swords, arrows, lances, cuirasses and helmets, harness for horses, bracelets, etc.; these were generally embellished with geometrical designs (circles, semicircles, crosses), and were of considerable elegance. To this period also perhaps belong the curious heads of bulls found in Costig. The dead were buried in coffins of stone and wood, in earthen jars, tombs of flag-stones or slate, or merely in ditches. It is indubitable that the exploitation of minerals already existed at this time, and perhaps also an alphabetic script was now first introduced. Iron was substituted for bronze, though at the beginning of its use there appeared a medley of objects in iron, copper, and bronze. It is thought that the exploitation and use of iron was borrowed by the Spaniards from foreign races, perhaps from Africa. What is certain is that the appearance of this metal coincides with the presence of innumerable objects of exotic origin in tombs and in places showing signs of habitation. The source of these objects can be determined upon with a certain exactitude, for in many ruins of villages belonging to the end of the Bronze Age, particularly in Andalucía, traces have been found of struggles which seem to indicate invasions and wars of new settlers.

Articles characteristic of the beginning of the Iron Age are: triangular daggers, found in different burial grounds (Aguilar de Anguita, Olmedo, and others) and, later on, short swords with sharp points, and long swords with rounded points; these were found in various parts of Eastern Aragon and Castille.

With the introduction and use of iron we come to an end of the primitive times, of which we have no written historical evidence, and enter upon ages of which we already know something from Greek and Roman writers.

10. *Phœnician Colonization.* Apart from others whom we can deduce with a certain verisimilitude (Assyrio-Chaldeans, Egyptians, Libyans), the oldest colonists of Spain of whom we have certain knowledge are the Phœnicians, inhabitants of the Western coasts of Asia (North of Palestine), and specially devoted to navigation and commerce. Reliable traditions speak of the foundation of a Phœnician colony in Cadiz in the 11th century B.C., whence one may infer that the relations of these foreigners with the people who lived in Spain began at an even earlier date. And as the Phœnicians are the first (so far as we know) to have written an account of their journeys and discoveries in Spain, it is considered that with them begin the historic times of the Peninsula; for all the earlier times (§§ 6-9) are called prehistoric—it would be better to say *prehistoriographic*—because we have no written records of them. Yet, as the information collected by the Phœnicians has not come down to us directly, but translated and modified in later times, it is not possible to learn what peoples they met with in Spain, nor the state of civilization of these peoples.

The Phœnicians established themselves on almost the whole of the coast of the Peninsula, especially in Andalucía, where, as in Murcia, they advanced for some distance inland. They also became dominant in the Balearic Islands, notably in Ibiza. Their colonies, which were trading ventures, were either founded by the State, or by the great mercantile families of Phœnicia. Generally they were situated on islands, near the coast, or on promontories easy of defence and having a natural port. The Phœnician influence lasted for several centuries, and, in certain regions, was so pronounced that long afterwards they were still known as Phœnician States, when the nucleus of the population of these places was already Spanish.

The Phœnicians contributed notably to Spanish civilization, introducing and disseminating their language and script, money (unknown till then), the industry of salting meats, and of salt-mines. They also brought to Spain many objects produced by the art and industry of the other countries (Asiatic and African) whose commerce they exploited. They greatly developed the mines in Spain, and, if they did not teach the natives to work them themselves, at least the beds of ore, copper, silver, lead, iron, and perhaps tin, benefited greatly by Phœnician mining. They also taught their religion.

The centre of the Phœnician colonies was Cadiz, where, according to certain ancient authors, some colonists constructed a sumptuous temple to their god Melkart, with columns made, or at any rate faced, with gold and silver. Tombs of theirs have recently been discovered, funeral statues (the anthropoid sarcophagus of Cadiz), jewellery in gold and silver, of oriental design (Aliseda), objects of ivory with pictures, and vases of glass, *e.g.* that of Aliseda, with hieroglyphic inscriptions.

11. *Greek Colonization.* After the Phœnicians, but at a very early date not exactly determinable, there also arrived on the shores of the Peninsula men of another seafaring race, the Greeks—rivals of the Phœnicians in exploiting the commerce of the Mediterranean. Yet the most ancient references to their relations with Spain, which have come down to our day in Greek authors, are not earlier than the 7th century B.C. (630 B.C.), although Hesiod makes mention of Spain in the 8th century. Whenever it began, Greek colonization established itself in rivalry with that of the Phœnicians, and not without sanguinary encounters on all the shores of Spain, especially on the East coast (Catalonia and Valencia). Their principal settlements in the Eastern regions were Emporion (market) in the province of Gerona; Hemeroscopion, facing the Balearic Islands, in the province of Valencia; Artemisium or Dianium (Denia) and Alonai. Frequent communication was maintained with the Southern region, as is proved by the accounts of Tartessos and King Argantonius.

A Greek traveller of the 5th century B.C., Pytheas, made a tour round the Peninsula by sea, and his narrative forms the most ancient written account of the Spaniards that we possess.

The Greek colonies, like the Phœnician, were either private, founded by great mercantile houses, or official, founded by the Government of that Republic to which the emigrants belonged.

The civilizing influence of the Greek colonies was considerable. The first money to be coined in Spain (at Emporion and Rhodas) was Greek in type and had a wide circulation in Europe. The Greeks also developed agriculture, introducing or furthering the cultivation of the vine and olive. They founded schools and academies, such as that of a certain Asclepides in Andalucía, and contributed above all to the artistic culture of the natives, to architecture (of which there are no remains), sculpture (reflections of which are noted, with more or less certainty, in various Spanish statues found recently), in pottery, in mosaics, and in other industrial arts. It is thought that they also introduced the theatre. In the legislative sphere their greatest influence seems to have been in Mercantile Law.

12. *The Celtic Invasion.* A little later than the Greeks, but also at a very uncertain date (6th, 5th, or 4th century), and perhaps at two different periods, there invaded Spain, by way of the Pyrenees, numerous tribes of a people who formerly inhabited the centre of Europe—the Celts. It seems that these new invaders, whose civilization was very primitive, met with great resistance in some regions, on the part of the tribes who had lived in Spain since a remote date; whereas, in other parts, either because of the gentleness or feebleness of the inhabitants, or because the region was uninhabited, they were able to establish themselves without resistance. Thus it happened that the Peninsula was divided between the Celts and the earlier inhabitants —to whom, in the mass, ancient authors gave the name of Iberians, a term employed for the first time in the 6th century B.C. by a Greek traveller, Scylax. Under this denomination were grouped tribes who had a right to the name, and others who had lived in Spain before the Iberian Invasion (§ 13).

The division was probably as follows: the regions next

to the Pyrenees, the Eastern Mediterranean zone, and part of the South, continued to be inhabited solely by the Iberians; the North-West (Galicia) and almost the whole of Portugal were dominated by the Celts; and in the rest of the Peninsula both elements were inextricably mingled. To the mixed people thus resulting, ancient authors have given the name of Celtiberians, and they indicate as their principal territory Celtiberia, a region of uncertain limits, which includes part of the modern Castille and Aragon. But it is not certain that all the so-called Celtiberians were really a mixed race, nor that the mixture was in all cases a result of the coming of the conquering Celts.

Celtic civilization was rudimentary, probably very similar to that of the Iberians, and certainly inferior to that of the men of Tartessos, who had already received (*e.g.*, on the Andalucían coast) many foreign influences—those of the Phœnicians and other Eastern peoples. Thus it follows (at least in their respective territories, some centuries later (§ 18)) that it is impossible, in the majority of cases, to determine from the mass of involved information that we possess to-day, what things are properly Celtic and what Iberian.

We know that the type of dagger known as *herradura* (horse-shoe) belongs exclusively to the Celts.

13. *The Iberians*. Another primitive invading race was that which the Greeks knew by the name of Iberians, of whom we have already made mention. It is not really known by what route they came into Spain, nor whence, although the opinion most accepted to-day is that they came originally from Western Asia, perhaps from Mesopotamia, and, immediately, from Northern Africa. Setting aside the hypothesis that they came in the remote period of the Neolithic Age, it seems possible to affirm that by the 6th century B.C. the Iberians already inhabited part of the Peninsula to the East, and a good portion of South-Eastern France. The Gauls ejected them from this at the end of the 5th or the beginning of the 4th century. In the 3rd century a number of tribes, undoubtedly Iberian, are

IBERIAN BRONZE FIGURES

Photo, Arxiv Mas.

known in the Mediterranean zone, from Catalonia to Valencia, and it also appears that they penetrated the central plateau and extended far into the centre of Portugal.

Classical authors of the Roman epoch describe them physically as men of short stature, spare, and long-headed (dolichocephalic), and morally as men of a very independent, noble, hospitable, and religious spirit, but also with defects such as arrogance and laziness.

As for their civilization, these same authors have handed down to us numerous accounts, supported in modern times by archaeological discoveries, referring to their dwellings, arms, arts, industries, and writing.

According to the classical authors, two unequal zones were distinguishable in the civilization of the tribes or groups of tribes whose common characteristic was their free manner of life. One of these zones was composed of the southern region (the bed of the Guadalquivir), inhabited by the Turdetani or Tartesians, and its extension to the South-East, in the region of the Turduli and of the Contestani; the other, corresponding to the rest of the Peninsula, was inhabited by Iberians and Celts, and probably, in certain districts, by remains of pre-Iberian tribes (prehistoric), which certain authors call Ligures, a generic name of doubtful accuracy.

The first zone was, in the opinion of these classical authors, the more civilized. Its population, which had attained a notable degree of economic well-being, knew and practised extensively agriculture, industry, and commerce by land and sea. They possessed a literature of their own, and annals, poems, and laws in verse, said to be very ancient. They were gentle in their behaviour, friendly, and welcomed foreign influences. To them refer the aforementioned Greek comments on Tartessos, that being the name they gave to the region of the Turdetani.

The peoples of the second zone were very backward, characterized by primitive customs, incessant wars, a generally hostile attitude to strangers, and a poor economic condition.

C

This vast difference between the two zones, along with certain details of character and spirit, has induced various modern historians to consider at any rate the Turdetani as a people of different stock from the Iberians.

Modern archaeological discoveries allow us to be more precise about the state of civilization and to distinguish four or five zones. The more advanced of these, to judge by the artistic remains which are left there, are: the South-Eastern region (the modern provinces of Murcia, Alicante, and Albacete, with extensions towards the North and along the coast) and that of Andalucía. The period of its highest culture appears to have been the 4th and 5th centuries B.C. The Carthaginian conquest (§ 16), which began and established itself chiefly in these regions, wiped out these indigenous civilizations which the Romans, in their turn, completely absorbed. Second in importance to them is the zone of the valley of the Ebro (Aragonese and Catalan districts), and that of the central plateau or Celtiberia, which flourished in the 3rd and 2nd centuries, and came to an end with the capture, in 133 B.C., of Numantia—the most important Celtiberian city of which we know to-day. That is to say, it came to an end through the imposition of the military and political power of Rome.

Finally we come to the rest of the Peninsula, and especially the North, which even to-day is little known archaeologically, and which the classical writers signalled as the poorest and most backward of all the regions.

The civilization of the South-Eastern zone reveals itself as the most powerful and the most perfect. Remains of numerous settlements, temples, and burial-places, already studied, show an abundant population and a notable degree of social development, and at the same time a religious spirit. The most important city which excavations in this zone have revealed is Meca, province of Albacete, in whose ruins have been found roads for carts, cut out in the rock, and great reservoirs and caverns. It seems that second after Meca in importance is the recent discovery of Minateda, also in the province of Albacete, and perhaps the fortifi-

Photo, Arxiv Mas.

" THE LADY OF ELCHE "
(From a cast in the Museum of Fine Arts, Barcelona)

cations found in Peña de Carochita (Torremanzanas, Alicante). Other buildings of equal importance are the temple or sanctuary of Cerro de los Santos, Albacete, and the necropolis of Archena (Murcia). The sculpture, although much influenced by oriental and primitive Hellenic models brought by the Phœnicians and Greeks, creates a type of its own, and reaches great technical perfection. Its culminating work is the bust known as the " *Lady of Elche*," because it was found in that place in the province of Alicante. Notable also are the bronze statues of warriors and other human figures, and those of idols and sphinxes and animals. There have also been unearthed jewellery and precious metals (among them, and the best of them, the diadem found at Javea, Alicante) and arms, with incrustations in precious metals. The pottery of this zone is the most beautiful of any found in Iberia. It is distinguished by its variety and its masterly decoration, at times purely geometrical, at others, of flowers and formalized animals (*e.g.*, on the vases of Archena and Elche) and warriors (Archena).

The remains met with in the Andalucían zone are fortified cities like that of Osma, sanctuaries like that of Despeñaperros and Castellar (Jaén); a necropolis, such as that of Almedinilla or that of Setefilla (Lora del Río, Seville); and ceramic ware with purely geometrical designs, which, on a basis of foreign influence, has been able to create a type of its own, thus manifesting one of the characteristics of the Spanish spirit, whose assimilations almost always rise above pure imitation, printing on them the seal of the race.

In Niebla have been discovered also examples with human forms and figures in relief, in which the pottery is mixed with metal (bronze) and which seem to exhibit exotic influences.

The civilization of the basin of the Ebro, revealed by archaeological remains, shows numerous towns (provinces of Teruel, Lérida, and to the south of Saragossa). Those of the 3rd century are more important than the earlier ones; among them, that of San Antonio de Calaceite had walls and a tower. We do not know of any sculpture, but there are pictures on steles, which are perhaps funereal. Offensive and defensive arms, in iron and bronze, are notable. Among the former are the curved sword, called Iberian (Latin *falcata*), and the long, two-edged sword which we have indicated in § 9. Among the latter, those which deserve mention are shields, covered with iron, and a bronze breast-plate, found in Calaceite. As regards pottery, which began with simple geometric designs, it developed later a character of its own, adding to former *motifs* those of conventionalized flowers, and sometimes very imperfect human figures.

Finally, the Iberian civilization of the plateau is richly represented in Numantia, where excavations have revealed to us the disposition of the streets and the means of paving them, the construction of houses and cellars, arms, and, above all, a very varied decorative pottery, with a character of its own, especially in its geometrical designs. On contemplating these remains, expressive of the genius of those Iberian tribes who for so long resisted invasion, and above all the Roman absorption, we can understand the great significance which the fall of Numantia h for Iberian culture, even more than for its political in dence.

Since then the civilization of Spain changed irection radically, yet without entirely losing the elements created by the Iberian and Celtic inhabitants and those anterior to these two groups.

14. *Social and Political Organization of the Iberian Peoples.* A Greek author of the 1st century B.C., Strabo, visited our Peninsula and wrote a *Geography*, making use of his own observations and those of other writers before him. He gives the most complete picture of the organization and life of the natives at that time and also, in part, before the Roman domination. Basing ourselves chiefly on Strabo, we can therefore form a rough idea of the particular characteristics of the life of the Iberians and Celts.

These two peoples were divided into tribes, independent of each other except when, for reasons of war, those nearest

to each other united temporarily, constituting a federation.
The most renowned of these tribes or federations were the
following: the *Callaïci* or *Gallaeci*, who occupied the territory indicated by their name; the *Astures*, who inhabited
part of the modern Asturias and of León; the *Cantabri* on
the coast between Villaviciosa and Castro-Urdiales; the
Vascones from the Basque provinces, Navarre, and part of
Aragon; the *Cerretani, Indigetes*, and others in Catalonia;
the *Edetani* in Valencia and the South-East of Aragon; the
Contestani in Alicante and Murcia; the *Turdetani* in the
South of Estremadura and West of Andalucía; the *Turduli*
in the centre and South of the same district; the *Lusitani*
in almost the whole of Portugal and part of Estremadura;
the *Celtiberians* (§ 12); the *Vaccaei* in the North of Old
Castille; the *Vettones* between the Douro and the Guadiana;
the *Carpetani* in Toledo and part of Madrid and Guadalajara; and the *Oretani* in the region of Ciudad Real.

The type of social life of these peoples varied according
to their degree of civilization, the conditions of the land,
and other circumstances. Most of them lived in little
villages or scattered over the fields, like the *Celtici* (who
occupied the South of Portugal), the *Gallaeci*, and the
Astures. Among others, such as the *Turdetani* there were
great urban communities (towns). Villagers who, from
their lack of importance or their scattered rural existence,
had no fortifications of their own (like Calaceite, Numantia,
etc., § 13), took refuge in case of war in towers or fortified
places, common to several villages and at times corresponding to the capital of the tribe or district.

Marriage among the Iberians and Spanish Celts was
generally monogamous, though cases of polygamy are
found in various tribes. The ceremonies with which it was
celebrated varied according to the locality, being in certain
tribes (among the Lusitani) very similar to Greek marriage.
The head of the family was usually the father, but among
the Cantabri it is believed that this was the mother, or at
least that she and the other women had the privilege of
intervention in the government of the family.

But the family was not the chief social organization in those days. This was the *gentilitas*, that is to say, a group formed by various families, either inter-related or who recognized a common stock.

The *gentilitas* was ruled by an assembly, or by a chief or patriarch, with authority over the *gentiles*, which extended to penal matters, for they were all united by common duties and rights. Each *gentilitas* worshipped particular gods—which were probably in their origin ancestors—lived all in one village, with a name of its own.

The *gentilitas* included also foreigners, received or adopted (clients), and slaves taken in war, bought, or obtained by other means. Among the freemen there existed a division into patricians and plebeians—the former being the wealthiest and strongest, and held public and military offices. The majority of the plebeians seem to have lived as clients of the nobles.

The union of different *gentilitates* formed a tribe, a group chiefly political in character. Some were governed by a king or a chief—sometimes elective, sometimes hereditary —and by assemblies. Others were governed by a variety of institutions (two magistrates, a council of ten, etc.). The assemblies, where they existed, were two: one, composed of patricians (Senate) formed probably by the chiefs of the *gentilitates* or by powerful individuals, the other, a popular assembly. The names given here to these political institutions are those used by the Latin authors.

The forms of property among the Spaniards of those days varied very considerably. In certain tribes the existence of personal property is clearly seen (*e.g.*, among the Lusitani); in others, communal ownership, including a common working in the fields and a subsequent common division of the crops, was the rule (*e.g.*, among the Vaccaei).

15. *Religion and Customs.* Apart from the gods of the *gentilitas* there were others, either particular to each tribe, or common to several tribes, whose cult therefore spread over wide districts. It seems that in certain places there was Moon-worship. The Lusitani sacrificed on their

altars animals and men (prisoners of war) whose entrails they examined, so as to learn by their movements whether the omens were good.

Strabo says that in the North and North-West the men wore black and used as defensive arms, shields and cuirasses of canvas and chain-mail, helmets of leather with three points, and, as offensive arms, lances and daggers or knives. The women preferred bright colours. The principal food of these people consisted of bread, made of acorn-flour, butter, and a sort of beer or cider. The Celtiberians ate mainly flesh, clad themselves with more luxury and lived in greater comfort. Their helmets were of bronze. The Lusitani anointed their bodies with oil and perfume, allowed their hair to grow long, and wore a kind of mitre when they went into battle.

According to Strabo and other authors of antiquity, the distinctive traits of the Spanish character were, as we have indicated above: physical hardiness, heroic valour, a love of liberty, lack of discipline, and a loyalty to the point of sacrificing life itself. Their courage and their excellent military qualities made them eagerly sought for as mercenaries, and thus we see them taking parts in the wars in Sicily, Africa, Greece and, later, Italy. In the Iberian sanctuaries of the Sierra Morena votive offerings have been found, representing infantry, armed with the curved sword and helmet, and cavalry, with shield and two lances.

The Basques demand a separate paragraph, because, although they are included in the foregoing remarks in the aggregation of the Iberian peoples, yet, though they have been supposed for some time to have belonged to them, it is uncertain whether they really did so, and strictly speaking, the problem of their origin is still unsolved. It is certain that, as described to us by the classical authors, they offer certain Iberian characteristics, in civilization and customs; but they also possess others, totally un-Iberian. What seems most evident about the Basques is their distinctness from the other peoples of the Peninsula.

Perhaps they are the only survivors in historic times of the prehistoric tribes of the caves of the Pyrenees.

16. *The Carthaginian Conquest.* The Phœnicians founded a colony called Carthage on the North coast of Africa (Tunis) at about the beginning of the 9th century B.C. It prospered rapidly. By the 7th century it was the most important of all the cities of Phœnician origin on the Western basin of the Mediterranean. It was given over chiefly to commerce and its sailors made important voyages of discovery—among them that of Himilco, who sailed round the Peninsula. In this way, extensive commercial relationships were established with new countries. It is thought that the Carthaginians gained possession of the Island of Ibiza in fairly remote times. But their definite settling in the Peninsula dates from the 6th century, when, bitter warfare having arisen between the Phœnicians of Cadiz and the neighbouring indigenous tribes, the former called in the Carthaginians to their aid. The armed intervention of these people soon became a true subjugation of the primitive Phœnician colonies; and, not content with this, they extended their colonization and so began upon the veritable military conquest of Spain. This undertaking was carried out by several generals, belonging to a Carthaginian family, the Barcas or Barcidae, who enjoyed great prestige in Carthage. Hamilcar Barca's conquest began in 236 B.C., and, by the end of the 3rd century, thanks to the continuous efforts of this general, his son-in-law, Hasdrubal, and his son Hannibal, and not without furious resistance on the part of the Spaniards, the Carthaginians dominated more or less securely almost the whole Peninsula as far as the Douro and the Ebro, except the Eastern coasts (from the Cape of Nao), which remained under Greek influence. They also occupied the Balearic Isles, amongst which Ibiza offers many traces of their domination. The Barcidae established a capital in New Carthage (Cartagena), erecting great buildings, military and civil (the gate, the temple of Melkart, walls, storehouses, etc.), and made it a centre of Spanish commerce.

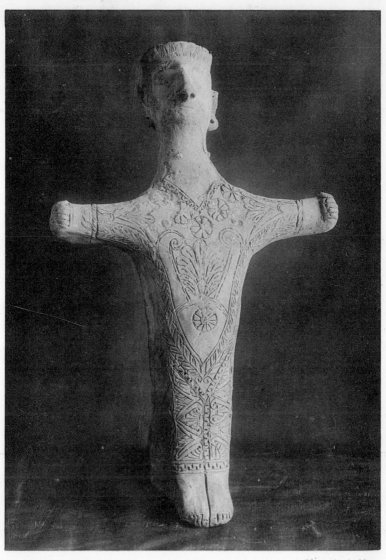

CARTHAGINIAN TERRA-COTTA FIGURE
(From Ibiza)

17. *The Civilizing Influence of the Carthaginians.* The principal aim of Carthaginian colonization, apart from commercial development, was to acquire men for the army and gold for the exchequer. The Barcidae turned their attention chiefly to these two things. They recruited therefore among the Spaniards a large part of their army, and levied heavy taxes upon the civilians. They respected the independence of the Spaniards in all other matters, and even endeavoured to become intimate with them, by means of mixed marriages. They exploited energetically the silver mines of the regions of Murcia and Andalucía, and perhaps also others in other parts of the Peninsula. They also established mints, where they made great quantities of coins. The industry of salting also progressed greatly in their time. Besides New Carthage, other important commercial centres of theirs were Cadiz (Agadir) and Ibiza (Ebussus), which, along with Málaga and other cities coined money. The Carthaginians greatly forwarded public works, constructing palaces, forts, temples, and roads; but all that has come down to our days are certain tombs, objects of trade, coins, and an inscription found in Villaricos. Their alphabet and their religion spread throughout the Peninsula, as did also their customs, which, in certain points, persisted for several centuries—such as, for example, the shape of and inscription on their coins. But though, in some ways, they introduced new elements of civilization into Spain, in others they diverted and probably perverted, the natural and true development of the natives, especially in the South and South-East.

II

THE ROMAN INFLUENCE

(3RD CENTURY B.C.—5TH CENTURY A.D.)

18. *Roman Expansion in Spain*

A T the end of the 3rd century B.C. (218 B.C.) Roman troops landed for the first time in Spain, to fight against the Carthaginians. The motive of this war was the well-known question of Saguntum, a city which the Romans held to be an ally of theirs, and which Hannibal attacked. A few years later (206), the Carthaginians, routed in the whole Peninsula, were driven out, and their domination came to an end. During this struggle the ancient Greek colonies and many of the Phœnician colonies helped the Romans, while the Spanish tribes took sides, some fighting for the Barcas and others for the new invaders.

Once these were victorious they meditated the conquest in their turn of the Iberians and the Celts. The tribes of the East and South submitted easily enough, but those of the Centre, North, and West, on the contrary, put up a stubborn resistance, which lasted for a long time. Until the beginning of the 1st century A.D., the Romans could not say that they were the military masters of the Peninsula, and even then they had to crush a formidable insurrection in the tribes which occupied the regions of Asturias and Cantabria. After this date there were only unimportant risings on the part of the Spaniards.

The policy pursued by the Romans in their conquest was not purely military. Where they found great resistance they adopted harsh and cruel measures, exiling to remote places whole sections of the population, destroying towns, exterminating their inhabitants, mutilating their young men of military age, or selling them as slaves. If, on the

contrary, they were well received, they made treaties of
alliance, recognized the independence of the friendly
tribes, and respected their rights more or less fully, according to the degree of their friendliness and the confidence
they deserved; or they bestowed honours and distinctions,
which flattered the vanity of the natives and their desire to
enter into relations socially and politically with their new
masters, whose power and culture dazzled them. At the
same time, the Romans made efforts to introduce into the
Peninsula elements from their own country in three ways:
by bringing over colonists and workmen for the mines and
industries, by distributing lands to their ex-soldiers, so that
they should establish themselves in Spain and found
cities, and finally by favouring indirectly intermarriage
between the Romans and the Spaniards. At the same time
they continued the organization of their colonial government by dividing the Peninsula into *provinces* with governors,
judges, and other functionaries, and by the promulgation
of special laws (§ 21).

19. *Romanization.* The result of all these methods was
that, by the end of the 1st century a great part of the
Spanish population had become Romanized, *i.e.*, had conformed to the type of life and civilization of the Romans.
The region in which this assimilation was most prompt was
the South (Andalucía), that is to say, the most pacific
region, and that which had come into widest and most
intimate contact with former colonists. At this time all
the important cities of Andalucía (Baetica) represented the
Roman type almost completely, and from the 2nd century
even the small towns had lost the original characteristics of
their buildings and their way of life. In the South of
Portugal also Roman influence took deep root. In the
East it was slower, except in the great settlements such as
Cartagena, Saguntum and Tarragona, and in general in
the coastal zone. As regards the regions of the Centre and
North, they continued to be antagonistic to Roman culture
for much longer, and maintained more or less intact their
laws, customs, language, political and family organization;

this was especially so in the rural districts, remote from towns and densely populated areas, and in mountainous places, difficult of access. They were the cause of frequent wars, until in 133 the fall of Numantia (as already stated) subjected to the invaders these regions which had been so refractory to Romanization. In the coastal districts of the North and West, Roman life developed more easily, as is attested by the many villas, remains of which have been met with in Asturias, Galicia, Portugal, and other places.

Romanization thus became complete in a territorial sense, and though uneven, it was in some places intense and equalled or even surpassed that in any other country dominated by Rome, with the exception of Italy. To this is due the fact that Spain gave to the government and culture of Rome (§ 25) notable heads of the State such as the Emperors Trajan and Hadrian (who, like Vespasian, Titus, Nerva, Marcus Aurelius, Diocletian, and others, greatly forwarded the progress of the Peninsula), together with poets, philosophers and orators. But even in the regions most influenced, certain elements of the indigenous civilization persisted, e.g., the language (as seen in sepulchral inscriptions and coins), religion, and customs (§ 14).

20. *Colonial Organization.* The Roman authorities implanted in the Peninsula the political and administrative institutions of their country, although this was not so in every region, on account of the autonomy which certain tribes and native towns enjoyed (§ 14). Those who were under the political power of governors and also paid tribute were called *stipendiarii*; if they were exempt from tribute, *immunes*; and if they enjoyed independence, *libri* and *foederati*. These were only obliged to assist the Romans with soldiers and ships. But since the Romans at one and the same time founded settlements of their own citizens (§ 19) or induced the natives to conform to their type, two new classes of cities arose, the *coloniae* and the *municipia*, with slight differences of organization.

In principle, a distinction should be clearly drawn between towns of the native type and those of Roman type, not only because of their customs and language, but also because the Romans did not concede to foreigners the civil and political rights which belonged to the citizens of the metropolis. But as time went on this exclusive policy was changed, and as a special privilege the natives were allowed to enjoy some or all of the Roman rights; and many towns and many individuals approximated to, or equalled, the juridical condition of the conquerors. Thus a Roman Emperor (Vespasian) conceded to all natives who came to hold certain public municipal offices the privilege of acquiring the status of a Roman citizen; Caracalla gave many Spaniards the privileges of citizenship simply by a decree. In this way the juridical unity of Spain was realized (though it never achieved completeness) and almost all the native towns adopted the regimen proper to the Romans.

21. *Municipal Government and the Assemblies.* The system commonly employed in the government of towns of the Roman type is known as the *regimen municipale*. According to this the inhabitants of each municipium were divided into three classes: residents (*cives*); temporary residents (*incolae*) and the floating population (*hospites* or *adventores*). The first two classes formed the *populus*, who for certain political and administrative purposes constituted a Popular Assembly. Until the 2nd century this Assembly elected the authorities or higher magistrates of the town, which election was carried out by voting, in a form analogous to that used in Spain to-day for the election of Town-Councillors. They also discussed the general interests of the town, and passed resolutions concerning it.

The municipal magistrates were four: two *duumviri* and two *aediles*. The former fulfilled administrative, judicial and military functions, and were of a higher standing than the *aediles*. These latter were responsible for the urban police and public order at spectacles. The treasury officials were called *quaestores*, and those charged with the drawing up of the census, electoral lists, etc., *quinquennales*. There was also a Municipal Council (*curia*), like Spanish town-councils of to-day, except that it was not the people who elected it, but the magistrates.

When a *colonia* or *municipium* was founded, it was customary to dictate a law and ordinances, for those who had to rule it in the future. These were engraved in bronze, according to the Roman custom, and exposed to public view. Of these laws, those of Osuna, Málaga and Salpensa have come down to us, though not in a complete form.

In the villages or rural municipalities (*vicus*), dependent to a great extent on those of the towns, there also existed Assemblies of residents, who deliberated upon various points concerned with their interests and administration.

Finally, the Roman citizens of each province were accustomed to unite annually in an Assembly, with the aim of celebrating religious festivals. When these were over, the Assembly changed into a meeting of a political and administrative body (*concilium*), one of whose principal duties was to legalize or censure the acts of the governor, with the power of denouncing him to the central powers. This became necessary by reason of the dishonesty in administrative matters which existed in the provinces.

The Roman municipal regimen was, then, for several centuries, a school of citizenship and of political education for the Spanish people.

22. *Decadence of the Power of Rome.* All these institutions, and especially the municipal regimen, as long as they functioned in liberty, inspired by the general interest of the citizens, formed the mainspring of the dominion and greatness of Rome. Unhappily, the great political upheavals produced by the succession to the throne, each of which was more violent than the last, and the enormous development of centralization and bureaucracy, which only bred dishonesty, led at last to decadence and disorganization.

Little by little the autonomy of the municipalities was diminished, and the functions of the Assemblies curtailed, as were those of the *duumvirs* and other functionaries, who were replaced by special delegates from the Emperor (*procuratores* and *praefecti*). Taxes were increased. All was subordinated to the aim of increasing the revenue, and members of the Curia were therefore made responsible for all default in payment of taxes. As a result of these methods, many men ceased to be *curiales*; but, as such abstention did not suit the State, the office of *Curialis* or *Decurio* was made obligatory and hereditary for every individual and family which by reason of its economic position could offer guarantees for the collection of taxes. As the citizens invented subterfuges to elude this tyranny, new laws were made barring their road of escape. Thus, what had once been an honour became, in fact, an unwelcome duty, and all desire to administer the *curiales* in loyalty to the municipality disappeared.

At the same time all civil liberties were restricted; many offices were made hereditary, and manual labourers were obliged to organize themselves in corporations, supervised by the State and subject to heavy taxes, while economic inequalities grew enormously, separating the classes more widely from one another and accentuating the dependence and misery of the poor.

Some Emperors tried, at the beginning of the 4th century —in face of the formidable barbarian menace (§ 29) which was slowly invading the Roman territories—to inspire public spirit once more, creating new functionaries, protecting the poorer classes and tax-payers from administrative dishonesty, reinforcing the functions of the provincial Assemblies, etc. But all these methods proved insufficient, in face of the marked decadence which had already begun to make itself felt.

23. *Social and Political Effects of the Roman Occupation.* The Roman domination produced three principal effects on the Spanish population: (1) *Political Unity*, imposing upon the tribes of the Peninsula for the first time the pressure of a central government, which fused the separate groups and reduced to a large extent the isolation in which they had lived before, facilitating their mutual relations, mingling them, and producing solidarity among them by means of common aspirations. (2) *Juridical Unity*, super-

imposing upon the institutions of the Iberians and Celts (§§ 14 and 15) Roman Law, which modified the institutions of family life and property, the laws of heredity, and the general economic order. It caused the disappearance of the *gentilitates*, giving personal rights to each member of the family, introducing the principle of private property, in opposition to the collective ownership maintained by certain tribes (*e.g.*, the Vaccaei). (3) *Diffusion of all forms of material civilization* (principally roads, public works, industry and commerce) *and of intellectual culture* (schools, literature, science), endowing the whole population with a common language, Latin, which became general in the Peninsula, and prepared the way for the later development of a national language (§ 47).

24. *Spanish-Roman Material Civilization.* Like all colonists, the Romans brought to Spain the latest products of their material civilization. They gave a great impulse to industry, especially to mining and the salting of fish, based on industries that already existed (§ 10); to agriculture, by encouraging the cultivation of cereals, the olive and the vine, whose products were exported in great quantities, and were much in demand; finally to pasturing, which became famous in the flocks of Baetica, from whose wool a celebrated cloth was manufactured. Other stuffs were made in various places, from flax and esparto-grass. Maritime commerce, already important in earlier times as we know (§ 13) progressed greatly, until the ships of the Turdetani were the largest and most numerous of all those that sailed the Mediterranean. In the coast of the South-East and North-West there were many excellent ports, natural and artificial, often lighted by lighthouses, such as that at Corunna.

To facilitate communications in the interior, the Romans improved and widened the existing roads, creating a system of Roman roads which crossed the whole Peninsula and were remarkable for their durability. Many of them were constructed by soldiers, and we still find not a few remains of them in various regions. To the same end, many bridges

ROMAN AQUEDUCT, SEGOVIA

were constructed, certain of which are in use to this day, such as the magnificent bridge of Alcántara (Estremadura). For the water-supply of the towns, great aqueducts were raised, such as those of Segovia and Mérida; and for their adornment, statues, triumphal and commemorative arches, palaces, etc. Many traces of Roman fortifications remain, *e.g.*, at León, Seville, etc.; they were remarkable for their strength and beauty. The permanent camps were walled, and formed veritable cities. One of these walled camps was the origin of León.

The Romans also organized river-navigation, in boats of shallow draught, on the Baetis (Guadalquivir), as far as Córdoba, and on the Guadiana, the Tagus, and other rivers.

For mercantile transactions and the service of the State the Romans coined money, replacing the ancient Phœnician and Carthaginian coins by Roman. But they allowed many indigenous cities to go on coining their own, with their own signs and inscriptions in Iberian and Phœnician letters.

25. *Intellectual Civilization.* In the intellectual order the Romans distinguished themselves above all as cultivators of the sciences—of law (jurisprudence) and of the practical sciences (agriculture, surveying, etc.). In other kinds of culture they imitated the Greeks. In this way, under a Roman dress, Greek influence spread through all the provinces, leaving its mark on the civilization of the world.

Roman public education comprised two grades: the primary school (*schola*, *ludus literarius*), and what we can properly call secondary and higher education (*artes* and *disciplinae liberales*). This latter contained two groups: the *trivium* (grammar, rhetoric, and dialectic), and the *quadrivium* (arithmetic, geometry, " music " and astronomy). There were several of these schools in Spain. The Romans also founded special schools for the study of Jurisprudence, but it is not proved that there were any of these in the Peninsula.

The Spaniards absorbed Roman culture to such a degree

D

that many of them figure among the most distinguished
men of science and letters of that time—writing in the most
elegant Latin. The chief of these are: the Cordovan,
L. A. Seneca, a moral philosopher whose doctrines were
not unlike those of Christianity; Quintilian, native of
Calahorra, professor and author of the best Latin treatise
on rhetoric; Lucan, a Cordovan poet and orator; Martial,
satiric poet, born in Calatayud; the Andalusians, Columella
and Pomponius Mela, the former, a writer on agriculture,
the latter, a Cosmographer; and certain political orators
and lawyers. Caius Julius Hyginus, director of the Palatine
Library, in the time of Augustus, was also a Spaniard, as
were several Emperors, already noted, certain of whom
were renowned for their learning in the sciences and arts.
The so-called Silver Age of Roman literature, which lasted
from the beginning of the 1st century until A.D. 117, is full
of Spanish names, whose spirit informed the culture of all
this epoch.

Alongside of this literature, Latin but pagan, there
developed a Christian literature, also in Latin, whose principal representatives were the religious poets Juvencus and
Prudentius, the latter a native of Tarragona or Calahorra.

As regards the literature in native dialects, not a single
work is known. Strabo affirms that such existed, though he
does not state whether this was before or during the Roman
Occupation. At any rate they were eclipsed by the writing
in Latin, which, as the result of Romanization, was the
most widespread idiom. The people did not speak the
same language as the men of letters, but debased forms of
it, which made up what was known as (*sermo rustica*), in
which the words and phrases exhibited modifications and
new and impure forms.

26. *Monuments.* The Romans gave a great impulse to
public works of all kinds, in which they displayed their
artistic culture—largely inherited from the Greeks—and
which intermingled with forms that had already been
introduced into Spain (§ 11). Many such works have
come down to us, as well as numerous examples of artistic

Photo, Arxiv Mas.

THE " BULLS " OF GUISANDO : near Avila

objects. We will cite as examples, beyond those which have already been enumerated in another context (§ 27): the Temple of Mars at Mérida; the triumphal arches of Bará (Tarragona), Martorell and Cabanes; the tomb, said to be that of a lady called Cornelia, at Bará; the *barros saguntinos*, that is to say, objects in pottery, of the Roman type, made in Saguntum, Tarragona and other places, the mosaics of Gerona, Nova (León), Elche, Moncada, and elsewhere; the silver cup with bas-reliefs of Otañes (Castro-Urdiales); the silver disc of Theodosius, found in Almendralejo, and numerous statues of gods, emperors, and other personages, among them the head of the goddess Roma, found in Itálica; the Mercury of Saguntum; the Trajan and the supposed Hadrian of Itálica, and many others. We only know the name of one Spanish-Roman sculptor, who signed himself Caius Antelius Aulinus (Mérida).

The Iberians and Celts also continued to make what they needed in their own manner, which was very distinct from the Roman. The chief objects of this indigenous art are: tombs, with statues (such as those of warriors, found in Galicia and Portugal), bas-reliefs and paintings; bronze idols with human forms, and the statues of quadrupeds (bulls, wild boars, pigs, and horses), examples of which are the celebrated bulls of Guisando (Avila) and those found in other places in Castille. Many of these monuments have Iberian inscriptions.

III

CHRISTIANITY

27. *Christianity*

THE Romans, though they had organized religion as a real part of their administration, dependent upon the State, were not intolerant, and accepted the gods of other peoples without scruple, and without putting any obstacle in the way of the most varied cults. In Spain they respected the religious ideas of the natives, though they never ceased to propagate their own, which, as a result of Romanization, became widespread in the Peninsula. Thus Jupiter, Diana, Ceres, Venus, and other gods worshipped by the Romans, came to be popular divinities in Spain.

But the Christian religion came to birth in the time of Augustus, that is to say, when the military conquest of the Peninsula was complete (§ 18). It was soon preached there by St. Paul and some of his disciples, as it is believed, so that already in the 2nd century, and still more in the 3rd, there were numerous Christian communities in Spain. These, like all others of their kind, suffered from the effects of the persecution which Nero, Domitian, and other Emperors waged against the Christians, sealing their faith with many martyrs in Barcelona, Valencia, Toledo, Saragossa, and other places. Religious peace was restored at the beginning of the 4th century, and soon after the Christian Church became an official institution protected by the State. The number of proselytes grew with extraordinary rapidity, while at the same time ecclesiastical administration was organized. Many bishoprics were created and certain Councils met (those of Illiberis, Saragossa and Toledo) and were distinguished by the rigidity of their ideas and the orthodoxy of their doctrines. One Spanish bishop, Hosius, was President of the Council of Nicæa, and enjoyed great prestige in the Christian world. In this way the Spaniards contributed energetically to the establishment and consolidation of the doctrines peculiar to the Catholic Church.

Yet the ancient religious beliefs of the Iberians, Celts, and Romans were not entirely obliterated. They persisted in many places, either in their original form, or producing, within Christianity itself, doctrines in disagreement with the doctrine that was considered legitimate and orthodox. Such deviations were known as heresies; the chief of them was that of Priscilian and his followers, who lived in Galicia; it continued until the 6th century.

28. *Social and Political Effects.* With its doctrines of peace and charity, of indifference to earthly possessions, of love of one's neighbour, of purity and simplicity of life, the Christian religion held the seed of a radical transformation of the Roman world. Yet its influence was limited, as regards social and political institutions. Various causes contributed to this—the evolutionary, internal, ethical meaning of its propaganda, and of what one might call its policy in the early centuries, which disdained all violent self-imposition, and clearly separated its sphere of action from the political power; the great difficulty that always exists in transforming a change of individual belief into a change of social conduct; the fact that the Church, as a human institution, was obliged to rely on the established social order at the time of its birth—because of all this, though Christianity preached brotherhood and counselled landowners to free their slaves, or at least to better their condition (it did not suppress slavery) rather, on the contrary, it adapted itself to it. Thus, the priests and the Churches possessed slaves, as did the ancient Romans. And though they demanded a vow of poverty as a condition of spiritual salvation, and the apostles and certain early Christians had all things in common, the new religion did not change the existing forms of property, nor did it cast from its bosom the rich and those who held land.

Thus the Church itself accumulated lands, flocks and houses, and many of the clergy dedicated themselves to commerce, although this was forbidden. Finally, Christianity did not try to change the political order in the slightest degree, though it fiercely denounced despotism, and preached the theory that kings should be the guardians and not the owners of their people.

But though Christianity could not insist upon all the ideals that made up its doctrines, it always preached them as counsels of perfection, and succeeded in attracting to them individual men. Those who followed them formed a group of elect, who withdrew from the world, renounced all the riches and comforts of life, and broke the ties of family and friendship. Thus there came into being anchorites, hermits, and, lastly, monks, who lived in communities, with a triple vow of poverty, chastity, and obedience, and were dedicated above all to the salvation of their souls. Yet these same monks, as we shall see, adapted themselves in part to the conditions of ordinary life. Their communities, if not the individual monks, possessed slaves, property and, as time went on, even political power. Of the social influence obtained by certain of them, and by the whole Church, we shall speak elsewhere.

The Christians built themselves special monuments, which differ in some respects from those of the pagans. Yet in type they were copied from these, as is seen in the *lucernarias*, entirely Roman, but with Christian insignia. Their most remarkable constructions are their sepulchres, such as the 4th century tomb which can be seen in the Archaeological museum at Barcelona, that of Albuera, Berja, and many others.

IV

THE DOMINATION OF THE VISIGOTHS

(5TH-8TH CENTURIES)

29. *The Barbarians in Spain*

THE Roman domination came to an end in Spain, as in all the other Provinces of the Empire, through the invasion of the Barbarians, inhabitants of Northern Europe, who slowly invaded the lands of the Centre and South. In Spain there were two invasions: that of the Suevi, Vandals and Alani, in 409, who wrested from Roman rule the greater part of Galicia, Lusitania, the Carthaginense and Baetica; and that of the Visigoths, who, in 414, took possession of certain parts of Catalonia. Later the Visigoths entered into an alliance with the Roman Emperors, renounced their conquests in Spain, and fought against the other barbarians, so as to drive them out, yet with intervals in which they fought for their own hand. The destruction of the Western Roman Empire in 476 made the Visigoths entirely independent. Some years before, they had conquered and politically annihilated the Alani; they caused the Vandals to emigrate to Africa (429) and in 585 they also succeeded in destroying the kingdom of the Suevi in Galicia. In 554 there had come into the Peninsula, as auxiliaries in a political revolution, troops of the Eastern Roman Empire (Byzantium), who, as a reward for their help, occupied for about a hundred years the greater part of Andalucía and the provinces of the East Coast. In the beginning of the 7th century the Gothic king Suintila drove them out of Spain. This episode of Byzantine domination was not without importance in the civilization of Spain. Nevertheless, the greater part of the new element was Germanic.

30. *Civilization of the Visigoths.*   The culture of the Germanic tribes was inferior to that of the Romans; yet it was not non-existent.   The earliest mention we find of them is in the 4th century B.C.   Divided into tribes, like the Iberians and the Celts, they lived as nomads, for the most part, given over to hunting and the rearing of flocks and herds.   Later they formed villages or small fixed settlements, and began to cultivate the ground.   Their civilization grew through contact with the Romans.   Towards the end of the 1st century they already built houses of brick, inhabited by a whole family.   They had also changed their primitive arms of stone and wood for arms of metal.

There were distinctions between the aristocracy, the people, and the slaves.   The last, together with the women, carried on the work of agriculture.   The men were generally tall, strong and fair-haired, and were given over to hunting and warfare.   They wore their hair long as a sign of freedom.

The nucleus of society was the family, and groups of families of the same stock formed separate units.   They were governed at times by elected kings, at times by assemblies or councils, of a varying number of members.   Certain Germanic peoples had two assemblies, one aristocratic and the other popular.

Within the family the father enjoyed absolute power over his sons, and marriage was carried out by purchase of this power, which the suitor effected by giving, according to his means, a certain quantity of horses, arms, etc., to the father.

Their religious ideas, like those of the Romans, admitted certain gods who were personifications of natural forces, and whose cults were very similar to those practised by the Iberians.   But almost all the Germanic tribes were soon converted to Christianity.

Of all these the Visigoths were the most cultured, because, before coming to Spain, they had lived for a long time in peaceful contact with the Eastern Romans (from 270 to the end of the 4th century).   To this influence was due their

conversion to Arianism, a sect which denied the divinity
of Christ, the mystery of the Trinity, and other dogmas of
the Roman Church.

Yet their civilization was much less than that of the
Romanized Spaniards, and many of its characteristics
differed widely.

31. *Attitude towards the Spaniards.* The influence of the
Visigoths in Spain was, on the whole, very small, except in
the realm of politics, where, thanks to their position of
conquerors, they could impose their will. Yet, like almost
all the ancient peoples, they respected to a great extent the
juridical and social independence of the vanquished,
recognizing their social order and their laws to be of Roman
origin. At the beginning of the 6th century these laws were
revised and collected in a code, known as that of Alaric,
because of the king who ordered and authorized its preparation. The Visigoths, for their part, also formulated
a code of laws, based on Germanic customs, clauses of which
were applied to the relations between the Visigoths and the
mixed Visigothic-Spanish-Roman population. Euric was
the king who ordered this codification, which was later
corrected and amplified by other kings.

The Germanic tribes in Spain put into practice the law
of partition which held sway in the last centuries of Roman
occupation, in favour of the auxiliary troops of the Empire.
Two-thirds of the land and half the houses were given
to the victorious troops, and also perhaps part of the
slaves and agricultural implements. It is certain that the
Suevi made this division in the North-West. The Visigoths
are thought not to have carried it out entirely, but in part.

As regards religion, though there were cases of intolerance against Roman Catholics (due more to political
reasons than to differences of creed) the Visigothic kings
generally respected the faithful and their clergy. There
was a popular proverb to the effect that the conquerors
paid equal reverence to the heathen altars and to those
of the Church, and a priest of Marseilles of the 5th century,
Salvianus, writes in praise of the tolerance of the Visigoths,

and of the respect in which they held a religion not their own.

As regards Spanish participation in the Government, though naturally most of the public posts were reserved for the Visigoths, Euric and other kings gave places, sometimes very important ones, to persons of indigenous or Roman stock. The provincial aristocracy, that is to say, rich people who collected taxes (§ 21), succeeded in entering all political organizations, side by side with the Visigothic lords.

32. *Conversion to Catholicism: its Consequences.* Yet the difference in religion kept up an eternal suspicion between the two races, the conquering and the conquered, among whom mixed marriage was prohibited, by a law of Roman origin. These religious differences had a great influence on certain civil upheavals in which the Catholics always sided with the opposition to the civil power, and were openly at war with the Byzantines. It was, therefore, in the interests of the Gothic monarchy that such a cause of strife should disappear, and this desire, together with the preaching of certain Catholic bishops, led to the conversion of King Reccared (587 or 589) and of many nobles, who abjured Arianism. At the same time, the Roman Catholic Church was raised to an official standing.

Many of the Visigoths, notwithstanding, remained faithful to their own religion, and provoked more than once serious revolts. As the result of Reccared's action, the Spanish-Roman population came into closer union with the powers of state, and the higher clergy began to intervene directly in the government of the country, by means of the Councils of Toledo. These were deliberative assemblies, which the king summoned freely, and at which were present bishops, abbots, and those nobles who held high positions in the administration. The king consulted them upon the laws which he proposed, and on the measures of government which he thought necessary, while the council merely gave its opinion.

The clergy present had also the privilege of proposing

laws; but the adoption of these proposals and of the opinion of the Council on matters about which the king had consulted it, depended solely on the will of the monarch, who, in important matters, always acted as he had proposed to do. Yet many of the decisions of the Council are merely a reflection of the juridical and moral doctrines of the Church.

33. *Juridical Unity.* The conversion of Reccared was not sufficient of itself to effect political unity. Other bonds were needed to unite the two races. So the ban on mixed marriages was removed, and King Chindaswinth, after having abolished, as is thought, the code of Alaric, mingled the Roman and Germanic elements of the code of Euric and imposed this as the common law on all subjects of both races. Yet the majority of the laws contained in this new code were inspired by the customs of the Visigoths, those of the Romans being forgotten. This was so in the distinction between social classes, and the relations of overlords and their subordinates (*buccelarii*) and slaves; in the forms of property; in part, in the laws of inheritance, and in the constitution of the family. Thus the dowry was generally paid by the bridegroom to the bride's father as a price of purchase of power over her. The following customs became general: common rights over property acquired during marriage; usufruct by the widow; the common ownership of hills and woods, and other juridical forms, which were foreign to the Roman type, and were more similar to the Iberian. This similarity was especially noticeable in the penal code, which left a great deal of freedom to private initiative in the punishing or pardoning of offences. This could be done either by vengeance, or by pecuniary indemnification, agreed upon between the offender and the offended or his family. This closed the road to any punishment on the part of the State.

This new code, which was revised by King Receswinth, and the Latin text of which has come down to us under the name of "*Liber Iudiciorum*," was added to by later kings, and continued to hold good in Spain after the disappearance of Visigothic rule (§ 46).

34. *Social Inequality.* The part of the Roman tradition which the Visigoths did not change was that of social inequality (§ 22). They continued the economic and personal subordination of the poor, small-holders, industrial workers, and in general every free man who did not belong to the nobility, especially among the rural population. The principal cause of this dependence, in which the mass of the people ranged themselves under the privileged classes, was the insecurity of life, and the fact that there was constant fighting in those times, while the State was not vigorous enough to protect its citizens. Thus those who lacked the strength to make themselves respected on their own account sought a protector or patron, agreeing to serve him, or paying him fixed dues, in exchange for his protection. When a man who entered into such an agreement was a freeman and a soldier, he was called *buccelarius* and received from his lord arms and goods, and the right to break such a pact when he wished. In distinction from these, there existed a class of labourers (*coloni*), who never left their overlord's land, which they cultivated, and for which they paid him rent. This class began in the time of the Roman occupation, and developed greatly in the days which we are studying now.

Slavery was so general an institution that even the churches and monasteries, as we have already said, possessed slaves of their own, both for the cultivation of their lands and for personal service.

The Jews, of whom there were great numbers in Spain, suffered severely under the Visigoths. Until Reccared's time their religious liberty was respected, but their fate soon changed rapidly. A king called Sisebut obliged them to be baptized, under pain of expulsion. Many were converted and others fled, coming back to Spain years later. But at the Eighth Council of Toledo laws of persecution were again passed and these were more strictly enforced at the end of the 7th century.

35. *Culture.* The fall of the Roman Empire, and the invasion of the Germanic peoples, produced everywhere a

decline in intellectual development. The Visigoths did not hold learning in much account, though certain of their kings and nobles are known to have collected important libraries. The true cultured class was the clergy, who nursed the remains of Latin science and literature in the primary and higher schools of the churches. Hence it came about that the most illustrious men of these times were always priests. The chief of them was Saint Isidore, Archbishop of Seville, who, in a characteristic manner united in his own person all the learning of his age. He was the author of many books of morality and history, and of a sort of encyclopædia or compendium of Graeco-Roman knowledge, known as the " *Etymologies.*" Mention should also be made of Orosius, author of the first universal history.

Though the Visigoths continued to use their own language and script for some time, they ended by abandoning them (especially after the conversion of Reccared) and by adopting Latin.

The Jews, on their part, had academies of their own, chiefly of a religious character, in which the professor read and commented upon the sacred writings in their national language, Hebrew. Hebrew, along with Chaldean, was also cultivated by the Catholic clergy. Thus Oriental, as well as Græco-Roman, literature, began to have an influence in Spain.

The Byzantines made their influence felt, not only by their domination in the South and South-East, where the descendants of the ancient Greek colonies continued to speak their language, but also by the constant communication between the Visigothic clergy and that of the East. This influence was felt most of all in the arts.

Of these we have found very few authenticated remains, but such as there are present important modifications or degenerations of the Roman type, and constitute what is known as Visigothic art. Mention may be made of certain capitals, found in Toledo, Mérida, Córdoba and other places; stones with reliefs, such as those of Ecija and Mértola; crowns and crosses of gold, ornamented with precious stones of a distinctly Oriental type, and coins also of gold.

As regards buildings, though much mention of them remains in writing, in general they have not come down to us in a state of preservation. Among those supposed to date from the Visigoths are the Church of San Juan at Baños de Cerrato (7th century?) ; that of San Miguel at Tarrasa (6th century); that of the Cristo de la Luz (Toledo), at any rate in its foundations and design; and that of San Román de la Hornija, destroyed by later reconstructions. It appears that not all these attributions are well-founded. Yet it is interesting to note certain salient characteristics of these churches. The general plan of the Basilica is of a Latin or Byzantine type (Greek Cross). The presbytery is usually of a horseshoe shape, as are also the arches leading into the nave. The horseshoe arch was already known to the Spanish-Romans, and belonged, therefore, in Spain to an older tradition than that of the Muslims.

Visigothic fortifications were similar in type to those of the Romans, as is seen in certain remains of them that have been found : Ercavica or Cabeza del Griego, Evora (Portugal, dating from the reign of King Sisebut), Toledo (said to date from King Wamba), and Córdoba, the so-called Puerta de Sevilla, which perhaps goes back to the 6th century.

Photo, Arxiu Mas.

CÓRDOBA: THE MOSQUE

V

MUSLIM DOMINATION

(8TH-11TH CENTURIES)

36. *The Muslim Hegemony*

AT the beginning of the 8th century (A.D. 711), Muslim
troops from Africa invaded the Peninsula and six
years later they were the lords of all Spain, except certain
small districts in the North (parts of Cantabria and the
Pyrenees). The conquerors made their political centre at
Córdoba, where the governor (*amīr*) resided, depending
upon the Caliph, who held his court in Asia. This situation
changed in A.D. 758, with the revolt of a noble of royal
stock, 'Abdu'r-Raḥmān I, who arrived in Spain from the
East and set up an independent kingdom, one of the most
prosperous and respected in the world.

Until the beginning of the 11th century (A.D. 1031) this
power held sway and constituted the most important political and civilizing force in the Peninsula, although certain
groups of Christians had begun the reconquest of the
country, and either alone, or with the help of foreigners,
founded the new kingdoms of Asturias-Galicia, León-
Castille, Navarre, and the Condado (Earldom) of Barcelona. The territories occupied by these kingdoms were,
until the above date, very small compared with those
occupied by the Muslims, and their culture was very scanty,
without life of its own.

37. *Attitude towards the Spanish People.* The new conquerors represented an element very different from the
Roman or Visigothic—not only in their religion, but in their
whole attitude to life. Like the Visigoths, however, they
did not try entirely to destroy the personality of the con-

47

quered. In spite of the intransigent character of certain
Muslims (*i.e.*, the Berbers, or Moors, inhabitants of North-
West Africa), and in spite of the cruelty revealed in some of
their campaigns (that of Aragon, for example), in general
they respected the religious ideas and practices of the
Spanish people, their laws, customs, and, to a great degree,
even their property. Thanks to this tolerance, and to the
liberty conceded to all their subjects and slaves who embraced the religion of Islam, they did not meet with much
resistance on the part of the inhabitants. Moreover, a
considerable number of Spaniards found themselves living
in their former districts and towns, subject only to the
political domination of the Muslims and to the payment of
tribute. These people were called *Mozárabes* (Ar. *musta'rib*,
" would-be Arab "). The toleration practised by the
conquerors in matters of religion only changed once, and
that for a short period.

Many Christians were converted to the new religion,
constituting a class of renegades who, though in bad odour
with the pure Muslims, had the strongest influence in
politics, and promoted certain formidable revolts.

The Jews also gained by the change of masters, as the
Muslims abolished the restrictive laws of the Visigoths.

38. *Government and Social Organization.* The Muslim Spanish State was a hereditary, absolute monarchy. The
amīr, latterly caliph, had under him various ministers or
viziers (*wazīr*), heads of different branches of the administration (*dīwān*) presided over by the prime minister (*hājib*).
A provincial governor was termed a *wālī*. There was a
council of state (Arabic *mashwāra*, Spanish *mexuar*); and the
organization of justice was highly developed, consisting of
judges (*qāḍī*) and other officers: *zalmedina*, or *zabalmedina*,
magistrate [Ar. *sāhib al-madīna*, master of the city] and
mustasāf [police-officer] who acted either in judicial matters
or in other kinds of business which lay in their charge.

The army commander was called the Kaid (Ar. *al-qā'id*,
Sp. *alcaide*), and the most common form of warfare
was the raid (Ar. *al-ghāra*, Sp. *algara*), carried out in

spring for the destruction of crops and the taking of booty. There also existed a species of military order [volunteers who lived on the frontier in a fortified camp] known as *ribāṭ*, Sp. *rápita*. Almanzor (Al-Manṣūr, 10th century), reorganized the army, substituting a system of regiments for the former tribal units.

The same social classes existed as among all peoples of that time: patricians, plebeians, and slaves. The last were labourers or personal servants. Distinct from these were the *eunuchs*, in personal attendance on the caliph and his wives, and those dedicated to military service. Among them, certain men, in spite of their position, came to occupy high political posts and to possess great riches and slaves of their own.

The Muslim family was polygamous. Each man might have as many as four legitimate wives, and as many concubines as his fortune allowed. But the first wife could exact from her husband a promise that he would have no others, under threat of divorce. Within the home, though the woman was subject to the man, she enjoyed a fair amount of liberty, including that of disposing of her goods without the permission of her husband.

All the fundamental laws of the social and political organization of the Muslims are contained (along with religious precepts and legends) in the Koran (*al-qur'ān*), and in the Sunna, or tradition of the Prophet. In Spain, the most copious work on the Sunna is the *Muwaṭṭa'* [" the thing made easy "] of Mālik ibn Anas (8th century).

39. *Muslim Culture.* The Spanish Muslims were eager for learning. Although there was no system of public instruction, as we understand it to-day, private schools abounded in every town—either foundation schools, with endowments of their own, or schools subscribed to by the pupils themselves. The first grade included reading the Koran and writing, poetry, examples of letter-writing and grammar. Higher education included the religious traditions, and a commentary on the Koran; grammar, medicine, philosophy, jurisprudence and literature, which included his-

tory, etc. Although the Muslims had received the basis of most of these subjects from classical antiquity, especially from Greece, through the Byzantines and the Romanized settlements of Asia and Egypt, they gave them an original and very powerful development, and so became the most cultivated people of those times.

The branches of learning chiefly cultivated were: poetry, history, philosophy, law and the natural sciences. Among the poets there were certain illustrious women. The language in which literary and scientific works were written was naturally Arabic, but the existence of a vulgar tongue, much mixed with Latin and romance words, can be affirmed (§ 48). This was employed even for official purposes. The Spanish Muslims cultivated popular poetry, sung by minstrels. Its metrical forms, which we know chiefly from the Song-book or *Cancionero* of Abencuzmán (Ibn Quzmān, 1126-1150), must have had an influence upon the Provençal lyric (which in its turn had an influence on Christian Spain); and its effects are particularly noticeable in the *Cantigas* of Alfonso el Sabio (§ 54). Similarly, it seems probable that the music of the popular singers of Andalucía spread very quickly through the rest of the Peninsula, and thence, later, to the whole of Europe.

The Jews also distinguished themselves greatly in poetry, philosophy, and medicine, contributing to the splendour of the society in which they lived.

Not less important than letters were the arts, in which the Muslims were disciples of the ancient Asiatic peoples (Chaldeans, Assyrians, Persians) and of the Byzantines. They succeeded, however, in inventing new forms. These are seen above all in their architecture, which differs greatly in style from any architecture known until then in Spain. The principal buildings of Arab or Muslim architecture are those dedicated to religion, the Mosques (Ar. *masjid*, Sp. *mezquita*). These generally consisted of an entrance court, a tower or minaret (Ar. *al-manāra*, Sp. *alminar*) from which the muezzin (Ar. *al-mu'addhin*, Sp. *almuédano*) announced the hours of prayer in a loud voice.

CÓRDOBA, FROM THE ROOF OF THE MOSQUE

(The tower was rebuilt in the 17th cent.)

Photo, Arxiv Mas.

CÓRDOBA: THE MOSQUE
Arches built by 'Abdu'r-raḥmān II

Within, there were several naves and a vaulted niche (*mihrāb*), without any image but facing towards Mecca [and, while standing before the niche, the *imām* directed the prayers of the faithful]. The finest example of a Spanish mosque is that of Córdoba, built between the 8th and 10th centuries, in which Arab architects utilized much material from former Christian and Roman constructions. The fundamental traits of Arabic building and decoration are: the horse-shoe arch, although, as has already been pointed out (§ 35), this was not a Muslim invention and dates from much earlier; columns, often taken from earlier buildings; the cupola, over a square base; arabesques or plaques of marble or plaster, incised with geometrical or floral designs, with a red or blue ground and gold relief; glass mosaics (ante-chamber of the Miḥrab) and glazed tiles in relief, which adorned the walls. As examples of civil buildings of this epoch should be mentioned the palaces of Medina Azzahra and of Alamiría (Córdoba), whose remains show us plans and methods of construction and decoration that are very remarkable. The artistic industries which flourished especially were pottery (plates and dishes with golden lustre; coloured tiles, etc.); work in gold (lamps, the hilts and scabbards of swords, jewel chests with carved plaques of precious metals and ivory) and textiles (wool and silk, tapestries, etc.).

40. *The Variety of Muslim Life.* The admirable development of scientific, literary, and artistic culture in Spain under the Muslims, rested on a firm basis of general prosperity in all classes. The Muslims encouraged the progress of agriculture, both by bettering the conditions of the agricultural labourers (the greater number of them, Mozárabes, § 37), by introducing new crops (rice, pomegranates, sugar cane), and by extending and regulating the system of irrigation. They also stimulated stock-raising and mining, and both established and developed to a great degree the textile industries of wool and silk (Córdoba, Málaga, and Almería), of esparto grass (Murcia), glass (Almería), writing-paper instead of parchment (Játiva), arms (Al-

meríca, Murcia, Seville, Toledo, Granada, and Córdoba), plain tanned and embossed leather (Córdoba), worked ivory, glass (invented in the 9th century), and other industries. In connection with this industrial movement there was great commercial activity, especially in the Mediterranean. For the Muslim fleets were the greatest of those days, and their chief ports of import and export were Seville, Málaga and Almería. The principal markets for Spanish products were North-West Africa, Egypt, Constantinople, the shores of the Black Sea (by which communication with Central Asia and India was later established), and those of Western Asia (Palestine, etc.). To cope with the vast exchange operations of so active a commercial life, the Caliphs struck numerous coins in gold, silver, and copper, whose basic types were the *dīnār* (gold) worth about 8*s.* 4*d.*, and the *dirhem* (silver), about 10*d.* By the beginning of the 10th century the public revenues had risen to the equivalent of about $2\frac{1}{2}$ million sterling.

The economic prosperity and political power were reflected in the luxury and wealth of civil life. Córdoba came to have 200,000 houses, 600 mosques, and 900 public baths. The streets were paved with stone, and water was brought to the town by means of conduits. The houses, whose façades showed but few windows, expressed their love of cleanliness on the outside by whitewash that was always fresh, and within by their fountains, their white walls, their gay decorations; and the life lived within them must have been very pleasant. The palaces of the Caliph, the nobles and the great landowners were sumptuous, as were also the mosques. The chief of these had twenty-one doors and 1,293 columns of marble and jasper, with gilded capitals. Its pulpit was of marble and precious stones, and hundreds of lamps illuminated it, many of them of silver. Travellers from all parts of the world came ceaselessly to visit the city and its surroundings, and other parts of the Spanish Caliphate: Muslims, from Africa and Asia, and Europeans, Frenchmen, Italians and Spaniards from the North. Thanks to the religious toleration of which we have spoken, foreign monks were frequently to be seen in Córdoba, and were given hospitality in the various monasteries in the neighbourhood.

41. *The Christian Kingdoms. Their Relations with the Muslims.* The Christian kingdoms established in the North of Spain were composed of indigenous and Visigothic elements, while in certain regions (Navarre and Catalonia) there were French strains. They were far from being on the same level—economic or intellectual—as the Cordovan kingdom. Although these kingdoms stretched, in the Centre and West, to the range of the Carpeto-Vetónica and the Douro, and to the East as far as the Ebro (Navarre) and the Llobregat (Catalonia), and though certain of their monarchs and leaders achieved great things, they were almost always over-ruled by the political power of the Caliphs, who not only caused them to recoil more than once before their onslaughts, but who also frequently intervened in the rôle of auxiliaries and arbitrators. The Caliphs' help was sought by the Christians themselves in the civil wars of Asturias, León, Castille, etc.—wars which arose over the succession to the throne, or through quarrels between the kings and the nobility. This subordination of the Christian kingdoms to the Muslims, resulting from the feebleness of the former and their inevitable recognition of superiority of the latter, brought about very close relations between the two, in spite of frequent wars. In periods of peace, or in places where there was no fighting for the moment, Christians and Muslims visited one another constantly, trading and intermarrying, for in those days neither side showed any acute feeling of religious intolerance. The upper classes and the kings themselves set the example, as is seen in the marriage of the daughter of the Aragonese Count, Aznar Galindo, with the Moorish governor of Huesca, Muḥammad Ataghil; that of a son of this marriage with a daughter of the King of Navarre; that of a granddaughter of the Christian commander, Iñigo Arista, with the Córdovan prince, 'Abdu'llāh, grandfather of the Caliph, 'Abdu'rrahmān III; that of Alfonso VI with

Zaida, daughter of the Muslim King of Seville (at the end of the 11th century), and perhaps the two marriages of the famous Almanzor (al-Manṣūr) with Christian princesses. It is interesting to note that, although disparity of religion was no obstacle to these unions, there were cases in which the Christian woman abjured her religion, with the consent of her family, and went over to Islam.

On the other hand, Christians abounded in Muslim towns, not only as Mozárabes, properly speaking (§ 37), but as temporary emigrants, and above all as soldiers in the service of the Caliphs. They sometimes even held high positions as public functionaries. Almanzor had in his pay several battalions of men from León, Castille, and Navarre, and certain counts of the kingdom of León helped him in his campaigns. Similarly, it was not unusual for Muslim troops to fight side by side with Christian troops, either against other Christians or against Muslims. Along the frontier marches the mixture was even greater. Here the Muslims who knew Spanish were called by their Christian neighbours *Moros latinados* or *Latinos*, whereas Christians who spoke Arabic were called *Cristianos algaraviados*.

To these strong reasons for reciprocal influence two others of extraordinary importance were added as time went on. As the Christians advanced towards the South, recovering some of the lands inhabited by the Muslims, there increased continually in the population of the kingdoms of León, Castille, Navarre, etc., three groups of newcomers: conquered Muslims, who either became slaves or remained at liberty in their own districts, but under the sovereignty of Christian kings, preserving, to a great extent, their own laws, customs, religion, etc. These were called *Mudéjares* (Ar. *mudajjan*, " left behind "). Secondly, Mozárabes (§ 38), who entered into relations with their co-religionaries, freeing themselves from Muslim domination. Thirdly, the Jews. These three groups, having been educated in Muslim territories, formed nuclei of influences of Arabic culture in the Christian countries.

42. *Muslim Influences on Culture.* This influence reacted

upon every sphere of life. Yet visible evidence of it is rare before the 11th century. A Cordovan writer of the 9th century, the martyr Alvaro (San Alvaro de Córdoba), mentions how strong it was amongst the Mozárabes. He says: " Many of my co-religionaries read the poems and stories of the Arabs, and study the writings of Muhammadan theologians and philosophers, not in order to refute them, but to learn how to express themselves most elegantly and correctly in the Arabic tongue. Alas! All the young Christians who become notable for their talents know only the language and literature of the Arabs, read and study Arabic books with zeal, and at enormous cost form great libraries of them, and everywhere proclaim aloud that their literature is worthy of admiration."

Arabic also penetrated to the Christian kingdoms, giving many words to the Romance languages then beginning to develop (§ 47), adding also mixed words, or altering Latin words through the influence of Arabic writing. In Christian documents of this time it is not unusual to see the signature of a Muslim, and in all probability some of them, above all treaties and communications of an international character, were written in Arabic. This is known to have been so later.

In the sphere of law and in administrative organization it is also certain that the spirit of imitation, stimulated by the superiority of certain Muslim institutions and the force of the customs acquired by the Mudéjares (§ 41), and Mozárabes, had their influence on the Christian kingdoms, but this also was little visible until the 11th century. Nevertheless, according to modern investigators, that of popular Arab music had already made itself felt in various countries in the 10th century (§ 39).

In order to explain why the Christians of the North were the most influenced by contact with the two peoples, one must not forget that the Northern regions, in which the reconquest began, were among the poorest, least populated (as is proved by the efforts of the kings to attract inhabitants), and the least thoroughly Romanized.

43. *The Mozárabes and their Contribution to Spanish Civilization.* On their part, the Mozárabes, the renegades, and those Christians who were living temporarily in Muslim territory also contributed certain elements of civilization, especially in the intellectual sphere. They translated Latin works (the Bible, the Canonical books); they compiled certain original books in Arabic; they brought manuscripts of Latin authors to the Mozarabic libraries, as did San Eulogio (9th century); they modified and enriched Arabic by forms borrowed from the Latin (*aljamía*, " foreign " or non-Arabic speech), which was spoken by the Mozárabes, certain of whose words and turns of speech passed into Spanish Arabic. Influences of Roman and Visigothic art may also have passed into Muslim architecture, both through the use of old materials (columns, capitals, etc.) and in technical constructive methods of building.

It is indubitable from the text of S. Alvaro quoted above that ecclesiastical schools of the Visigothic tradition (*i.e,* of the Catholic Visigoths), were still carried on by the Mozárabes in the cities of the Caliphate, thanks to Muslim toleration. These must have diffused something of their culture in the society around them. The names of certain Abbots who were directors of these schools stand out, *e.g.,* Spera-in-deo, Sampson, and others.

Furthermore, as the Reconquest advanced, and the Mozárabes entered anew into the territories and social life of the independent Christians, they brought with them and disseminated all that they had preserved of their ancient culture, together with what they had assimilated from the Muslims. To them, doubtless, and to the Mudéjares, is due a considerable part of the wealth of words of Arabic origin which were to be met with in Spanish, and which still persist. Alongside of this contribution, and as unmistakable, is their contribution to art. They created in the North, and in part of the centre of Spain a Christian architecture, much influenced by the Arabs, which a modern historian and art-critic had justifiably called

MOZARABIC ARCHITECTURE

San Miguel de Escalada, Burgos

" Mozarabic Architecture." Among the more or less complete examples of this style that remain to us are the Church
of San Miguel de Escalada (León), the work of monks who
had come from Córdoba; that of San Baudel de Berlanga
(Soria), that of Santa María de Melque (Toledo), those of
Lebeña, Peñalba, Celanova, and others. The architectural characteristics of these churches are the almost exclusive use of the horse-shoe arch and of a system of vaulting,
which did not exclude the occasional use of wooden roofs,
such as existed in the old basilicas. Many of these Mozarabic churches, constructed from the 9th to 11th centuries, were destroyed later by the invasions of the fanatical
Almorávides and Almohades. The most southerly of those
that remain to-day is that already mentioned at Melque
(early 10th century). This, together with that of San
Baudel (late 10th century), represents the most genuine
type of this style of architecture.

Upon the industrial arts (work in gold and other metals,
and in marble, and miniatures), the Mozárabes also set
their seal.

44. *European Influences.* But the Muslims were not alone
in influencing the Christian kings, and in giving an impulse
to their civilization. In Navarre, Catalonia, and Aragon,
especially in the two former, the Franks (who with Charlemagne and Saint Louis aided the first steps of the Reconquest) contributed many elements of their culture and social
and political organization.

It is true that the Spaniards, in their turn, contributed
in certain respects to Frankish civilization, thanks to the
personal assistance at the Court of Charlemagne of a
Spanish priest, Teodolfo, a continuer of the classical education of San Isidoro (§ 36), and one of the most illustrious
teachers of the Carlovingian reign. But the case of Teodolfo
is isolated, and entirely personal, although his influence is
reflected in other spheres than that directly subjected to
his spiritual guidance, as, for example, in the religious
architecture of certain districts of France. The greatest
number of Spaniards of those days, especially the refugees

in the new independent centres which were at war with the Muslims had, as we have already seen, scant culture and primitive organization. It was logical that they should try to imitate and assimilate all that they saw that might be profitable to them among the foreign peoples with whom they came in contact. This happened with the Franks in the districts which we have named. Their most recognizable influence was in politico-social organization; manors (*señorios*), counties (*condados*), laws, etc., §§ 45 and 46); in writing (the form of lettering known as French); in literature, in the plastic arts and in coins. The two chief instruments of Frankish influence were their domination in the districts already mentioned, and the clergy (especially the regular clergy), who often travelled, keeping up relations with foreign countries and continued to be the most cultured class.

Once Catalonia was independent, commercial and naval activity in the Mediterranean was extended, and this brought about contact with another people, the Italians, whose characteristics are already noticeable at this period, especially in architecture.

The Asturio-Leonese kingdom had also relations with European elements, but in a different form. The clergy, pilgrims, and foreign adventurers who were encouraged to take part with the Spanish troops in wars against the Muslims, were the means of introducing foreign customs and influences. Their centre seems at this time to have been Santiago de Compostela, famous in Europe because it possessed the tomb of the Apostle St. James, where pilgrims from all countries came together. The number of pilgrims was already very great in the 9th and 10th centuries, and produced a very flourishing industrial life there, with the acquisition of new inhabitants, chiefly of French origin.

It is thought that the Normans also left influences on architecture, although their sojourn in Galicia was brief, and of a purely military nature.

45. *Principles of Social Reconstruction of the Christian Monarchs*. The result of all these factors, intensified by the

necessities of a country which was beginning a new life
with scanty means, and by the survival among the inhabitants of older institutions (Hispano-Roman and Gothic),
is that the new Christian kingdoms offer an original frame-
work of institutions and culture, which varies greatly in
different localities.

Taking the general lines of these institutions, we may say
that the social basis of those times continued to be the
inequality of classes, much accentuated by the feeling of
dependence of the masses (the poor and the small-holders)
towards the minority (the nobility), who were the landlords and holders of public offices. A new element was the
institution of the clergy as a civil class, with prerogatives
and economic influence equal to that of the nobles.
Indeed, the kings and their subjects made great concessions of land to the churches and monasteries, granting
to the Bishops, Chapters and Abbots rights and powers
over the people, freemen or slaves, who lived there.
The relation which united freemen—whether nobles of
small fortunes or plebeians—with the rich men and the
privileged clergy was called *encomienda* or patronage (*cf.*
the relations between the *buccelarii* and their overlord, § 34).
Those under patronage gave at times, in exchange for
protection, all or part of the produce of their land, and
were always obliged to render their patrons certain services
and to pay certain taxes. But like the *buccelarii*, they could
break this dependence and seek also another patron, if
their original one did not suit them. Such also was the situation in which both the holders of lands and of industries
found themselves. With both types the social and economic dependence became so strong—owing to the turbu-
lence of the age, and the real difficulty of moving from one
place to another without running grave risks—that there
came about a really servile relationship, in which the protected, especially the plebeians, were usually no better
off than the old *coloni* (§ 22). They are called by various
names in the documents of the period (*criationes*, *familias*,
cassatas, *siervos*, etc.), and they formed the majority of

the rural population, were sold with the land that they cultivated and could not possess goods that were really their own; nor could they marry people of their own station who belonged to a different overlord. The hardships of their situation made them often rebel against their "protectors."

Such was the law until the 9th century in most of the lands of the Centre and West (Asturias, Galicia, León and Castille). But already, at the beginning of the 10th century, things changed greatly. Owing to the increase of population and to the greater security, the overlords became afraid and mitigated their tyranny. They offered the serfs possibilities of extricating themselves from their dependence. Many of them bettered their condition, either by obtaining their liberty or by diminishing the obligations that weighed upon them. Thus there grew up an intermediate class, which was called *juniores*, some members of which were only obliged to pay a personal tax to the overlord (*juniores de cabeza*); while others cultivated his lands as before, but might possess goods of their own and change their place of residence, although if they transferred themselves to lands belonging to the king or of another noble, they lost all their goods.

In Catalonia things happened differently. Thanks to the division of conquered territories made by the Frankish kings, there grew up alongside of the great landed proprietors a group of small independent proprietors (*allodiales* and *beneficiarii*) who constituted, as it were, a rural middle class, which existed right up to the end of the period of which we are now writing. On the other hand, the slaves born of the old *coloni*, and freedmen of the Visigothic epoch, instead of bettering their condition, as those in Castille were doing, went from bad to worse, and constituted the class that was later called *remensas* (§ 64). The clergy enjoyed wide privileges, as has already been stated. As great proprietors of lands and slaves the outstanding monasteries then were those of Bañolas, Amer, Roda, Camprodón, and others. These institutions helped greatly in the repopulation of the country, in its cultivation and in

the construction of castles for its defence—three things
essential in this part of Spain (as they were later to be in
others) because, thanks to the wars against the Muslims,
the land remained deserted and unpeopled, and as repopulation proceeded it was necessary to defend it from
fresh onslaughts. The name Catalonia was derived from
the abundance of castles and the military regime, as had
happened earlier with the name Castille. Before the 12th
century the Catalan district was called " Marca His-
panica "—the Spanish marches.

Of Navarre and Aragon little is known before the 11th
century.

46. *Political Organization.* In Asturias, and in the kingdoms derived from it, the monarchic form of government
of the Visigoths continued, along with the councils and
laws of the *Liber Iudiciorum* (or *Fuero Juzgo*). But the
kings lacked the authority and power which they had
enjoyed before. The small extent of their territories
in the early centuries, and the sparseness of population,
did not permit of their levying large taxes, nor of
keeping an army of their own. On the contrary, they
had to rely, for the carrying out of the Reconquest,
upon the nobles and upon any persons capable of
carrying arms or of leading men in war. Those who
lent their aid demanded privileges in return, or else
rebelled against the king and put the crown in jeopardy.
In order to pacify these rebellions, by removing the causes
of them, and also to attract partisans for themselves, the
monarchs gave lands to the nobles and clergy and waived
their claim to certain rights which before had belonged to
the kings alone, such as the right of collecting tribute from
the people, administering justice within certain limits,
giving certain laws, arming themselves in war, and even
coining money. This quasi-voluntary renunciation on the
part of the kings resulted in certain great lords, temporal
and spiritual, becoming petty kings within the limits of
their dominions (*señorios*, *tenencias*). Moreover, they were
exempt from paying tribute (as were sometimes also all

the men dependent upon them), and they might leave the service of their king and go off in search of another. Such action was termed *desnaturarse*. On his part, the king could banish those of his subjects who fell into disgrace, which was what happened to the Cid. It was this very exile which was the cause of the military expeditions which led the Cid to the conquest of Valencia, and gave him so great a reputation amongst the Muslims as a leader. The nobles lived in castles, solidly fortified, and in sites impregnable or very difficult of access, and from thence they menaced the power of the kings, sallied forth to war against other nobles, and also, frequently enough, to rob the people who journeyed on the roads.

Yet the monarchy did not entirely abandon its fundamental attributes. The concessions made were always revocable and had exceptions, which allowed of royal intervention.

The kings seized every favourable occasion to proclaim their right to establish royal judges in the towns and *alfoces* [the districts under their administration, Arabic, *al-hauz*], to enrol troops and command the army, and to promulgate laws, collect tribute and coin money.

At the same time, so as to ingratiate themselves with the populace, the natural enemy of the nobles, and to attract groups of the population and gain loyal subjects, they granted to various cities and towns privileges similar to those already accorded to the nobles and clergy. They were made, to a large extent, autonomous, and were exempted from tribute and service. Certain of them considered themselves to be places of sanctuary, so that any man who managed to reach them became entirely free, even if he were the escaped slave of a nobleman, or a criminal condemned by the law. All these factors led to the gradual development of the *municipios*, and their primitive form of government was by popular assembly (*concilium*, Spanish, *consejo*), whose executive representatives were a judge (*judex, juez*), and various *jurados, fieles* and *veedores*; this, however, did not exclude the functioning of royal jurisdiction at the same time. The document by which the king authorized such privileges received the name of *fuero*; and the charter which regulated the establishing of a town on the basis of territorial concessions to the inhabitants was generally called *carta puebla*. The nobles also could grant *fueros* and *cartas* in their lands, but only with the consent of the king.

Territory which belonged neither to the nobles nor clergy, nor to the *municipios*, was divided for purposes of government into districts (*mandationes*), presided over by a count (*conde*), whom the king appointed at will, and who exercised judicial, military and administrative functions, aided by a viscount (*vicario*) and an assembly of residents (*vecinos*).

In Catalonia, the Franks also divided the land into *condados* (counties), under the suzerainty of the monarch. The counts were at first merely delegates, who could be removed at will; but later the office became hereditary. That of Barcelona was considered as the most important, and carried the title of marquis. But gradually, as they declared themselves independent of the Frankish monarchy, the various *condados* remained without any closer relationship among themselves than the memory of the ancient supremacy of Barcelona, which maintained a certain prestige. As time went on, the great conquests achieved by the counts of Barcelona in territories occupied by the Muslims, and their annexation of certain of the original *condados*, changed these counts, *de facto*, into sovereigns of the whole territory, or at least established their political hegemony in Christian Catalonia.

The territories of Navarre and Aragon were more tardy in establishing a central power. At first every noble or great landowner fought for his own hand against the Muslims without any true organization of their forces. Later, at an uncertain date, they recognized a leader, whose monarchic qualities were accentuated as time went on. At the beginning of the 11th century the monarchy of Navarre was the most powerful of the Peninsula.

47. *Economic Life.* The hazards of those times did not allow of any great development in industry and commerce, nor even in agriculture, on account of the pillage and havoc of war. Moreover, the territories in which the Reconquest began were little suited for agriculture, being mountainous, cold, and wet. But the kings managed to stimulate cultivation by means of concessions to agriculturalists (especially in Catalonia), and by the right of *adprisión* or *presura*, according to which any man who ploughed uncultivated land could hold it lawfully, and even acquire it for his own. Other great promoters of agriculture were the monks, especially those of St. Benedict, who, throughout the Peninsula, dedicated themselves to tilling the soil. According to contemporary documents, the principal products of the Centre and West were wine, millet, oats, beans, honey, wax, wheat, and flax. The olive was unknown in Castille until later. In certain parts of Catalonia agriculture made a certain amount of progress.

As regards industry, the development was very limited. The most important trades seem to have been in Galicia—fishing and the salting of fish—a very old tradition (§§ 10-13); silversmith's work, and jet (*azabache*) for making the holy objects bought by the pilgrims to Santiago. The industries in connection with the elementary necessities of life (baking, shoe-making, spinning, and weaving) were, for the most part, carried on at home, and the production was small. In Catalonia they must have been more advanced, judging by the importance of Barcelona, already noted by the 10th century, both in commerce and as a port. Many of the industrial workers, especially the simple operatives, were slaves. They began to form guilds (*cofradías*) according to their trades. Articles of prime necessity were taxed in the majority of places, as were also the day labourers. Money was scarce, and either preserved the Roman types or was of Muslim or Frankish origin, and imported from abroad.

48. *Culture.* In spite of the elements mentioned above (§§ 43 and 44), culture was very deficient. This may be

MOZARABIC ART. BEATUS' COMMENTARY ON THE APOCALYPSE (975)

(*Gerona Cathedral*)

explained not only by the decadence of the old Roman civilization in the time of the Visigoths, but also by the new disturbances produced by the Muslim conquest, and by the difficulties that life offered in Christian territories, so that the chief care of the people was to defend their life and land from their enemies and to re-occupy the country. The clergy, especially the regular clergy (monks), who spent a more peaceful and retired life, was the class best able to dedicate itself to study and that which achieved the highest degree of culture. In the monasteries and churches were assembled the scanty libraries of the time, the monks dedicating themselves to copying on parchment rare or important books, and to compiling new ones, principally religious and historical (the *Cronicones* and *Crónicas*). The richest of these libraries seem to have been those of Oviedo, León, San Zacarías (Navarre), Ripoll, Vich, and, later on, others in León and Castille. The old Visigothic religious schools were continued (§ 35). That of the Bishop of Vich, Atón, was famous and received foreign students, chief among whom should be mentioned the monk Gerbert, who pursued his studies there, then went to Córdoba, was later secretary to Hugh Capet, and finally ascended the Papal throne under the name of Silvester II. In the last years of the 10th century and the beginning of the 11th, the school of Ripoll was also important, chiefly on account of the great qualities of Oliva, its Abbot and Bishop of Vich. Amongst the various studies then pursued in Catalonia, that of mathematics achieved a certain development. But the majority of the people, including the nobles, could neither read nor write. Amongst the more notable importers of Oriental culture was the Rabbi, Menahem ben Saruk (10th century), of the Synagogue of Tortosa.

The language in which books and documents were written and which was generally spoken, continued to be Latin, but it was a Latin already much modified and corrupted. The new forms which words acquired produced little by little the birth of new regional dialects: *Gallego* (Galician), *Leonés-Castellano*, *Aragonés*, *Catalán*, etc., which

F

were called *romances*.   The earliest writings known to employ many words of *romance castellano* date from the 10th and
11th centuries.   The current of formation of the new idiom
which these documents reveal was arrested at about the
middle of the 11th century by the Latin influence of the
Cluniac monks, but it began again later (§ 52).   To this
early stage of *romance castellano* belong the first epic poems,
cantares de gesta or " chansons de geste," inspired by the
most outstanding national figures, such as Count Fernán
González, in Castille, or by particularly typical and tragic
episodes in the annals of the time, such as that connected
with the *Infantes de Lara*.   The original versions of these
poems have been lost; but, recast and renewed later on,
they have come down in a fragmentary state to our own
time.

As regards Catalan, the first document known to us in
which it was employed seems to have been composed at a
later period than that with which we are now dealing (§ 54).

49.   *Architecture and Other Arts.   Dress*.   As was natural under
the circumstances, life, both public and private, took on a
very modest and little cultured aspect.   The buildings reveal
this, in the first place.   Certain constructions remained
from the Roman and Visigothic epoch, and were more or
less in ruin, their preservation depending upon their degree
of usefulness.   Those which were newly constructed were
small in size and scant in comfort.   The majority of them
were made of wood, or at least had wooden roofs.   In the
churches, monasteries, and palaces (the three most important types of building), the walls were of stone and the
roofs vaulted, while outside, to counteract the pressure of
the roofs, were buttresses.   Both the form of construction
and the ornaments preserved the old Roman or Visigothic
models, but in a degenerated form, and showing Byzantine
(§ 35), Arab, Frankish, and Italian influences (these last in
Catalonia).   The horse-shoe arch (§ 39), is common in
Asturian and Castilian churches.   In the Asturian churches
of the 11th century are already to be met that novelty and
variety of construction and decoration which single them

MOZARABIC ARCHITECTURE
(San Pedro de la Nave, Zamora)

out above others: Santa María de Naranco, San Miguel de Lillo, Santa Cristina de Lena, and, later on, the primitive basilicas of Santiago, Valdediós, Escalada, Sahagún, etc. In these, as in others further South (in the territories which belonged to the kingdom of León and of the future kingdom of Castille), influences of the older Spanish style of the Visigothic period are visible—that of those Spanish workmen who had been retained in the Muslim dominions; for, as we have already said, great social liberty was allowed them until the end of the 11th century, except in the period of Cordovan intolerance of the middle of the 9th. For this reason these antique churches have been called Mozarabic (§ 43). From the 10th century onwards until the end of the 11th, all the churches which we know in the Peninsula repeat and improve, with regional and local modifications—produced by the various influences already noted—the architectural directions begun in Asturias in the 9th century, with the addition of certain new elements, such as the rounded exterior apse (*e.g.*, San Cugat del Vallés), and the arched roof in the basilicas of Roman type as in Ripoll and Valdediós, etc.

Arabic influence is especially noticeable in gold and silversmith's work (coffers for relics, crosses, etc.), while French and Irish influences appear in the miniature-painting of manuscripts and in the frescos which once adorned the inside walls of churches and palaces. Clothes, very simple at first, but richer as time went on, also reveal foreign influences. So does the enamel work and sculpture, of which we have valuable examples in the doors of churches and sepulchres, frontals of altars, and retables (*retablos*). The chief public amusement was the chase, to which the kings and nobles were especially addicted. The people had their dances and songs, which were dedicated to recounting either pious legends (appearances of the Virgin or Saints), or to warlike episodes. There were very frequent quarrels, crimes, and robberies in desert places. Amongst the superstitions which most influenced the life of the time must be counted the "judgments of God" (taken from the Germanic peoples) or *pruebas vulgares*, which consisted in submitting the judgment on a criminal case to a duel between two people (*duelo judicial*), or to a chance circumstance (seizing a red-hot iron without being burnt, dipping the hand in boiling water, etc.).

Photo, Arxiv Mas.

HISPANO-MORESQUE POTTERY
(*Manises, Valencia, 14th cent.*)

VI

HEGEMONY PASSES TO THE CHRISTIAN KING-DOMS, AND A DISTINCTIVE NATIONAL CULTURE IS DEVELOPED

(11TH-15TH CENTURIES)

50. *Political Changes*

FROM the 11th century onwards the political situation of the Peninsula changed radically, with important consequences to all social life and culture. The Caliphate of Córdoba disappeared, breaking up into various " party-kingdoms " (Ar. *ṭā'ifa*, Sp. *taifa*), which, divided and at war amongst themselves, naturally offered less resistance than formerly to the attacks of the Christians. These took possession of Toledo in A.D. 1085, and of Saragossa in A.D. 1118, advancing also far in the South of Catalonia. Two new invasions by Berbers from Africa, the Almorávides and Almohades (" the Marabouts " and the " Unitarians ") momentarily checked the Christian advance at the end of the 11th and in the 12th centuries. But these were eventually overcome, and in the 13th century the King of Castille took possession of Córdoba, Seville, and, in general, all the North and West of Andalucía, while the King of Aragon conquered the kingdom of Valencia, Murcia, and the Balearic Isles. These facts transferred the political hegemony to the Christian element, in whose territories there came about an increase of population, wealth, and culture.

In the Christian states the following modifications took place: in the North West and Centre three kingdoms were formed: León (with Asturias and Galicia), Portugal, and Castille. The two former were definitely united in the 13th century; Castille declared itself independent in the middle of the 12th century and declined to unite with León. The territories of Navarre were divided into two kingdoms : Navarre and Aragon. The latter joined with Catalonia under one sovereign in the first half of the 12th century, to separate no more, and conquered extensive territories in Southern Italy (Sicily and Naples). The Basque provinces—autonomous, although under the influence either of Navarre or Castille, came definitely under the suzerainty of the King of Castille in 1200 (Guipúzcoa), in 1332 (Alava), and in 1370 (Biscay).

The Muslims became restricted to the kingdom of Granada, which included part of the province of that name, along with those of Almería and Málaga, as far as Gibraltar.

51. *Muslim Culture of this Period.* In spite of the changes indicated, and the political disorganization of the Muslim territories, their civilization not only maintained its former high level for a long time, but even grew in certain directions, and exercised an increasing influence on the Christian kingdoms. Industry and commerce continued in great prosperity until the 13th century, Córdoba, Seville, Almería, Valencia, and Mallorca excelled as mercantile centres, and had close relations with Italy, Africa, and the ports of the Asiatic coasts.

The most notable and abundant products of agriculture and commerce were: sugar-cane (Valencia and Seville), oil (Andalucía), silk (Granada), tanned leather (Córdoba), paper made from rags (Játiva), tapestry (Chinchilla and Cuenca), goldsmith's work, arms and ceramic ware (Seville, Mallorca, Valencia, etc.). After the Christian conquests of the 13th century commerce and industry remained in the hands of the Muslims (*Mudéjares*), who had made acts of submission. But these declined later, being partly assimilated by the Christians, or modified by them— as we shall see.

In architecture and its complementary arts the Muslims of Granada created a new type, related to that of Morocco,

GRANADA: THE ALHAMBRA. THE COURT OF LIONS

Photo, Arxiv Mas.

GRANADA: GENERALIFE

and characterized by the splendour of its decorative detail. The most famous and pre-eminent example of this is the Alhambra of Granada. The inhabitants of Granada also continued the flourishing tradition of certain industries, above all, agriculture, silk, goldsmith's work, and pottery.

But the sphere in which the Muslims chiefly shone during the two periods of the kingdoms of *Taifas* (11th to 13th centuries), was that of science and literature, and more especially in philosophy, medicine, astronomy, and mathematics, and in poetry and history. The Jews, numerous in Muslim districts, contributed greatly to this scientific and literary movement, which flourished most brilliantly in the 12th and 13th centuries. Their most illustrious representatives, both by reason of the importance of their doctrines and the influence they exercised all over Europe, were the Muslim philosophers Averroes, Avempace, and Abentofail (Ibn Ṭufayl), with the Jewish savants Ben Gabriol [known to the Latins as Avicebron], Ben Ezra, and Maimonides.

The principal service rendered to European culture by Muslim Spain was the transmission of Greek science— both philosophy (Plato, Aristotle, Empedocles) and other branches of learning, in a form that was partly a distortion, partly a restoration of the original. Thus they began the renaissance of classical civilization, which had been obscured since the destruction of the Roman Empire. Attracted by this novel method, many foreign students, French, English, German, and others, came to Spain and worked in the Arab schools, diffusing later throughout Europe the knowledge they had acquired. This movement was assisted also by the voyages of certain of the above-mentioned savants, especially Ben Ezra (1070-1139), who was in Italy, France, and England, and spread the ideas of the Spanish Jews in these countries.

It is to be noted that the majority of the Muslim and Jewish men of science in this, the most resplendent, epoch of their culture to which we now refer, lived in Christian territory, where they took refuge from the persecution to

which they were submitted by orthodox Muslim theologians and by the fanatical "Unitarian" emperors. Thanks
to this, their contact with the Christians and their influence
upon them were much greater than before, showing not
only an interest in Greek science, but an original mys-
tical philosophy. This was heterodox to a great extent as
regards Islamic dogma, but it counted among its disciples
some of the great Catholic writers. The three philosophers
who had the greatest influence on Spain in this sense were
Algazel (al-Ghazālī), Abenhazam (Ibn Ḥazm), and the
Murcian, Ibn 'Arabī.

From the 13th century onwards the philosophical movement declined noticeably, and although the monarchs of
Granada continued to patronize culture, founding schools
or academies, and a university at Granada itself, intellectual predominance escaped from the hands of the Muslims.
The most illustrious writers of this period were historians,
geographers, and political writers, and chief among them
were Benaljatib (Ibn al-Khatīb) of Loja, Aben Said (Ibn
Sa'id) al Maghribī, and the jurists Ibn Salmūn and Ibn
'Asām, whose doctrines became celebrated outside of Spain,
and enjoyed authority in the African Tribunals.

52. *Elements of Civilization in the Christian Kingdoms.* The
Christian kingdoms of the Peninsula formed a meeting
place of two great currents: on the one hand, the Muslim
and Jewish, which may be called the *Oriental*, from the
Asiatic origin of both Islam and Judaism; and on the other
the *European*, which, if it drew nourishment in part from the
former (§ 51), yet gradually acquired an original development, which grew more powerful as Muslim culture
declined.

The European current took the following main directions.
French influence was represented first by the monks of
Cluny, who, at the beginning of the 11th century, entered
Spain at the call of the King of Navarre and spread throughout Aragon, Catalonia, and Castille (from 1033), producing amongst other results: a literary revival of Latin
(to which we have already referred in § 48), the recrud-

GRANADA SILK, 15TH CENT.

escence of a baronial regime in the French sense, and Roman Catholic unity in discipline and cult. Other agents of *French* influence were the many adventurers (some of them of noble birth) who assisted King Alfonso VI in his wars against the Muslims, and the travellers of all classes who came to Castille, especially after the conquest of Toledo. The *Italian* influence had begun some centuries earlier, in the North East (§ 44). It increased as Catalan trade grew in the Mediterranean, particularly through the political relations between Italy and the Counts of Barcelona and the Kings of Aragon. *Flemish* and *German* influence, the vehicle of which was the active commerce between the Cantabrian coasts and Flanders, spread later to the rest of the Peninsula, especially in the sphere of the plastic arts.

The Italian influence acted first on Catalonia, Aragon, Valencia, and Mallorca. Its effect was later in Castille, where it did not make itself felt in certain spheres until the 15th century. For their part, the Spaniards furthered these external influences from within, by temporary emigrations, chiefly in search of foreign centres of learning. The majority of the great men of Spain, from the 12th to the 15th centuries, studied at French and Italian universities, and many held professorial posts there, earning general esteem in the learned world.

The main characteristic of this period in Spain is manifestly a great thirst to know and assimilate the elements of culture offered to the Spanish people by contact with foreigners, and especially with the Muslims and Jews.

The culminating examples of this intellectual incorporation of Oriental influences with Christian culture should be mentioned. Once having conquered Toledo, Alfonso VI (1072-1109) created there a centre of translators of Oriental books, among whom there figured many Jews, some baptized, others not. Toledo offered at that time the outward appearance of a Muslim city, in dress, customs, art, and even in the current language. The initiative of Alfonso VI was upheld in the succeeding reigns and found its apogee in that of Alfonso VII (1130-1150), for this monarch welcomed the Jews who had been expelled from Muslim territory (§ 51). The representative figure of this intense intellectual activity was the Archbishop of Toledo, Raimundo, who inspired and patronized the translation into *romance castellano* and Latin of some of the most noted classical works (Aristotle, Euclid, Galen, etc.), annotated and glossed by Muslims, as also the original writings of certain Arabic and Jewish thinkers. The most important collaborators of the Archbishop in this work of culture seem to have been Canon Marco, Archdeacon Domingo González or Gundisalvo, and Juan Hispalense. Gundisalvo also composed (in Latin) various original philosophical works, much influenced by Oriental learning. The cultural effect of this labour was not limited to Spain. It affected all Europe, not only by the circulation of books from Toledo, but also by the attraction which the Spanish centre held for foreign savants and for students from Italy, France, Germany, and England. The translations of Muslim works, made expressly for these wandering scholars, served to disseminate throughout Europe the Oriental culture which was available in Spain; they show a breadth of view which forms a contrast to those examples of the unreasoning hatred for new things, shown by the Council of Tours (1169), and Paris (1209), which forbade the monks to read works on physics.

The third important landmark in this movement of assimilation was the reign of Alfonso X (" the learned ") (1252-1284), who founded in Murcia and Seville academies and schools of philosophy and languages, which attracted and employed Muslim and Jewish scholars, as well as the most cultured Christians of the epoch. The school of Murcia was directed by the Arab philosopher, Muhammad " el Ricotí."

At the same time Muslim and Jewish influences had the same effect in the other Christian kingdoms, as in Toledo, Seville, and Murcia. Thus in Saragossa (in the last days of the Muslim domination of this city) flourished Avem-

VIEW OF SALAMANCA

Photo, Arxiu Mas.

pace, whose name we have already mentioned. In Barcelona worked the Jewish poet and jurist, Isaac ben Reuben, and the philosophers of the same race, Judah ben Barzilai (*d.* 1130), and Hasdai Crescas (*d.* 1410), and the mathematician Abraham ben Hiyya; in Tortosa was the Muslim savant Ibn Abī-Randaqa. Again, independent of the work of translation carried on in the aforementioned centres, Muslim science produced some of the works which stand highest, and which most influenced Spain and other countries, such as Averroes (commentaries on Aristotle), Abenarabi (Ibn ʿArabī), and Abentofail (Ibn Ṭufayl).

It was at this time that the first universities were founded in Castille (Palencia, 1212 or 1214; Salamanca, Valladolid), with the collaboration of Spanish professors and others brought from France and Italy. From the 13th to the 15th centuries these institutions increased considerably throughout the Peninsula. They were either of municipal origin or were founded by private initiative (the donations, legacies, etc., of bishops, abbots, nobles). The first Catalan university was established in 1300, in Lérida, by Jaime II.

Alongside of this creation of centres of higher education went the creation of libraries, many new ones being founded in monasteries, cathedrals and convents, in palaces of the kings and private houses of nobles. Thus the love of books developed, and great value was attached to them. This may be seen from the beauty of the manuscripts, and the rapid development of miniature-painting and bookbinding.

The interest in scientific and literary culture was considerable among the clergy and nobility. This was especially so among the latter in the 14th and 15th centuries, in Castille, where many great lords dedicated themselves to the writing of poetry, history, treatises on doctrine, and to translating books from Arabic, Latin, French, and Italian. As a contrast to all this, the establishments of popular education were few and defective, in spite of the proposals of certain monarchs and the foundation of certain municipal and monastic schools. The truth is that at that time there existed no aspiration, such as we feel nowadays, towards a general culture which should include all classes.

The concrete result of all these influences we shall see, in every degree of social and individual life, in the following paragraphs.

53. *Directions of Literary Culture. Epic Poetry.* At the beginning of this period, almost all the literary work was in Latin, including poems, religious or historical, of which we find examples in Castille (*e.g.*, the *Cantar del Cid*), and in Catalonia (the funeral song of Borrel III, Count of Barcelona, *d.* 1018).

As regards Castille (in which we now include the Leonese districts and those lands conquered by both kingdoms towards the South) we have already indicated the Latin reaction which occurred in the middle of the 11th century and paralysed the employment in literature of the new mother tongue. But the spiritual movement to which the formation of these new languages corresponded was far too deep-rooted to be crushed in this way at birth. The Romance languages continued to grow and enrich themselves in everyday life and common speech, without being able to reveal their literary qualities, owing to the preponderance of the Latinisms of French origin introduced by the monks of Cluny. But, growing strong in their obscure development they profited by the movement towards independence which began in literature at the end of the 12th century, in the centres of ecclesiastical culture, and perhaps also by the greater stability of civil institutions and by the growth of patriotic feeling. At length the Romance dialects reacted against Latin and took rapid and definite command of literary creation, both in poetry, law, and philosophy. Thus the 12th century saw the appearance of a new literature written in the new languages, which almost at once produced notable works in Castille, Galicia, Catalonia and, later, in León.

In Castille this literature adopted the form of epic songs, already existing in the foregoing centuries (§ 48), and which now produced both new versions of ancient poems (such as

MUDÉJAR BOOKBINDING
(15*th cent.*)
(*University Library, Salamanca*)

that of the Seven Infantes of Lara), and new works, such as the two poems of the Cid, which have come down to us; one (*Poema del Mio Cid*) belonging to the middle of the 12th century, and the other (*Crónica del Cid*) probably somewhat later. All these are characterized by their patriotic sentiments and are the expression of the life and ideals of the aristocratic and military class of the age. As the influence of these poems spread to other parts of Spain, they were adapted to the demands of local sentiment, as for example in León, where the poems of the fictitious Bernardo del Carpio (mid-13th century) expressed Leonese national feeling. At the same time, the epics in both dialects (Castille and León) extended their subjects to heroes who did not represent their respective regions, but were common traditional legends, such as that of the Visigothic king Don Rodrigo (12th century, perhaps preceded by earlier songs of Mozarabic origin), and themes from the French epic (Charlemagne and the twelve peers of France), which had been carried all over central and western Spain by the popular ballad singers (*juglares*). Some of these singers came with French knights who were auxiliaries of Alfonso VI in the campaigns which culminated in the capture of Toledo (§ 50); others followed the " Pilgrims' Way " to Santiago, spreading their own literature and, at times, allowing themselves also to be influenced by Spanish themes, as seems to have been the case with Witiza and Don Rodrigo.

This invasion of the heroes and themes of the French epic (which took place when the Castilian epic had already given indubitable proofs of its existence and originality), is what led to a belief that the early chivalrous poetry in the Castilian dialect was nothing but an imitation of the French. It has already been seen that this was not so, as regards the subject-matter. As regards the verse, although the irregular metre in those texts which we know makes considerable use of a line of fourteen syllables, it finally evolved a Spanish type—lines of sixteen syllables, with assonance, and a break in the middle.

This was not the only direction of Castilian poetry. Its more erudite side, which also allowed itself to be influenced by French models of a non-heroic type (moral and religious), gave rise in the 12th century to a school which called itself *Mester de Clerecía*, superior in technique to the earlier and contemporary popular school, and using themes either purely pious (lives of the saints, etc.), or remote reflections of Greek or Latin works (*e.g.*, the History of Alexander the Great). In the 14th and 15th centuries the popular lyric (in tune with the national life, in which the middle class of citizens was already much to the fore), became democratic and sought inspiration in general themes, such as love, which not only inspired new works, but also prompted the *juglares* of the time to re-mould and re-fashion the ancient heroic ballads, bringing them into line with contemporary ideas and feelings. Fragments of these renovations are the early popular ballads called *romances* handed down by oral tradition in all the lands where Castilian is spoken. The themes that seem most to have interested the men of these times, and which therefore appear in the *romances* (or fragments of romances), which modern specialists consider to be original, were: Bernardo del Carpio, the Cid, Fernán González, Infantes de Lara, and the siege of Zamora (episode of Vellido Dolfos). It was thus that the ancient poetry of the " Cantares de Gesta " became really popular in its diffusion and its themes, though in its original form it was the poetry of the nobility and was destined to die, when it had completed its social and military functions, as happened also in France. It must be added that the *juglares* or public singers who spread this literature amongst the masses, mingled with it the erudite poems of the *Mester de Clerecía*. Thus it happened that the two literary currents, although of fundamentally different origin, met in a common artistic and educative reaction on the masses of the populace, with whose sentiments they were largely in accord, but to which they also gave strength and direction.

The new poetic form of these episodes was enriched later—towards the 15th century—with another series, not derived from the ancient *cantares*, but original as regards subjects. It manifested itself by treating in the popular Spanish manner, with new details and new characteristics, certain national personages, men and women, who had either already been used by the older *juglares* or had been taken from the French epic. Such are, in the former group, the figure of Doña Lambra, taken from the Infantes de Lara, and the episode of the oath in Santa Gadea; and, as regards the second group, Charlemagne, Roland, El Conde de Irlos, El Marqués de Mantua, Valdovinos, Gaiferos, and many others which Don Quixote quoted and used repeatedly, and who are still living personages at the poetic basis of the Spanish national soul.

Others were added to them who were neither legendary nor borrowed, such as the Castilian King Don Pedro the Cruel (1350-1369). Almost at the same time ballad poetry was invaded by subjects inspired by the wars against the Moors on the frontiers of the kingdom of Granada (§ 50), in which the inevitable Moorish influence is expressed, and which give birth to the early *romances fronterizos*. The earliest of these which we possess to-day seems to be that referring to the defence of Baeza in 1368. To this group also belongs the well-known ballad of Abenamar (Ibn Aḥmār) inspired by the beauty of the Moorish city of Granada, which the Castilian king, Juan II, contemplated at the head of his troops, on a June day in 1421, sixty-one years before it fell into the hands of the Catholic kings.

It remains to be said that both the poems or fragments of heroic poems and the *romances* which derived from them, were recited to the accompaniment of instruments by the *juglares*, giving rise to a form of our national popular music which was much enriched in later centuries, and echoes of which are still found in the traditional songs of many districts of Spain. At the same time religious music, which also became popular, took on forms which deserve to be called Spanish (although in those centuries it differed according to locality), and to which numerous references exist in contemporary documents.

54. *Provençal Influence and the Schools of the 14th and 15th Centuries.* A new element of French origin came to change profoundly the direction of literary history, giving it another road and other genres. The school of the troubadours of Provence, born in the Midi of France, essentially lyric and erotic (*i.e.*, inspired by themes of love and the ideals of chivalry), learned, correct, and unashamed. The Provençal poets, who used the idiom of their country, related to Catalan, influenced first Catalonia and Aragon in the 12th century, and then, later, Castille and Galicia. Its apogee was reached in the 13th century, when many troubadours came to Spain. The consequences of this new influence were very various in the different regions.

In Catalonia it spread in great purity (that is to say, preserving its characteristics and without modifying them through its contact with local life), until the 15th century, when a really Catalan school arose—Provençal though it was in origin. This was at a time when the use of the national language was making itself felt in scientific works, and in general in all prose literature, which was turning its back on Latin. The classic age of Catalan poetry (in which Valencia and Mallorca should be included), covered the 14th and 15th centuries, at the end of which it began to disappear. The first Catalan poet of whom mention is made is Ot de Montcada (11th century), and the earliest literary text known (the *Homilies d'Organyá*), date from the end of the 12th century.

In Castille the Provençal style did not take such root; but in Galicia it suffered an important change, for the Provençal or Limousine language was replaced by Gallego-Portuguese, and the romantic and learned characters of the troubadours' verse were supplemented by those of the popular poetry of the region (perhaps Celtic in origin), realistic, satiric, and even licentious. The new Galician school soon reached perfection, imposed itself throughout Castille, modifying the *romance*, and held sway from mid-13th to mid-14th century. The best poets of this time wrote in Galician. The masterpieces of Galician literature of

Photo, Arxiv Mas.

THE WALLS OF AVILA

this period were the *Cantigas de Santa Maria*, a compila-
tion of four hundred and seventeen religious poems of
a legendary nature (tales of miracles of the Virgin), which
have come down to our day with the music to which they
were sung in the churches, in which Arabic influences have
been discerned (§ 39).

But the Castilian element (in language and in spirit),
was more inclined to the epic than to the lyric, as we have
already seen. It owed its influence to the ancient *Mester de
Clerecía*, and to the didactic books translated from the
Arabic. It continued to work in obscurity until, in the
14th century it broke new ground for itself, setting Galician
influence aside, although taking from it certain inspired
themes and a great variety of metres. From the time of
Alfonso XI (1312-1350), Castilian poetry continued to gain
ground throughout Spain, and triumphed completely in
the 15th century.

The meeting of all these currents produced three distinct
literary streams: one, didactic and moral, derived straight
from the *Mester de Clerecía*; a second, popular, derived
from the *romances*, mainly epic in character, which we have
already mentioned; and the third, satiric, derived from the
Galician and Provençal schools, free both in theme and
expression. Alongside of the Castilian poetry, Castilian
prose developed; it had a hard struggle with Latin and
managed, in the 13th century, to gain much ground in
didactic literature (books of history, morality, and religion),
science (philosophy, mathematics, astronomy, medicine,
etc.), and legislature (the municipal statute laws of Alfonso
X were drawn up in Aragonés).

The most illustrious writers of the various schools mentioned are: of the *Mester de Clerecía* (13th century), Berceo;
of the Galician lyric, King Alfonso X; of the Provençal
lyric in Castille, Don Enrique de Villena (15th century);
of the new Castilian school, with influences from all the
foregoing types, Juan Ruiz (Archpriest of Hita), the Chan-
cellor Ayala, the Marques de Santillana, and others who
also figure in later schools (§ 54); of Catalan Provençal

writers, Alfonso II (the first Spanish troubadour), Guillem
de Bergadá, Guerau de Cabrera, Vidal de Besalú, Cerveri
de Gerona, considered as the last of the troubadours, and
one of the most popular (1250-1280). Of the Catalan
school proper, the most outstanding examples are Jordi
de San Jordi, Andréu Febrer, Corella, Ausías March, and
Jaime Roig.

55. *The Classical Renaissance and Italian Influences.* But
whilst these interesting events were taking place in Spanish
literature, there was a renaissance of the ancient influence
of the classical authors (Greek and Latin), who, for centuries,
had had much weight in Europe (§§ 11 and 25). Apart
from the impulse which the Muslim authors may have
given them, the principal factor which hastened the restoration of classical studies in the Peninsula was Italy, where,
through various favourable circumstances, they had already
developed to a considerable extent.

We have already seen why the Spaniards (especially
those of the East) came into frequent contact with Italy.
And the Italians did not limit themselves to disinterring
and revealing texts of forgotten classical authors, but, inspired by these and by the ideas of the age, they had created
a rich and important literature, as early as the 13th century. They brought to Spain both the originals and their
translations from the Latin and Greek, and the works of
their own poets and prose writers, especially Dante,
Petrarch, and Boccaccio.

Thereupon a twofold current was set up in Spain. On
the one hand it was purely classical, with the reading
and translation into Castilian and Catalan of Virgil,
Ovid, Lucan, Homer, Livy, Plutarch and other ancient
authors; and on the other it was Italian, with a great dis-
semination of the above-quoted authors. Both currents
attained great force in Catalonia and Aragon, from the end
of the 14th century. The first seemed to be the more
prominent in the 15th century, through the personal influence of Alfonso V of Aragon (1416-1458), who transferred his court to Naples and there gave great impulse

to Latin studies. Latin predominated again in official documents, in correspondence, in didactic works and even in poetry, in spite of the importance of the Catalan school; and Latinists, in this renaissance sense, were amongst the Spaniards who shone most at this time in Italy, France, and Spain, as polemists in philosophy and in literature. Such were the Bishop Pedro García, who carried on stubborn arguments with the famous Pico de la Mirandola; the Catalan Gareth or Garreth, commonly called Chariteo, and the renowned Fernando de Córdoba, master of medicine and the liberal arts, poet, musician, painter and polyglot, and a man of happy and tenacious memory, who achieved fame in Paris and was much extolled by the great Italian humanist, Valla. But this mode was ephemeral, and the real Italian influences conquered, and set their seal on writers in all the regions; and at the same time the Castilian school spread with great vigour throughout Aragon and Catalonia, not only on account of the origin of the kings of Aragon from Ferdinand I (1410), but also through the emigration of many Castilians (nobles and poets), to territories in Aragon and Catalonia and to the Court of Naples. Many Catalan writers of the 15th century were already bilingual, and thus was prepared the final victory of the Castilian element throughout the Peninsula.

The Italian influence proper began in the Western regions at the end of the 14th century, Seville being its centre. There an Italian, Micer Francisco Imperial, began to publish imitations of Dante. Naturally a struggle began between the partisans of the new school and those of old Castilian, which had developed from Galician and the *Mester de Clerecía*. The former prevailed, making its way into all literature, and changing its form and basis. The climax of this influence, which gave a new extension to Castilian production and continued to hold sway in Castille for many centuries, corresponds to the 15th century, and particularly to the first half—*i.e.*, the reign of Juan II (1412-1454), a great patron of culture and specially of literature, like Alfonso V of Aragon. The principal Italianate writers of Castille are: the above-mentioned Marqués de Santillana, Juan de Mena, Pérez de Gúzman, Jorge Manrique, and Caravajal or Carvajales; this last is famous, not only for his lyric poems, but also for having imitated the old epic *romances*.

All that has been said hitherto applies mainly to poetry. The same influences were at work upon prose. The main results in Castille, Catalonia, and Aragon were the appearance of " *libros de Caballería* " (books of chivalry), a species of novel in which were recounted the adventures in war and in love of wandering knights, with a large proportion of fantastic elements; the first *novelas amatorias*, erotic and sentimental tales under Italian influence; the great advance upon the old *Crónicas*, which became real histories, according to the classical model, and the beginning of preceptive literature (rhetorical and poetic). Amongst the historical productions of the 13th century, stands out the first General Chronicle of Spain, by Alfonso X. It is peculiar in that its text is formed, in part, of fragments of epic poems, some of which refer to the Cid and complete the manuscript of the *Poem of My Cid* (§ 53), which we possess to-day. This is a very important fact in literary history. At the same time there developed a vast production of religious and moral works, emanating from the clergy.

56. *Cultivation of the Sciences*. The main activity of the Spanish spirit at this time was directed towards literature, but scientific studies were not entirely neglected and certain Spaniards gained fame, especially in law, and Catholic theology.

We have seen that among the Oriental works which were translated in Toledo (11th century), both in the reign of Alfonso X and of his father, Ferdinand III, philosophy and ethics abounded. The first produced no appreciable movement in Castille for the time being. In Catalonia the Muslim influence was concentrated in the great Catholic thinker, Raimundo Lulio (Raymund Lully), who gathered many elements of Arabic mysticism, though interpreting them in a Christian sense. The writings of Lulio formed a school and gave birth to various teaching establishments which, during many years, disseminated his thought in the Eastern regions and in Mallorca; but none of his disciples and followers had the same importance.

Books of morality of Eastern origin, written almost always in the form of tales or apologues, when they had any offspring in Castilian or Catalan literature, were converted to Catholicism. They were superseded at last by the ascetic and pious writings of the clergy. Part of this production took on a political character, in the form either of treatises on government or of counsels to the kings and governors.

In juridical science, the main influences came from Italy, and were in the tradition of Roman Law. The most notable jurists of the time are Romanists who had been brought up on the writings of the Italian commentators, and who were translated and repeatedly plagiarized. The most important monument of this kind is the sort of encyclopaedia, edited under the direction of Alfonso X, and known under the name of " *Las Siete Partidas.*" The reading of this work spread, in the Castilian text and in translations, throughout the Universities and Schools of Law. But even here one is constantly aware of that national complexion which Spanish thought had already assumed, both in the elements of traditional Castilian law, which *Las Partidas* contains, and in the divergences from Justinian law, which characterize them (*e.g.*, the conception of the State and of the function of Monarchy), and also in important innovations in the penal code, which are very modern and humane in sentiment, and amongst which figure the separation of the sexes in prison, the punishment of those who wrongfully used those undergoing sentences, the institution of forced labour as a means of utilizing prisoners in work for the public good, and the fixing of a maximum period for the duration of law-suits. In other branches of legislation, particularly in that which to-day we call " social," Spanish law, both in Castille and in the other kingdoms, shows important innovations, such as the prevention of disease and the safeguarding of life (as we see from the *Fuero Viejo*), the ordinances for labour (*Ordenanzas de Menestrales*), etc.

At the same time the jurists, lay and clerical, cultivated the Canon, or Church, law, distinguishing themselves in this very Spanish branch of study, both at the Papal court and in the Universities of the Peninsula, and abroad (Bologna, Paris). From the interplay of these two currents there arose a curious theologico-political literature, directed chiefly towards the discussion of the relations between Church and State. The chief representative of this is the Catalonian Franciscan, Francisco Eximinis or Jiménez, Bishop of Elna. The main thesis of these writings is that the civil power (the kings) should be subordinated to the ecclesiastical power (the Pope), who is declared to be "the general lord and monarch of all the world, both by divine and temporal right." Alongside of this doctrine they were wont to expound others, of a more democratic sentiment.

Theology proper had also many and good exponents in Castille and Aragon. Certain bishops distinguished themselves at the Council of Basle (1431-1437), at Rome, and at Avignon. Outstanding among them were : the famous professor of theology at the University of Paris, Guido de Terrena, native of Perpignan (then a city of the crown of Aragon); Cardinal Juan de Torquemada and Cardinal Don Gil de Albornoz, celebrated for many reasons, who founded in Bologna (1364) the College of San Clemente, for Spanish students, which still exists. Furthermore, the dramatic episode of Pope Luna (Benedict XIII), whom the Church resolved to depose for reasons of its own convenience, shows in its juridical development that Canon law was on the side of the Spanish Pope, and also that the cultivation of this branch of the law had, among the group faithful to Luna, and masters of their subject, unshakable defenders of the purest, if not for the moment of the most applicable, doctrine, as regards the election of the Pope.

Finally, in the domain of religious oratory, which in the 13th and 14th centuries acquired special importance through the polemics against the Jews and Muslims, and the consequent conversion of both, the Valencians Fr. Pedro Nicolás Pascual (1227-1300) and Fr. Vicente Ferrer (1357-1417), both excelled and were both canonized by the Church. The Catalan Dominican, Fr. Ramón Martí (13th century), distinguished himself in the literature of apologists and in that of the defence of Catholic theology against Oriental influences.

As regards the exact and natural sciences, the Spaniards lived almost exclusively on translations of Oriental books, which were widespread in the 13th and 14th centuries, through the efforts of Alfonso X. Thus the doctors, mathematicians, astronomers, and chemists of Castille and Aragon contented themselves with applying and developing the doctrines of their Greek and Muslim masters, until, in the mid-15th century, there began to appear a realistic and experimental tendency in medicine, which modified the old doctrines and set up chairs of anatomy and surgery. Characteristic of this age were the fantastic derivations of astronomy and chemistry, called astrology and alchemy, the former resulting in the study of the stars in connection with the particular life of individuals, and in divining the future, and the latter in seeking the " Philosopher's Stone," or the method of preparing gold chemically. Many persons participated in both errors, amongst them, several monarchs—most of them Aragonese. Notable cultivators of these arts were Alfonso X in Castille, and Arnaldo de Vilanova in Catalonia.

The rise in esteem of the serious study of the exact sciences coincides with the appearance of cosmographers and cartographers of Mallorca and Catalonia of this age, who improved navigation and traced the first general maps with such accuracy that they were sought after in all the countries of Europe. Amongst them figured two of the Jewish family Cresques, to one of whom, Jafuda Cresques, Henry the Navigator of Portugal entrusted the direction of the nautical school which he had founded at Sagres.

57. *Industry and Commerce.* This notable advance in cosmography and cartography arose from the great development of industry and commerce, and in general, of the maritime relations of Spain in the Mediterranean and other seas. From the moment when the frontiers of the Christian states of the Peninsula stretched to the South of Andalucía and into Italy and Greece (through the success of Catalan and Aragonian captains), their economic life grew in importance, thanks to the following factors: growth of population amongst whom there figured many Muslims, Mozárabes, and Jews; greater stability and peace in political life, through the almost complete political annihilation of the Muslim element; and a greater contact with European countries. To these causes were added the civil liberty of a great part of the population, who could thus dedicate themselves with more enthusiasm and better results to work in the cities and municipalities, as we shall see.

The development of industries is attested by the formation of many guilds of mechanics (*cofradías* and *gremios*), and in the frequent legislation in this sphere. Records exist of the exportation of products and of commercial relations with Flanders and Germany (as regards the North), and with the countries of the Mediterranean (Catalonia, Mallorca, etc.). The earliest dates which we possess relate to Barcelona, which, ever since the 9th century, had had a commercial tradition (§ 47). This grew in the 11th and 12th and especially in the 13th centuries, through the conquests realized in the Peninsula and in Italy. The most flourishing industries seem to have been textiles of wool and cotton, leather, iron, glass, artistic work in metals and pottery. With this active maritime commerce, Barcelona became one of the chief ports of the Mediterranean from the 13th to the 15th centuries; but by this time certain industries—such as cloth—already appeared to be declining. Silk-weaving lasted only for a short time and was of small importance; so was agriculture, whose chief product was wine.

Photo, Arxiv Mas.

HISPANO-MORESQUE POTTERY

(*Manises plate,* 14*th cent.*)

Aragon had regions of great agricultural development, exporting oil, wine, rice, and saffron to Catalonia (by the Ebro), and to Flanders. But in other regions the poverty was extreme and lasted for many centuries. The chief industries were cattle-breeding, the curing of hides and woollen textiles (looms of Saragossa, Tarazona, Albarracín, Jaca, and Huesca).

Valencia was mainly an agricultural region, but it also developed the industries of cloth, silk, Spanish leather, paper, brass, and ceramic ware (plates with gold reflections) made by potters of Muslim origin. Its navy competed with that of Catalonia.

Mallorca was, from the 13th to the 15th centuries, one of the richest commercial centres of the Mediterranean, on the basis of extensive agricultural exploitation and an excellent system of irrigation; it also exported jewellery, ironwork, soap, paper, textiles, and pottery.

The Mallorcan mercantile marine was one of the most numerous of the 14th century, and carried produce throughout the Mediterranean and into the Atlantic. In the commercial and working population there were many foreigners (especially Italians), and also Muslims and Jews. Yet its fall came about very rapidly, through a number of complex causes: social wars (§ 64), plagues, floods, the incorporation with the Aragonese Crown (1344), which brought about an increase of tribute money, and the taking of Jaffa and Constantinople by the Turks (1453), which closed the commerce with the East. One of the trades which most enriched Mallorca was the slave trade. In Navarre, stock breeding had great importance, agriculture (olives and wine), was limited to small districts. The main industries were: the making of serge, Spanish leather, cured sheepskins and canvas for export.

The Basque provinces were mainly commercial centres, where they shipped a great part of the products of Aragon, Navarre, Castille, etc. The *fuero* of San Sebastian (1180) already contained mercantile laws. The ships of the Basque maritime towns (federated for this purpose with

those of Santander, Asturias, and Galicia) had an extraordinary importance, both mercantile and military, in the
Cantabrian and the northern seas, coming to blows often
enough with the English. The most important industries
of these provinces were: the extraction of iron from the
ore, and, as an outcome of this, manufacture in iron and
steel. At the Cantabrian ports foreign merchants were
welcome—French, English, and Flemish.

Finally, Castille seems to have maintained, even before
the 13th century, frequent commercial relationships with
Flanders and other countries, exporting iron, wool, grain,
hides, wax, spun yarn, quicksilver, tallow, wine, cumin,
and aniseed from the regions of Castille proper; oil, honey
and fruits from Andalucía; hides, wools, and wines from
Galicia; iron from Asturias. Apart from Santiago, whose
importance went on growing with the extension of pilgrim-
ages, the following grew into important commercial and
industrial centres from the 13th century: Seville (where
French, Italian and Portuguese ships from Africa put into
port); Toledo, Segovia, Zamora, Burgos, Valladolid,
Medina del Campo, and others. The agricultural and
industrial products which seem to have been most highly
developed during this time (13th to 16th centuries) are:
textiles, hides, ceramic ware and objects of iron and steel,
and objects made from these metals and from gold.
Cattle-breeding rose extraordinarily in importance, all
breeders joining in one association (the *Mesta*), and receiving great privileges.

Traders were represented abroad by consuls; they
established in the principal countries bureaux of commerce,
or exchanges, formed true mercantile colonies, such as those
in Bruges and Antwerp, from the end of the 15th century,
where there was a noticeable preponderance of Castilian
and Basque merchants. They facilitated their mutual relations by means of bills of exchange; the earliest of these
known are from Valencia and Mallorca.

The kings favoured these transactions, granting immunity of markets and fair-days, reducing the import

Photo, Arxiv. Mas.

ESTELLA: ROMANESQUE CLOISTER OF SAN PEDRO

duties, mending the roads, having new ones built, prose-
cuting robbers who infested the countryside, etc. But customs continued to exist at all the frontiers and even in the
towns (where toll was paid not only on food-stuffs, but on
raw material, such as the cocoon of the silk-worm), and also
a tax was levied on every sort of transaction (Ar. *al-qabāla*,
Sp. *alcabala*), so that industry and commerce struggled with
great obstacles, which prevented them from prospering.
Added to these were the monopoly exercised by the Crown
over the mines, salt, and fisheries; the rights of turn-pike
and bridge tolls, of passage, mills, kilns, etc., which many
nobles held in addition to the towns, and the excessive
regulations of work laid down in the ordinances of the trade-
guilds and in the general workmen's laws, which went so
far as to fix details of production. These, if they avoided
fraud to a great measure, on the other hand brought technique to a standstill, and made invention difficult.

Barcelona offers a distinctly protectionist character, at
this time, which militated even against the produce of other
parts of Catalonia. Valencia, on the other hand, had a
leaning towards free trade.

58. *Romanesque Art.* Perhaps the most eloquent testimony to the general progress, and to the growth of public
wealth, in the Christian kingdoms, is to be found in the fine
arts, and especially in architecture. Here also are seen the
various foreign influences that were at work in Spain.

Building, which had been comparatively scanty in the
foregoing centuries (§ 49), grew and enriched itself. Great
churches and palaces were constructed, and decorated with
statues, reliefs and paintings of great merit. The architecture of the 11th and 12th centuries has a special character, on account of which historians have signalized it as a
new type, which they call *Romanesque*, just as the new languages that sprang from Latin were called *romance*. In
effect this is nothing more than a new transformation of
Roman architecture. It bears within itself a great mingling
and variety of elements, which clearly demonstrate various
foreign influences (among them, Arabian, § 43), as well as

the influences of the particular inventions of the people of each locality. This Romanesque art flourished in all the Christian kingdoms. Its type in the regions of the Centre and West were different from those in Aragon and Catalonia, where in general it took on more robust forms, heavy proportions and clumsy ornamentation, revealing here (as in Navarre), mainly French influence, just as, in the districts of the East coast, Italian influences predominate. The roofs are already vaulted, of various shapes, with great pillars or columns; their capitals are worked in relief, with motives of leaves and fruit, human faces, and animals, sometimes made grotesque. Outside, the churches show a great wealth of sculptural decoration, especially in the porches, gargoyles, and even in the walls. The windows are still few, because the walls must necessarily be strong (in spite of the use of buttresses), and are provided with stained-glass.

There were many churches with several naves (three), each of which ended in a chapel (apse), generally round, both within and without. This form was modified in the regions that came under the influence of the Cistercian Order (end of 13th century), with the substitution of rectangular chapels for the circular apses, and later, by the ambulatory (*girola*), which necessitated a radiating series of chapels in the head or apse of the church. A representative type of the first style is the Catalan monastery of Santas Creus, and, of the second, that of Poblet. In Romanesque churches one frequently finds porches, cloisters, and towers, either of stone (attached or unattached to the main building), or of wood (the towers of Sahagún).

The principal examples of this style are: the *Pórtico de la Gloria* and the South doors of the Cathedral of Santiago, an admirable piece of Romanesque workmanship; the door and the Pantheon of the kings at San Isidoro of León; the monastery of Leyre (Navarre); the palace of Carracedo (León); the fine door of the monastery of Ripoll; the Cathedrals of Lérida, and Tarragona, and many cloisters and doorways of Catalonia, Aragon, and Valencia.

VALENCIA: THE EXCHANGE

(15th cent.)

In the other arts, the Romanesque type reflects the same distinctive characteristics. Sculpture (the decoration of the churches, and images of the cult), developed greatly, both in stone, marble, and wood. So did goldsmiths' work (chalices, crosses, crowns, reliquaries), and the carving of furniture, though in all these branches of art Oriental, French, and Italian influences are manifest.

59. *Gothic Art.* But already in the Romanesque constructions of the 13th century (*e.g.*, those mentioned above, at Santiago, Lérida, and Tarragona, and the monasteries of Santas Creus and Poblet, where the Gothic arch was used for the first time), are seen modifications which herald the advent of a new style. This is the art known as Gothic (*ojival*), and, from the middle of the 13th century, was superimposed on Romanesque art throughout the Peninsula. The chief characteristics of Gothic art are: the pointed arch (as distinct from the older rounded arch), which was used both as an element in construction and for beauty; the groined vault, which permitted of greater height and increased, by its support, the number of arches springing from the pillars; an extraordinary development of the buttress, which no longer backed against the wall, but stood clear and was joined to it by arches, which received the weight of the vaulting; a lessening of the thickness of the walls (since there was no longer such strain on them), and the insertion of many windows, with stained glass; a profusion of decoration in the porches, with reliefs and statues, either in high relief or standing quite clear of the wall; the polygonal apse, and the great importance of the towers, which usually ended in a spire, richly worked. As a result of all these things, Gothic buildings are very high, light, and richly adorned both with representations of people, human scenes, and animals, and with flowers, ivy leaves, holm oak, thistle, etc., and by symbolistic designs. In Spain certain of these general characteristics of Gothic art appear in modified form, especially the flying buttress, which was less important than in other countries; glass windows, except in one case, are fewer, and the

decrease of the thickness of the walls did not go as far as in other parts of Europe. It must be added that, as in Romanesque, so in Gothic, art, important regional modifications occurred, which made Castilian Gothic differ from that found in the Eastern and Mediterranean districts. In the 14th and 15th centuries architecture degenerated, through the exaggeration of decoration and the loss of primitive constructive vigour.

This is the period of the great Cathedrals of Spain and of the Castilian palaces, built by the kings and the great nobles. Almost all these buildings show a great admixture of styles on account of the period at which they were begun, and the slowness with which such colossal and costly work proceeded. In the following period, too, we find frequent cases of the admixture of Renaissance models with the earlier Romanesque and Gothic buildings. Hence arises the rich variety that characterizes many Spanish cathedrals. In Andalucía much the same thing happened, but here there is an admixture of Muslim elements, the most striking example of this being in Córdoba.

The most remarkable of Gothic church architecture in Spain is to be seen in the cathedrals of León (12th century), notable for the purity of its style and for its windows; Cuenca (13th century); Burgos (14th and 15th centuries); Toledo, Barcelona, interesting because of the signs it bears of Italian influence, and Palma de Mallorca. Some very beautiful and characteristically Gothic art is to be seen in the cloisters of these churches, and in many other cloisters, such as those of the monasteries of Santas Creus and Poblet. Amongst civil buildings the following must be mentioned: the Palace of the Duque de Infantado at Guadalajara, and that of Miraflores in Burgos; the so-called "Casa de los Picos" in Segovia and "Casa de las Conchas" in Salamanca; the Lonjas of Barcelona and Valencia; the Ayuntamiento and the Palace of the Diputación at Barcelona; the Catalan fortified palaces of Solivella and Palafolls, and that of Bellver in Mallorca. In military architecture, which advanced greatly in the 14th and 15th centuries, the

WROUGHT IRON " REJA "
(Barcelona Cathedral Cloister)

MUDÉJAR DECORATION, 14TH CENT.

(*Córdoba*)

Gothic type is seen in the walls of Avila, the towers of Serranos (Valencia), the castles of La Mota, Segovia, and others. Beautiful workmanship is also to be seen in the crosses that marked the entry into the confines of a town and in the *rollos* or pillars of justice, which used to stand in public squares.

As is natural, the new style was reflected in other arts as well as in architecture, and produced beautiful work in sculpture (figures for porches and tombs), carving in wood, especially choir stalls, and in certain ordinary articles of furniture, such as *bargueños* (a kind of bureau); also in marble (statues, decoration on arches, etc.), and in worked gold (especially reliquaries, processional crosses, little coffers for relics, image plates, etc.—an art which acquired great importance). Pottery continued to be influenced mainly by Muslim art.

60. *Mudéjar Art*. There also arose in Spain an entirely Peninsular art, which goes by the name of Mudéjar, the work of Muslims living in Christian territory (§§ 41 and 45). It is a combination of Gothic and Arabic elements, which gives it an original aspect. It is characterized on the outside by the use of brick-work in which decorations are traced, blind arcading, glazed tiles (Sp. *azulejo*, Ar. *az-zulaij*), and horse-shoe arches. Admirable examples of Mudéjar architecture are found in Toledo, Puerta del Sol (Gate of the Sun), Puerta de Bisagra, the Synagogues of Santa María la Blanca and the Tránsito, and other buildings), in Seville (the Alcázar), Saragossa (the leaning tower known as the *Torre Nueva*), in Calatayud (the bell-tower of Santa María), etc. Mudéjar art is also expressed in marvellous panelled ceilings, carved and painted; dados and ornamentation in plaster and coloured tiles; in ceramic (plates, vases, and enamelled tiles), in bookbindings (geometrical designs), and in certain details of sepulchral statues and in the tombs themselves.

61. *Painting*. In the early centuries painting on walls or on wood and linen was little practised, although many churches are known to have had their walls decorated with

frescoes, most of which have disappeared. On the other hand, painting on parchment attained great importance, as all books were illuminated. This work shows distinct influences (Mozarabic, traditional Visigothic, Italian, etc.), and came to produce real pictures of great merit from the 13th century onwards. The *Libro de los Testamentos* in the Cathedral of Oviedo is one of the principal monuments of this art, in its Spanish form, of the 12th century. Of equal merit in the 13th century are the miniatures of the Ripoll manuscript, and in that of the *Cantigas* of Alfonso X, in which latter both French and Mudéjar influences are recognizable. Painting on glass was practised from the 10th century onwards, and made obvious progress, its figures growing larger, more complicated, and more perfect until the magnificent glass work of the 13th, 14th, and 15th centuries was produced, which may be admired to-day in the cathedrals of León, Oviedo, and elsewhere.

From the 12th century the frescoes are more numerous and more important and reveal Byzantine, Italian, and Mudéjar influences, with two principal tendencies or schools: the Catalan (Pedret, Fenollar, San Miguel de la Seo, Tahull), and the Leonese (Panteón de los Reyes, at León). Those of San Baudilio de Berlanga (Soria), and those of Arlanza (Burgos), are also notable and extremely original. In the 14th century mural paintings showing French and Italian influences were produced (many of them remarkable, *e.g.*, those of Pedralbes, Pamplona, and San Miguel de Focer), and also some showing Mudéjar influence (the church of Maluenda, Saragossa). In the same century painting on wood developed, particularly for religious purposes (retables and statues). The three conflicting influences in this genre are: Italian, from the 14th century; French, especially in the North, Navarre, and upper Aragon; and Flemish, from the beginning of the 15th century. This last held sway especially in Castille, whereas the Italian influence is seen chiefly on the East coast. However, in Catalonia there was no lack of Flemish artists who passed on to the natives many elements

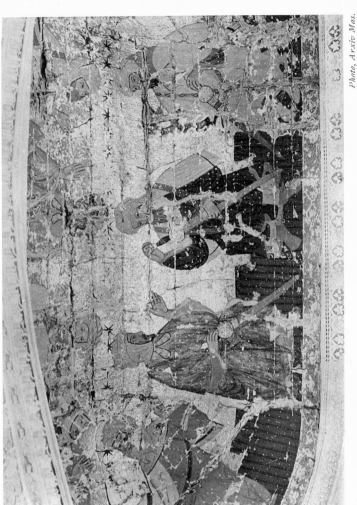

THE NASRITE KINGS OF GRANADA
(From a painting in the Alhambra)

LUIS DALMAU: THE VIRGIN AND THE COUNCILLORS
(*Barcelona, 15th cent.*)

of their art. An example of the meeting of Italian and Flemish influences, with the latter in preponderance, is the famous picture painted in tempera by the Catalan Luis Dalmau, known as *La Virgen de los Concelleres*. Purely Italian influence is represented in Catalonia by Ferrer Bassa and Pedro Serra, each in his different way, and later (second half of the 15th century), by Jaime Huguet, notable for the expressiveness of his faces and the influence exercised by his technique. A mixture of French and Italian influence is chiefly displayed by the Aragonese Lorenzo Zaragoza. In the 15th century the formation of a Valencian school is discernible, and reveals clearly a spirit of its own. In Valencia also Jaime Baco (Jacomart), who was inspired by the Flemish school, had considerable influence. He produced admirable paintings on wood (*retablos*), such as that of San Martín at Segorbe.

Yet from these conflicting influences, painters of a purely national stock began to emerge, with an assured originality which could shine by its own merits. Such is the painter Bartolomé de Cárdenas, a Cordovan by birth, who worked mainly in Aragon, and was popularly called Bartolomé Bermejo. Works representative of his art are the *Santo Domingo de Silos*, now in the Prado, and the *Piedad*, which is in the *Sala capitular* (chapter house) of the Cathedral of Barcelona. Of equal importance in the early history of true Spanish painting is a certain Maestro Alfonso. His origin is unknown and the only one of his works extant is an altar-piece at Bacelona, painted for the church of San Cucufate del Vallés.

As regards the two Castilles, we do not know of any painting done indubitably by Spanish hands until the end of the 15th century, when a certain Fernando Gallego, much influenced by the contemporary Dutch masters, made various interesting paintings on wood. He was followed by a Francisco Gallego (possibly his son), and by various anonymous painters, some of them noteworthy, *e.g.*, the man who was known as the Maestro de la Sisla (of the monastery of the Sisla, Toledo).

H

Andalusian painting, which was later to stand at the head of all Spanish art, revealed at this period neither any particular force nor any original traits. Its chief work is considered to be the *Annunciation* of Pedro of Córdoba.

In giving a comprehensive account of the period, we cannot ignore the presence in Spain of many foreign painters who accentuated and spread the influence of their various schools. Among them may be mentioned Van Eyck, Andrés Marcal, Niccolo, Paolo de San Leocadio, Pagano, and probably the Jorge Inglés (George the Englishman), who served the Marqués Iñigo de Santillana. Besides this personal contact with the painters, there were journeys abroad made by Spanish artists and also the importation of Flemish and Italian paintings, especially paintings on wood.

62. *Romanesque and Gothic Sculpture.* The 11th century saw the rise of an original form of sculpture in Spain, which took priority over the other countries of Europe. It began by sculpture in marble, which was derived originally from Muslim art of the foregoing centuries, especially the 10th, and culminated in the Crucifix of León, called that of Ferdinand I, and in the reliefs in the arch of San Millán de la Cogolla.

In imitation of these works, the Mudéjar and Spanish artists conceived, also in the 11th century, but in stone, what a modern critic has called " the most typical series in all Europe," which is represented in the capitals of the cloisters of Santo Domingo de Silos, and later in the reliefs in the same cloisters. This art spread later to the South of France.

In both marble and stone it continued to develop in the centuries that followed on the 11th. Outstanding examples are seen in stone in the reliefs of the Puerta de las Platerías, at Santiago de Galicia; the sculptured South doors of San Isidoro at León; those of Frómista and Jaca (cathedral); the sepulchre of the daughters of King Ramiro I, originally in Santa Cruz de Serós; the admirable and typical door of Ripoll (Gerona); various cloisters, such as those of San

ROMANESQUE SCULPTURE

The Gate of Glory, Santiago de Compostela

Cugat; the Holy Porch (*antecámara santa*) of Oviedo, and above all, the Pórtico de la Gloria at Santiago. We know the name of the sculptor of this last work. He was Maestro Mateo, and his self-portrait in stone figures in the same porch. We also know the names or the personalities of others, such as the Catalan Arnall Catell, who is called Maestro de Sepulcro de San Vicente, and others. Beside them worked foreign artists, *e.g.*, Maestro Eruchel, who seems to have been Mateo's teacher. The originality and skill of 12th century Spanish sculpture surpassed that of all its Christian contemporaries.

In the 13th century our sculpture declined and was deeply influenced by the French school; yet in the second half of the century it managed to range itself second only to its model, as is seen in the sculpture of the cathedrals of Burgos, León, and Toledo, which belong to this time, while in the 14th century, the cloisters of the Cathedral of Pamplona are noteworthy.

Italian influences followed upon the French, especially on the shores of the Mediterranean and in Aragon. Later came Mudéjar influences, and finally, Flemish-Burgundian. And, as in painting, there arose in the midst of these impositions of foreign styles certain examples of Spanish originality, such as the polychrome sculpture of Burgos, León, and Oviedo, and much of the Aragonese sculpture of the 16th century. At other times there are examples of a profound and inspired assimilation of foreign types, as in the case of the Aragonese Juan de la Huerta, called to France to make the tomb of John the Fearless, and Margaret of Bavaria at Dijon. In Catalonia there flourished an artist of the first rank, Pedro Juan de Vallfogona, author of the St. George of the Palacio de la Diputación of Barcelona and—with the collaboration of other artists—of the great *retablo* at Tarragona.

Finally, in the early part of the 15th century the Eastern regions of Spain began to be influenced by the new renaissance sculpture of Italy, especially through artists coming from there, and through the works sent from Italy.

63. *Social Evolution in Castille.*   While the wealth and culture of the separate Christian countries was increasing, the position of the social classes with regard to one another was changing also.   In Castille the manorial nobility (*nobleza señorial*) still had the chief say in matters of jurisdiction, by reason of their privileges, their power, and their lawless spirit, which was always opposed to the concentration of power represented by the kings.   But in economic matters the nobility lost ground, because of the development of commerce and industry, in which the nobles had no part.   They were also the poorer because free labour (compared with the former slave labour) diminished the profits of agriculture, which was the main source of their wealth.   In fact, the former slaves ended by emancipating themselves entirely; the *Juniores de Hereditate* enjoyed the right of changing masters without forfeiting their possessions, a change which began in certain districts in 1215, and spread later throughout the land.   Then, too, from the end of the 12th century all slaves succeeded in getting their tribute and their services fixed formally in writing; they could no longer be sold along with their overlord's land, and their marriages were recognized as valid, even though they had been celebrated without the consent of their overlords.   These advantages were not gained without a struggle, notwithstanding the support they met with in the towns, certain favourable interventions on the part of the kings, and the declaration of certain councils.   The nobles resisted as far as possible the pretentions of the servile class, and encounters that led to bloodshed came about frequently, such as those between the serfs and the monks of the Monastery of Sahagún in the 11th, 12th, and 13th centuries.   The liberation did not take place uniformly throughout Castilian territory, nor simultaneously for all the slaves.   Even in the 14th century legislation indicates the persistence of the class of *Juniores de Hereditate*.   The populace, though free in the sight of the law, continued to be subject to oppression from the nobility, as is shown by the repeated complaints made to the kings.

Photo, Arxiv Mas.

PAINTED WOODEN BOX

Those who were really free took refuge in the towns (*muni-cipios* or *consejos*), where, with the aid of the autonomy given them by *fuero*, there arose and multiplied a middle class of traders and manufacturers, possessed of movable wealth which they converted later (in competition with the nobles) into property in land. From the sons of this class arose mainly the *letrados*, that is to say, the university students who dedicated themselves to jurisprudence, influencing thus the government and the public administration, and so being employed by the kings. The *fueros* or municipal charters of Castille contain the recognition—at an earlier date and much more fully than the charters of any other mediaeval nation of Europe (*cf.* the Magna Carta of 1215) —of the fundamental liberties of man, irrespective of social position, though with that feeling for local privilege that was characteristic of the epoch.

As regards the clergy (apart from the landed clergy, who shared the same destiny as the nobility), they increased their class privileges and continued to accumulate land, thanks to donations. But the popular element, backed by the kings, began to set themselves against this tendency by seeking to acquire juridical equality, especially in the payment of taxes and the *fuero judicial*, and by a tendency to avoid the accumulation of property.

64. *The Social Classes in the rest of Spain.* Similar progress was not made in Catalonia and Aragon. In the former the old nobility, together with the *señores allodiales* (§ 45), the monasteries and churches, held almost all the land in their power. Dependent on these were their protégés (*emparats*), called *homes de paratge*, an intermediate class, and the *colonos* or slaves (*payeses*), overburdened with taxes and services, and forbidden to leave their land unless they redeemed themselves by paying down a sum of money. Hence they got the name of *payeses de remensa* or *redimentia*, which is already used in documents of the 12th century (§ 45). But since they could not redeem themselves in the majority of cases the abuses of the nobles were very great. The *payeses* ended by revolting, giving rise to a real civil

war, in the last third of the 15th century. The middle class established itself with great vigour in Barcelona, Tarragona, and other towns, with charters (*municipios con fuero*), under the hegemony of Barcelona; they enjoyed the same civil rights as were granted by the Castilian *fueros*.

In Aragon the nobility was divided into two classes, the first of which, that of the *ricos hombres*, were exceedingly powerful, and had more authority over their dominions than had the lords of Castille and Catalonia. Before the 13th century it was believed that the slaves (*vasallos de parada*) could freely change their place of domicile. But from then onwards their condition became worse and the rights of the nobles increased to such a degree that they were at perfect liberty to kill their slaves by hunger, thirst, or exposure. So much is revealed in the *cortes* of Huesca in 1245, and those of Saragossa in 1381. As was only natural, revolts broke out. The middle classes, less important here than in Castille, or Catalonia, gathered in the university towns, often making common cause with the nobles.

In Valencia there was no servile working class, except the Muslim slaves and *colonos* handed over to the conquerors. The middle classes and the people had the upper hand in the cities and important towns, whilst in the country the nobility was preponderant, with the laws and customs of the kingdom of Aragon.

The history of the social classes in Mallorca is very similar to that of Catalonia, with the difference that the seignorial element was represented, not by nobles or clergy, but by the burgesses and rich citizens of the capital. The exploitation of the country people gave rise to revolts and bloodshed in the end of the 14th and beginning of the 15th centuries.

In Navarre the situation was very similar to that in Aragon. Juridical inequality and servitude for the benefit of the nobility and clergy persisted for a long time.

65. *The Mudéjares and the Jews*. The great Christian conquests, from the 15th century onwards, led to the in-

MUDÉJAR CEILING IN THE ALJAFERIA, SARAGOSSA

clusion in the population of the various kingdoms of many
Muslims (*Mudéjares*) whose civil and political liberty was
respected in Christian Spain, and of many Jews who had
formerly resided in Muslim territory. The influx of the
Jews increased before the 13th century, by reason of the
persecution to which their savants and non-orthodox
writers were submitted by the Almohades (§ 51). They
were made welcome by the Christian kings in Toledo and
other places.

The juridical and social status of the *Mudéjares* and Jews
living in Christian Spanish territory was at first excellent,
and we have seen how profound was their intellectual influence. But from the end of the 14th century elements of
discord and opposition crept in between them and the
Christians. These were mainly inspired by the Church
and were based on religious differences; but they had
also an economic basis, for almost all the commerce and industry found itself in the hands of the *Mudéjares* or Jews.
This hostility was especially strong against the Jews, and
it culminated in popular tumults, which, in 1391, and at
other dates, resulted in the assault and sacking of the Jewish
quarters in the principal towns, with the death of many of
their inhabitants. Although the kings managed to suppress the brutal disorders and guaranteed their civil rights
to the Jews, and although the *Mudéjares* were not submitted to such violence, the result for both the one and the
other was a very real loss in social and juridical status by
the end of the period which we are now examining. Yet
we must distinguish between the condition of the free
Mudéjares, from those who were serfs (numerous in Aragon
and Valencia), and those who were personal slaves, taken
in war or purchased, and who made up a great part of the
serf-labourers in the reconquered regions. The condition
of these *Mudéjar* slaves was naturally worse than that of the
free *Mudéjares*.

66. *Political Evolution.* The main interest of the political
history of Spain from the 11th to the 15th centuries (1499),
lies in the twofold struggle of the Monarchy against the

nobility, and of the *municipios* against the great landlords, and partly also against the kings. The nobles and the *municipios* were alike in their hunger for privilege and autonomy, and were therefore naturally at loggerheads; but never had the middle classes and the populace opposed the authority of the king in Castille in the violent and un-reasoning manner which the nobles had always adopted out of a pure spirit of anarchy. And if, in Aragon, Cata-lonia and Valencia, those two classes took arms against the monarchy, the struggle (more or less purposeful), lasted only for a short while, and only a few of the *municipios* took part in it.

The Monarchy aspired, as was natural—given its charac-ter—to concentrate in its own hands, and exercise effectu-ally, all civil powers. The original struggle for the crown itself (which, as a continuation of Visigothic times, had disturbed the Asturio-Leonese kingdom from its beginning) was resolved in favour of hereditary succession of the first-born, whether male or female. In the 13th century Alfonso the Learned formulated this principle in legal terms. But there remained another crucial question, which impeded the growth of real power and the unification of civil and political life—the independent and anarchic spirit of the nobles, who, relying juridically on the system of feudal nobility, over-reached themselves at every step, disobeying the king, creating difficulties for him, disputing by force of arms his guardianship—if he were a minor—or his favour, in order to enjoy public offices. Also more than once they stirred up general revolts, such as that of the *Unión Aragon-esa*, which set in jeopardy the life and throne of Pedro IV. In the Aragon-Catalan Confederation the king established himself earlier than in Castille (mid-14th century), though he could not entirely destroy baronial power nor do away with the factions and private wars of the nobles. In Navarre the same thing happened until, at the end of the 15th century, the dynastic question of the Prince of Viana gave motives for a new war, based on the opposition be-tween the sense of privilege of the nobles and the *municipios* on the one hand, and royal absolutism on the other. From this struggle the first faction emerged weakened, and the Monarchy victorious.

In Castille the opposition between the two elements had more vicissitudes. The Monarchy had been gradually recovering all the attributes of sovereignty, with the gradual limitation of all the ancient privileges; but, in fact, it did not dominate the nobility, except when a king of great energy and extraordinary personal endowments sat on the throne. And even such an one did not enjoy his authority save at the cost of enormous energy and bloodshed, as happened in the days of Sancho IV, Alfonso XI, Pedro I, and Juan II (not through his own doings, but through his favourite, Don Alvaro). On the other hand, ground was lost to a notable extent when the king, either through weakness, or in favour of his own partisans, relaxed his resistance and conceded new privileges to the nobles, either in jurisdiction or in revenue, as did Enrique II and IV (15th century). This latter was dethroned by a faction of the nobles, who, with their ambitions and their private wars, disturbed the public peace throughout the kingdom.

67. *The Cortes and Democracy.* Yet in all parts central administration was being gradually organized, dependent on the king, with ramifications throughout his territory.

The legislative power, which had been wielded in earlier centuries by the monarch, assisted by his *concilium* of nobles and prelates (a continuation of the Councils of Toledo), grew more complicated, from the end of the 12th century in Aragon and León, and at a rather later date in the other kingdoms. A new assembly was instituted, in which deputies from the free *municipios* (*procuradores* and *personeros*), were incorporated as an essential element—in Castille, as the only essential element. This assembly took the name of Cortes, and was instituted earlier than were assemblies of analogous type in other countries of Europe. Although its proper function was the voting of taxes—which, as has been seen, were only paid by the people—it acquired in-

directly legislative authority, by means of petitions to the
kings for new laws or reforms of old ones.   The kings frequently acceded to this, either from a sense of justice, or
under force of public opinion, or to placate headstrong
elements and avoid disputes.   The periods of greatest influence and splendour of the Cortes of Castille were from
1188 to 1348, and from 1369 to 1406.   Their power declined with the growth of the royal power, and also on
account of the discord that arose between the deputies of
the people and the representatives of the nobles and clergy
in the Cortes, discord that weakened these assemblies in their
position as regards the king.   The popular element persisted almost alone from the beginning of the 15th century.

The Cortes of Aragon, Catalonia and Valencia had more
juridical rights than had those of Castille, including that
of electing a king if the hereditary line became extinct, as
happened at the death of Don Martín (*Parlamanto de Caspe*).
On the accession of a new monarch, or the renunciation of
the crown by the heir, the Cortes intervened, in Castille as
elsewhere, to give solemn recognition to the new king, and
to make him swear to respect the *fueros* and public liberties.
In all parts it was the king who, *de jure*, convoked the Cortes,
freely and without formal summons, and who indicated the
persons and *municipios* who were to be present, until by
custom, a certain number of these were fixed.

In Aragon, Catalonia, Valencia, and Navarre, the Cortes
were represented, when they were not sitting, by permanent deputation (*diputaciones*), which formed a kind of executive and fiscal commission.   That of Catalonia, which,
from 1365 onwards, was obliged to reside in Barcelona, took
the name of *Diputació del General* or *Generalidad*.   The Cortes
of Valencia was instituted in the 15th century.

68. *Organs of Government.*   The kings were aided in
executive matters by Councils (*Consejos*).   That of Castille
(*Concilium, Cort, Curia*) was in principle composed entirely
of nobles and prelates.   From the end of the 11th century
it is thought that representatives of the *municipios* were admitted to it.   It was modified at different times in the 14th

Photo, Arxiv Mas.

WROUGHT IRON CRUCIFIX
(*Catalan* [?] 14*th cent.*)

and 15th centuries, and by the end of the latter it consisted of a great number of members (*oidores*), nobles, ecclesiastics, and plebeians, and had rights of government, finance, and justice (Court of appeal). In Aragon and Catalonia there was also a royal Council (*consejo real*). One was formed in Navarre in the 14th and 15th centuries, and in 1364 it became a special council for questions of the Exchequer (*Cámara de comptos*). Governors represented the king in districts and provinces. They were either nobles or of the people, according to the epoch, and were called *Condes, Adelantados, Merinos, Bayles*, etc. The representatives of the kings in the towns were called *Alcaldes, Merinos, Sayones*, and their executive officers (constables), *alguaciles* and *zabalmedinas*.

The judicial power, or that part of it which was in the hands of the kings and which they managed to increase from year to year, was represented in Castille until the 13th century by a supreme royal tribunal (the above-mentioned *Consejo* or *Cort*), and by individual judges (*jueces*)—*i.e.*, the administrative functionaries already cited. From this date there began a tendency to separate the judicial and the administrative functions. Hierarchies of judges were created, the royal tribunal was reformed, etc. At the end of the 14th century, while the councils persisted, the first *Audiencia* was created in Segovia and a later one in Valladolid.

In Aragon there arose a special judge, called the *Justicia*, who at first accompanied the king, and whom later the nobles changed into a sort of mediator between themselves and the Monarch in cases of controversy or discord. This privileged position was modified in the time of Pedro IV, who created a separate royal tribunal or council; and though in 1441 the nobles and the *municipios*, in collaboration, made the office of *Justicia* permanent, so that the king could not change him at will, really he continued to be a royal dependant, under the inspection of a tribunal (tribunal of the sixteen) created by the Cortes. The two chief privileges of the *Justicia* were called the rights of *firmas* (signature) and *manifestación* (declaration) respectively, designed to protect the goods and the persons of the accused, or litigators, whilst the case or dispute was being tried; but these guarantees (which were often abused), only benefited the nobles and the middle classes. The lower classes never enjoyed them. A sign both of the centralizing of the monarchy and of the development of the protection of the weak against the nobles, is the legal order contained in the *Fueros generales* of Aragon, that presumptive defendants might no longer be disposed of and kept in prisons, fortresses, or houses of the nobles; to make up for this, communal or state prisons were instituted. In the event of a noble disobeying this law, the royal judge might require the handing over of the prisoner, and if the noble did not satisfy this demand, he was heavily fined. There was also in Aragon special provision for the protection of orphans, represented first in Valencia in 1337, by the appointment of a Father of the Orphans (*Padre de Huérfanos*), and later, in other places, of a General Father of Minors (*Padre general de Minores*).

Catalonia offers a special character in its government, by reason of the hegemony of Barcelona, and by the power acquired by the burghers in this and other cities of that kingdom. Apart from the *Diputación general*, or *Generalitat*, already mentioned, Barcelona had special powers, of great influence in that country: first consuls (a magistracy imitated from those in the South of France), then *pahers* (1249), and finally, *concelleres*, elected in a popular assembly. These last were assisted by the council of a hundred (*Consejo de Ciento*, or *Cien jurados*, 1265), representatives of all the free social classes. Its members enjoyed political, administrative, military, and mercantile rights.

The king was represented by the *lugarteniente* (deputy or lieutenant), the *Gobernador general* (Governor General, an office created in the 14th century), the *procuradores* (in the *comarcas* or districts), the *vegueros* and *sub-vegueros* (in the smaller demarcations, known as *veguerías*, and *sub-veguerías*), and the *bayles*, who figured in all the *municipios* in the country.

The Inquisition arose in Catalonia and Aragon in the 13th century, as a highly specialized tribunal of ecclesiastical character, designed to punish those guilty of heresy. For commercial matters there was established in Barcelona the so-called *Consulado de Mar*, an institution that was imitated in Valencia at the end of the 13th century (1283).

One other point must be noted at this period—the zeal with which the travelling royal jurists codified and worked for legislative unification, introducing new juridical principles, part of which were derived from the university studies of Justinian Roman law. This zeal existed chiefly (though with varying results), in Castille and Aragon. In Castille various complications were produced, projected codes and encyclopaedias, such as *Las Partidas* (§ 56). This activity progressed rapidly in the hands of legists and jurists, though it did not entirely oust the legislation that had arisen in foregoing centuries, and that had been based on social, political, and economic needs.

VII

END OF THE RECONQUEST. POLITICAL UNITY, THE BEGINNING OF SPIRITUAL GREATNESS

1479-1517

69. *Personal Union of the Christian Kingdoms*

DURING the foregoing centuries a desire had frequently been manifest to reduce the various kingdoms of Spain to unity, either through the hegemony of one of them, whose ruler should assume the title of Emperor, or by matrimonial alliance. This proposal was facilitated in mid-15th century by the marriage of Isabella, Infanta of Castille, and Ferdinand, hereditary Prince of Aragon, who succeeded to the throne in 1479. The grandson of these two, Charles V, united effectually and lawfully the Crowns of the two States, together with that of Navarre, the conquest of which was achieved by Ferdinand, who annexed it to Castille in 1515. This union of the three kingdoms under a single head did not, however, lessen the autonomy they had enjoyed when under their own kings. Neither the Cortes nor the Exchequer (*Hacienda pública*), nor the administration of justice, nor the military organization, nor the laws, either political or civil, of any one of them disappeared, nor were substituted by organizations or rules that were common to all three. The avenue by which this actually took place later was nevertheless opened, and it was logical that a more or less complete juridical and social unification should take place, in view of the tendency towards centralization displayed by all the monarchies of Europe; the new needs of the times gave rise to new legislation, which was naturally common to the three kingdoms in many points, and to more intimate and friendly contact between the citizens of the formerly separate kingdoms.

BIRTHPLACE OF ISABELLA OF CASTILLE

(Madrigal de las altas torres)

The monarchic unity was completed by the conquest of the Moorish kingdom of Granada in 1492, the year of the discovery of America. The conquest of this last Muslim kingdom in the Peninsula was celebrated in Rome (where the struggle against Turkish power, which was engrossing Europe, was represented by the Spanish Pope, Calixtus III), with feasts and with the publication of Latin laudatory poems. A little later, through inheritance from his father, Charles V received the imperial crown of the Holy Roman Empire, with much territory in the centre and west of Europe (Franche Condé, Luxembourg, Holland, Flanders) and rights of sovereignty in Italy.

70. *Crystallization of the National Ideal.* Although these results did not come about until rather later, their causes are already to be seen in the period we are examining, *i.e.*, in the reign of the so-called Catholic Monarchs (*Reyes católicos*). Their policy (*i.e.*, the energetic concentration and intensification of the foregoing tendencies), determined the path of the state, and thus of the nation, in the following two directions: *Imperialism*, the spirit of domination and preponderance in Europe; and *Religious Unity*. For some centuries these were the two predominant ideals in the ruling elements of Spain and in its social and political order.

The former was brought about by the Catholic Monarchs by means of matrimonial alliances. They married their children into the royal families in Europe; Portugal, Austria, France, and England. By conquest they gained Granada, parts of North Africa, Italy, and America. In these conquests their main opponents in Europe were the French.

Religious unity was achieved through the expulsion of the Jews, the forcible conversion of the *mudéjares* (or *moriscos*) from Castille, Granada, Navarre, and the Basque Provinces (1502), and by the establishment of the Inquisition in all the kingdoms. This was a religious tribunal, expressly dedicated to discovering and persecuting the heresies of the newly converted, whose faith was distrusted.

This tribunal was substantially the same as in the foregoing centuries, and, replacing the regular jurisdiction of the bishops in matters of faith and custom, it functioned in other kingdoms of Spain (in Aragon, as we have seen, since the beginning of the 13th century), for the persecution of those heresies which were then stirring in Spain as in the South of France and other European countries.

71. *The Inquisition.*   The Inquisition employed torture (as did all the tribunals in those days), to extract a confession from the accused; it kept those awaiting trial in solitary confinement; it kept secret the charges, and the names of the accuser and witnesses were not revealed to the accused.   This latter was allowed to choose a lawyer to defend him, who might object to judges whom he feared were prejudiced, draw up exculpatory speeches and, finally, might appeal against the sentence to the Pope.   The punishments meted out by the Inquisition were: public or private " reconciliation "; penance, more or less rigorous; subjection to the vigilance of the tribunals; the temporary or permanent use of a distinctive garb—a yellow tunic with a red cross (*sambenito*); temporary or lifelong imprisonment; fines or indemnification, and death at the stake— a punishment which had existed in the civil penal code of Castille since the 13th century.   Moreover, every sentence of death or imprisonment carried with it the confiscation of goods, which passed into the Royal Exchequer; but, as part of them were paid to the functionaries of the Inquisition, they came, in practice, to be ceded to them as remuneration, and this gave rise to great abuses.   When death at the stake took place, the criminal or criminals were handed over to the civil authorities, so that these might execute the sentence.   This was called *relajación al brazo civil* (turning over to the civil arm).   The solemn public act—in which, besides a great procession through the streets of the city, the sentences of the various condemned men were read, the abjurations and public " reconciliations " verified, and the handing over of the offender took place—was all called the *auto de fe*.   The

CASTLE OF SIMANCAS
(The " Record Office " of Spain)

burning took place later in the presence of a notary. If the offender had escaped, he was burnt in effigy; if he had died, the Inquisition might disinter and burn his remains. Sometimes also he was hanged first and burnt afterwards.

The rigour of the Spanish Inquisition was very great at first, and there were numerous appeals to the Pope. The number of accused was at times so large that they could not be contained in the prisons of the tribunal. In the first *auto de fe* celebrated in Seville, ten offenders were condemned to death at the stake; and, according to a contemporary, in the course of eight years, 700 men suffered this fate and 5,000 were condemned to prison and other punishments. In Avila, between 1490 and 1500, more than a hundred and thirteen were burnt. In one *auto de fe* alone, at Toledo, 1,200 accused appeared, and, in another, 750. In Jerez there was an *auto* which lasted three days.

72. *Absolutism and Centralization.* Along with these principles of policy, the Catholic monarchs set about intensifying the characteristics of the monarchic institution. Stronger, and with more personal energy than their predecessors, whose struggles (especially in Aragon and Catalonia) had prepared the way for them, they meant to remove all the obstacles which opposed the efficacy of royal authority.

Isabella's chief aim was to reduce the power of the nobility, which had become puffed up by its triumphs in the time of Henry IV (§ 63). Sometimes she took violent means, attacking the castles, imprisoning the great lords, despoiling them, or putting them to death. At other times, with the help of the Cortes and by legal means, she subdued them to the royal power and diminished their revenues which they had usurped or acquired from the Crown. As regards the middle classes, the road was easier. They were profoundly royalist in Castille, and in most of the other kingdoms. From among them were recruited the professional lawyers or *jurisconsultos*, who studied at the universities the Imperialist doctrines derived from Roman law. They had been politically broken by the internal

I

struggles of the *municipios*, and they longed for a strong power which could set the Administration in order. Of this the King and Queen took advantage. They ceased to give new *fueros* to the towns, though without apparently abolishing any; and they intervened more and more in municipal affairs, introducing new laws and ordinances, nominating delegates and royal officials, and substituting for the old, elective officers in the Council, others that were held for life, or were hereditary, and that were nominated by the Crown. As regards the Cortes, they did without it for the greater part of their reign, and not one met in Castille between 1492 and 1498, although during this time there occurred events of such national importance as the conquest of Granada, the discovery of America, the establishment of the new Inquisition, the expulsion of the Jews, and the forcible conversion of the Muslims. Moreover, because the *municipios* grumbled at the heavy costs of travelling for their deputies, there began the custom of paying them from the Royal Treasury—a new bond of dependence which prejudiced the free discharge of their duties. There were novelties in the Penal Code; at this time, 1480, was introduced the practice of visiting prisons to inspect the treatment given to the prisoners, and protect them against abuses of their gaolers. Then, too, began the application to the Colonies of the principle of hard labour for prisoners, as a means of using them profitably and guarding them from the dangers of idleness. This system had already been drawn up three centuries earlier, in the *Partidas* (§ 67). In civil matters Castilian legislation was reformed in various points, principally in regard to the rights of the family (*Leyes de Toro*). At this period, too, there appeared in Aragon the first law fixing the working day at eight hours (1593).

In Aragon Ferdinand followed a similar policy, seldom summoning the Cortes, omitting to consult them when further supplies were needed, or forcing them by threats to vote him money. In Catalonia the policy of the earlier kings had been to favour the lower classes, ordering that each one of their five *concelleres* (save the second, who be-

Photo, Arxiv Mas.

CASTLE OF MOMBELTRÁN, NEAR AVILA

longed, like the first, to the highest classes of the bourgeoisie)
should be elected from a separate class, so that each class
should be represented. Ferdinand the Catholic made
changes in the organization of the *municipio* of Barcelona,
whose *concelleres* had been originally nominated by the
Crown, and then by *insaculación* (drawing lots). He intervened more and more, by means of his officials and delegates, in the administration of other *municipios*. Again, the
generalidad suffered a change in its ancient system of election which was transformed into a mixture of election and
insaculación (1454), and, later, by *insaculación* alone (1493).
Yet its administrative, political, and military power remained essentially such as it had become in the foregoing
centuries.

73. *The Social Classes and the Reform of Customs.* The
Catholic monarchs also turned their attention to the social
order. We have already seen that in Aragon the ancient
rural servitude still existed, without any amelioration, and
that in Catalonia the *payeses de remensa* (§ 64) were profoundly discontented. Following the example of these, the
vasallos de parada (§ 64) in Aragon also rose in various places,
and the King intervened wholeheartedly for the bettering
of their condition. But either through a lack of vigour over
the enterprise, or because the nobility still, even in this
reign, enjoyed great power, Ferdinand was obliged to give
way and ended by abandoning the cause of the serfs, and
recognizing once again the old seignorial rights, including
that of punishment without trial. Many of these serfs were,
as we have said, Muslims.

In Catalonia things took a direction of their own. The
king resolutely supported the *remensas*, and on being recognized as arbitrator both by them and the overlords, he
issued a decree, known as the *Sentencia arbitral de Guadalupe*,
in virtue of which the abuses were abolished. The decree
recognized the freedom of the *payeses* to leave an estate
taking their goods with them, to purchase their freedom by
a sum of money, and deprived the landlords of the power
of criminal jurisdiction.

Personal slavery continued to be practised as hitherto. Slaves were generally acquired by purchase; although, as we shall see, Isabella decided that the American Indians could not be used as slaves.

The situation of the clergy needed much reform, both as regards their privileges (which were as disproportionate as those of the nobility), and as regards their conduct, which was in general very loose. Isabella tried to remedy both these things. She attacked their privileges because these tended to prejudice both the sovereignty and the revenues of the Crown. She attacked their immorality and—with the help of Cardinal Cisneros and various councils—the rule of various Franciscan Orders, driving out the rebels and shutting up monasteries. In Aragon, however, these reforms were not carried out at this time.

74. *Bureaucratic Organization.* The amplification of the functions of government and their growing centralization gave rise to a need for the organization of offices and of a series of new public servants. So the sovereigns, and especially Isabella, set their minds to this task. The ancient Council (*Consejo*), was reformed and was brought more under the control of the crown. Most of the places on it were given to the representatives of the middle classes, *i.e.*, to the *letrados*, the educated, and the vote was taken away from the nobles. The complication of governmental functions gave rise to the creation of new councils, such as that of the Inquisition, the Indies, the Army, and the Military Orders. In Aragon there were others, both for the kingdom of Aragon itself and for the dominions in Italy. Moreover, the offices of secretaries, scribes (*escribanos*), and accountants (*contadores*), were made uniform and regulated.

The administration of justice in Castille continued to be organized in the following hierarchy: the Royal Council (*Consejo Real*), *Audiencias* or chancellories (of which there were now three), *Alcaldes mayores*, and *Corregidores* (magistrates), and judges of various categories. In Navarre another *Audiencia* was created, and in Aragon the Royal Council or *Audiencia* continued to function. Ferdinand and

fernãda

hyſpana

yſabella

ſaluatorre

onceptõiB

maꝛie

THE DISCOVERY OF AMERICA BY CHRISTOPHER COLUMBUS

(Woodcut of 1494)

Isabella were much preoccupied in purifying the personnel of the Judicature, and in avoiding, or punishing, its traditional abuses. A special militia or civil guard, called the *Santa Hermandad* (holy brotherhood) was formed, with the special object of dealing with the numerous bandits who infested the country. This force came to number 2,000 men, and it destroyed the malefactors by swift and severe measures.

The Exchequer and the Army were also reorganized. Compulsory service existed alongside of voluntary recruitment. The Army was divided into companies or *capitanías* (500 men) and *coronelías* (12 companies); the artillery, which had come into use in the 14th century, was augmented and Army administration and health were promoted. The men who chiefly influenced these reforms were Gonzalo de Córdoba, called the *Gran Capitán*, Francisco Ramírez and Gonzalo de Ayora.

75. *The Discovery, Conquest, and Organization of the American Colonies.* The discovery of America was the result of the expedition carried out in 1492 by Columbus, with the concurrence and support of the Crown of Castille. Its aim was to reach India or the countries of the far East and Southern Asia, by the Western route, as the Portuguese were endeavouring to sail down the coast of Africa, and round the Cape of Good Hope. Columbus had tried in vain to interest various European sovereigns in his plan. Only in Spain were his ideas given consideration. Only there did the Crown show faith in him, and decide to supply the means by which his desires might be realized. Thus the expedition was made with Spanish gold, in Spanish ships, and with the concurrence of pilots and mariners from Spain. Moreover, the Crown made a contract with Columbus as to the juridical conditions which were to regulate any possible benefits of the voyage, and the administrative organization of the lands which might be occupied during it (*Capitulaciones de Santa Fe*). Certain islands situated at the entrance of the Gulf of Mexico, the Antilles, were discovered in 1492, and, a little later, much land on the conti-

nent itself.   In principle, the government of the country he had discovered was confided to Columbus, in accordance with the above-mentioned *capitulaciones*.   He was overlord, under the sovereignty of the King; and officials of the Exchequer and other departments accompanied all the expeditions which followed upon the original voyage of discovery.   Soon the Crown intervened afresh, since further discoveries rectified the original idea that the new lands were in Asia, and it was realized that what had been discovered was a new continent.   Thus there was applied to these new dominions the general system of government then current in Europe, especially in Spain, with governors nominated by the King, officials of the Exchequer to collect taxes, *alcaldes* (mayors) and *regidores* (magistrates), *municipios*, bishoprics, *audiencia*, etc.

In order to direct the affairs of America from the Capital, the " Supreme Council of the Indies " (*Consejo supremo de Indias*) was formed; while at Seville was established the so-called *Casa de Contratación*, a kind of custom-house, factory, tribunal, and scientific centre, where a commission of pilots gave nautical instruction and collected the information and memoranda sent home from the new territories.

In effect, the ruling of these growing colonies was a State department; and it was soon evident—both in the administrative order and in the economic, social, and cultural spheres of action—that the directing centres of Spain possessed a clear idea and an ample realization of the problems posed by the new lands and peoples which had entered the royal dominions, and had consequently come within the sphere of action of the Spanish people.

New international problems also arose over the discovery of the American territories.   The chief of these was the rivalry of the Crown of Portugal, for it will be remembered that the Portuguese were inspired with a similar idea of exploration to that of Columbus and the Catholic monarchs.   But this rivalry was resolved by the intervention of the Holy See, held then by a Spanish Pope, of the Valencian family of Borja (Borgia), Alexander VI.   The resolution was contained in four consecutive Bulls, of which the third (4th May 1493), was the most important. In it the Pope traced the so-called *línea de reparto*, or " Line of Alexander VI." This was an imaginary line which, drawn through the poles (*i.e.*, in the direction of the meridians of longitude, passed at 100 leagues from the Azores and from the Cape Verde Islands). The obvious insecurity of this line was resolved in principle by means of an agreement (Tordesillas, 1494), between the Crowns of Spain and Portugal. Pending the definite decision they agreed to recognize as belonging to the Spanish Crown all that lay to the West of this line, and to that of Portugal, all that lay to the East, including those parts of Africa already occupied, which had been ceded some years earlier by a Bull of Pope Calixtus III.

76. *Personal Treatment of the Indians. Negro Slaves.* Apart from the government and colonization of the American colonies (always called " The Indies " in Spain), there arose a question which in those days was of capital import- ance, given the current European attitude to barbarian peoples or savages, who were considered to be natural and proper objects of slavery. The Spanish State was the first to exchange these ideas for ideas of the juridical equality of mankind, and these became the basis of their colonial system. Consequently Queen Isabella—in spite of opinions to the contrary, and to the fact that Columbus himself had taken Indian slaves and was prepared to sell them in Spain —declared the natives of America to be free. The prin- ciple of freedom in the eyes of the law (with the sole ex- ception, and that a temporary one, of cannibals and those who made war on the Spaniards) was confirmed and regu- lated by later monarchs. This principle formed the basis of a legal ruling, which had no precedent in the history of colonization and no contemporary imitators. It was the most detailed and generous legislation for the protection of the natives that history has produced up to the present day.

But the needs of the Spanish emigrants in the exploitation of the mineral and agricultural wealth of the New World made it necessary to impose personal service on the Indians (as has happened in recent times in Africa and other centres of colonization). These obligations included that of performing manual labour under certain conditions (one of them being the *jornal*, or day's wages, which turned them into free workers). A system was also introduced of conceding to Spanish colonists certain fixed extensions of colonial territory, including the groups of Indians who lived on such territory, under the formal condition that the holders of concessions should protect and civilize the natives. This system was known as that of *repartimientos* or *encomiendas*.

But, as has continually happened in all colonizations, ancient and modern, such concessions gave rise to abuses among unscrupulous men, whose only idea was that of enriching themselves, no matter by what means; and, in conformity with the general ideas of the epoch, they looked upon it as natural that savage or inferior peoples should be slaves. As a result of this, many Indians were in actual fact slaves; others were hunted like wild beasts, with dogs, or were put to death, and those who were subject to Spanish masters (*encomendados*), were sometimes treated very harshly. Conscientious colonists protested against these abuses, which happened mainly in the Antilles, in the early years of colonization. They were constantly denounced to the King and Queen, who always tried to suppress them. A Dominican friar, living in the Antilles, Padre Las Casas, indignant at the impunity of the disobedient colonists, set off for Spain and went to King Ferdinand and Cardinal Cisneros, begging justice for the Indians. He was nominated their Protector, and was appointed to inspect the conduct of the colonists. But, though he was supported by the monks of his Order and by many other persons, he could achieve nothing effective on account of the opposition of the Hieronymite monks (who had also been ordered to conduct an inquiry), and the intrigues of the exploiters themselves, who were naturally eager that the abuses should not be corrected.

This question is vital at the present day as a basis of all judgment on colonization. Spanish America represented the eternal struggle between the principles of humanity and justice and the selfishness of the majority of mankind —a struggle which still goes on in our days, both in the occupation of lands inhabited by peoples of inferior civilization, and in colonization, with or without conquest, such as that which exists in the relations between workpeople and their employers. The singularity of the ruling classes in Spain at the end of the 15th century, and of all those who followed them (kings, governors, theologians, jurists, religious orders, as well as many of the *conquistadores*, administrators and colonists in America) was that they raised themselves spiritually above the practice common of their time, proclaiming ideas which contradicted it, trying to impose these ideas by means of legislation, and striving continually for their realization and for the punishment of those who transgressed them.

In this struggle the Spanish State, the missionary religious orders in general, and the other Spaniards who seconded such humane conduct, went as far as possible in making official repression and prevention efficacious and in furthering spiritual authority. They hurled themselves against those same obstacles which are met with in all similar attempts, even to-day. The scrupulousness with which they attempted to avoid abuses in the realm of external guarantees is attested, not only by the above-mentioned protective legislation in general, but also by the special legislation for labour, which developed in the following period (§ 84). This offers a model in this kind of legislation, which at that time found no parallel in any country. Thus it is understandable that the territories colonized by the Spaniards should be to-day those in which the Indian inhabitants have survived in the greatest numbers. It has been proved that the statistics of violent extermination given by Padre Las Casas in the heat of his generous defence of the Indians were inexact. Save in isolated cases in the Antilles, which have already been mentioned, the decline of the Indian inhabitants was not due to butchery nor to warfare, but to other causes, among them the effect produced (and still produced in modern colonies) by the introduction of European methods of labour, especially in the mines, upon the nature of the Indians, who were not accustomed to such hard work. And as regards this work, we have proofs that it was not so hard, and therefore not so hated by the Indians themselves, as we have been accustomed to believe.

The keenness of the feeling of justice towards inferior peoples was so great at this time in Spain itself that it was even manifested towards the Negroes. Padre Las Casas himself had suggested, as a compromise, that Negro slaves should be introduced to replace the Indians, who were to remain free. But he changed his opinion on this point in later years. Others, more advanced than he, preached against the treatment of the Negroes, practised by all the peoples of Europe, and begged for their liberation. Such were: Padre Avendaño, B. de Albornoz, Fray Pedro Claver (who was canonized later), and Padre Alfonso de Sandoval, writers and missionaries of the 16th and 17th centuries, and precursors of the whole anti-slavery movement. But though the liberty of the Indians had the support of the great majority of cultivated Spaniards, that of the Negroes was not so much in favour. Nevertheless, according to all the documentary evidence and the accounts of travellers, negro servitude was much more humane in our island and continental possessions than in those of other colonizing races.

77. *The Protection of Industry and Commerce*. The economic policy of the kings was protectionist. They tried to favour national industries and avoid the competition of certain foreign products, both by taxing or prohibiting imports and by making difficult the export of raw materials, such as wool. Thus there was an increase in the manufacture of cloth (Toledo, Seville, Murcia, Valencia, Barcelona, and other places), silk (Granada), leather, glazed tiles, arms and silver objects, apart from the production of wool (pro-

moted by great privileges granted to the stock-farmers),
wine, oil, iron, etc. In general, great industrial progress is
to be seen in Castille and neighbouring districts, Valencia,
Aragon, and Mallorca (in which certain manufactures
were revived), whereas in Barcelona, the decline of its
ancient splendour is already clearly to be seen. In all parts
the expulsion of the Jews caused harm to industry. The
protection of agriculture was much less, through the competition of stock-farming, and this, coupled with repeated
bad harvests, brought about great backwardness of production in the beginning of the 16th century. Wheat-flour
reached exorbitant prices in Castille and the bread had
to be made of various mixtures, or with flour made of
acorns, etc. On the other hand, the kings paid great attention to the working and products of the mines, especially to the gold and silver mines of America. At that time
it was thought that the principal wealth of a nation lay in
possessing much currency, which is why the export of money
was prohibited. But the kings also favoured agricultural
development in America and sent over seed, plants,
labourers, experts in irrigation, etc.

To encourage commerce, many privileges were given for
fairs and markets, and subsidies were granted to owners of
large ships. An attempt was made to limit the establishment of foreign merchants in Spain and their intervention
in America. All merchandise going to and from the Indies
was exempt from duty, and other similar measures were
taken. Commerce with America could only be carried on
from the ports of Cadiz and Seville.

78. *The Thirst for Culture and its Consequences.* The impulse given to culture in the foregoing centuries, with its
predominant tendencies towards studies in literature, law
and the applied sciences, increased during the reign of
Ferdinand and Isabella. The influence of Italy continued
to grow, and there were new needs caused by the discovery
of America. Eloquent manifestations of the thirst for
knowledge were: the private foundation of many university colleges, and professorships, especially in Castille (the

greatest of these was the University of Alcalá de Henares, founded by Cardinal Cisneros and dedicated especially to the study of classical languages and literature, and to philosophy); the appointment of notable scholars and teachers as tutors to the royal family and to the Queen herself; the protection given by many nobles and prelates to foreign professors, humanists, and men of letters, with whose help academies and free courses of instruction were organized, in the houses of the nobility. Furthermore, the tradition was maintained that our scholars should go abroad to perfect their culture in the universities of Italy and France. This is attested by the groups, or as they were then called, *Naciones*, of Spaniards which were found then and later at foreign centres of learning, and who sometimes left graphic expression of their presence in sketches painted on the walls of the buildings, *e.g.*, that of the University of Bologna.

All these things combined to produce a serious revival of Greek and Latin culture, and of Hebrew (which led to the study of the Bible and its translations); to the cultivation of Arabic and the initiation of a philosophical movement, which, on the basis of Plato and Aristotle, began to embody a rectification of classical philosophy. At the same time jurisprudence continued to develop, both in political, civil and canon law. Map-making and cosmography not only retained, but increased their old splendour, both in the schools of Catalonia and Mallorca and in the scientific centre of the *Casa de Contratación* at Seville (§ 75). Medicine resolutely entered upon the sound methods of investigation and experiment, reforming those methods learnt from the Muslims, and establishing the first chairs of anatomy and surgery.

In literature the classical Italian influence and the Castilian tongue triumphed fully, the latter even imposing itself on Catalan, Valencian, Portuguese, and even on several Italian poets. Stories of chivalry spread with the translation of *Amadis de Gaula* and the publication of other works derived from this, and from the amatory novels of

Italian type. But the two greatest literary creations of this time were the *Picaresque* novel, dealing with the customs of the poor—beggars and criminals—and the secular theatre. The former was due to the extraordinary merit and the influence of a book called *Tragicomedia de Calixto y Melibea*, commonly called *La Celestina*, written by Fernando de Rojas. The founders of the theatre were Juan de la Encina, Gil Vicente, and Torres Naharro, who treated of religious subjects (*e.g.*, the Nativity, etc.), and also of popular customs as exhibited by peasants, shepherds, etc. Till then the most important dramatic and musical-dramatic performances had been religious, and had been celebrated in the churches on important feast-days (Nativity, Holy Week, etc.). But, as is shown by Valencian documents of the end of the 14th century, there were already being played, at the Court of Aragon, comedies of manners, not with religious but with profane subjects.

Besides those already mentioned, the following were eminent in various branches of the sciences and literature at this time: Antonio de Nebrija, Doña Beatriz Galindo (a lady known as *La Latina*), Diego de Valera, the brothers Vergara, Hernán Alfonso de Herrera, Pedro Martínez de Osma, doctor Montalvo, Galíndez de Carvajal, López del Vivero, Juan de la Cosa, Sánchez Ciruelo (who wrote against judicial astrology, a superstition still very general then in Europe), Morales, and others. Outstanding as poets were Garci Sánchez de Badajoz, Pedro Manuel de Urrea, Guevara, the Valencians Crespi de Valldaura, Bernardo Fenollar and Fray Iñigo de Mendoza. Cardinal Cisneros deserves mention, not only as founder of the University of Alcalá de Henares, but also as a politician and as editor of the monumental Polyglot (or Complutensian) Bible, which was the first edition of the Bible text in Hebrew, Greek, Chaldean, and Latin, with grammars and vocabularies (1514-1517).

79. *The Fine Arts.* Along with this growth of scientific and literary culture there was a great advance in the artistic education of the Spanish people. This was largely due to

Italian and Flemish artists, who continued to visit the country in great numbers, and certain of whose masters exerted a powerful influence on many of our painters before the truly Spanish manner had come to its own.

In architecture and also in decorative sculpture and allied arts the mixture of the old Gothic and the classical Renaissance produced a new form called *Plateresque*, because in its exuberant decoration it resembled the filigree of silver workers. Typical examples of this work are the façade of San Pablo and the College of San Gregorio at Valladolid, and the façade of San Esteban at Salamanca. Along with this tendency, and at times confused with it, arose another, more national, type. This was a mixture of Gothic Renaissance and Mudéjar art (usually with this last in preponderance), which took on a special aspect of its own, and to which modern critics have given a special name, derived from the epoch at which it flourished, *i.e.*, *Isabelino*, or Isabella I. Typical amongst other examples of this style is the Chapel of the Vélez family at Murcia. Equally deserving of mention is the originality of the decoration of shields, applied by the artist Juan Guas to the *capilla mayor* of San Juan de los Reyes at Toledo. At the same time, in other buildings, Gothic forms continued to be used (*e.g.*, San Juan de los Reyes, and in the Chapel of the Condestable at Burgos). In the hospital of Santa Cruz at Toledo we find the Roman style, interpreted according to the Italian renaissance. A great many colleges, churches, palaces, and castles were built at this time, in one or other of these very diverse styles.

Mudéjar influences continued to inspire the artists, both in construction and decoration, apart from the abovementioned *Isabelino* style. Examples of this art are the interior of the Alcázar of Seville, the door and vaulting of the Chapter house in Toledo, the Church of San Juan de la Penitencia (founded by Cisneros in Toledo), and a room in what is now the *Archivo* at Alcalá.

In painting, Italian and Flemish influences combined, and, besides works expressing purely one or other of these

TOMB OF JUAN DE PADILLA, PAGE TO FERDINAND AND ISABELLA

(Burgos: Museo provincial)

influences, there was produced an eclectic school, in which characteristics of the Spanish school proper began to appear. The most notable native painters of this time were: the Castilians Fernando Rincón and Pedro González Berruguete; the Valencians (?) Rodrigo de Osuna and his son; the natives of La Mancha, Ferrando Yáñez, and Ferrando de Llanos, both disciples of Leonardo da Vinci; the Catalans, Huguet and the Vergós (father and two sons); the Aragonese, Bernat and Díaz de Oviedo; the Sevillians, Pedro de Córdoba and Alejo Fernández, and certain anonymous authors of admirable works. Amongst the foreign artists who were then in Spain may be mentioned: Sithium, Benson, Francisco de Amberes, Juan de Borgoña, and Francisco Niculoso Pisano, a worker in ceramics who settled in Triana (a suburb of Seville) with the nickname of *Ollero* (potter).

Three great schools of sculpture flourished—those of Burgos, Toledo, and Seville, and, independent of these, one which may be considered as a product of León. These three schools were the joint creation of native and foreign sculptors, and in them sometimes national, sometimes foreign, influences predominated. The most illustrious artists of Burgos were: Gil de Siloé, and Diego de la Cruz; in Toledo, Juan Alemán, Egas Comas, Juan Guas, Pablo Ortiz, Rodrigo Duque, and Sebastián Almonacid; in León, Fadrique Alemán. The names of the authors of some very important works are unknown, as, for example, the creators of the sepulchre of Alonso de Cartagena (Burgos), those of the Counts of Tendilla (Guadalajara), and that of the young man reading at Sigüenza, a masterpiece of the Toledan school. In Seville we know the names of Lorenzo Mercader or Mercadante, Pedro Millán, Dancart, and Jorge Fernández.

Apart from the works already mentioned, the following deserve special notice: *tombs*, those of Juan II, Queen Isabella, and the Infante Alfonso (Miraflores); that of Juan de Padilla (Burgos); those of Alvaro de Luna and his wife (Toledo); that of the Cardinal Cervantes (Seville) and that of Alfonso de Velasco and his wife (Guadalupe); *retablos*, those of the cathedrals of Seville and Toledo, and especially that in the Carthusian monastery of Miraflores, that of San Nicolás (Burgos) and others; *choir stalls*, those of Toledo, León, and Zamora. As regards *doors* with sculpture and statues, those of the churches of San Gregorio and San Pablo (Valladolid), the Colegial de Aranda and Puerta de los Leones, Toledo; the decoration of the church of San Juan de los Reyes and of the neighbouring monastery of the Santo Entierro (Holy Burial) at Toledo; the Apostles of the Parral; the Nativity of the door of San Miguel (Seville Cathedral); the saints of the door of the Bautismo (Seville); the Resurrection and Burial of Christ, which are in one of the chapels of the same cathedral, and the door of the Chapel Royal of Granada.

Amongst the so-called industrial arts, the following were pre-eminent: the reliquaries of the German, Enrique de Arfe, and of his sons and disciples and other artists (particularly those of León, now disappeared, and of Toledo and Barcelona); silver table-services, by which the silversmiths of Barcelona made their name, and other domestic pieces in gold; the iron *rejas* or screens at Burgos, Pamplona, and Toledo, textiles and embroidery (those of the *Tanto Monta*, and of Cisneros in Toledo, that of Roncesvalles, etc.), and the original application of tiles to altars and *retablos* (such as that of Queen Isabella in Seville), and to the façades of churches (the Church of Santa Paula at Seville).

At this time also the national school of music began to form. Its chief characteristic is the closeness with which the feeling of the melody follows that of the words. The three most notable musicians then were: Juan del Encina, Anchieta, and Peñalosa, protégés of the Catholic monarchs. Encina may be considered as the inventor of the mixed dramatic genre known as the *zarzuela*.

80. *Customs.* But along with these ideal manifestations which they had attained, the private lives of the Spanish people continued to reveal a terrible lack of morality, which was reflected in the literature and especially in the

HIGH ALTAR IN THE MONASTERY OF MIRAFLORES, BURGOS

(*By Gil de Siloë*, 1489-1493)

WROUGHT IRON " REJA "
(*Huesca Cathedral*)

thirst for luxury and ostentation in dress, furniture, adorn-
ments, and festivals. The monarchs themselves were guilty
of this also. Isabella loved to show herself in public,
richly attired, a thing which her confessor, Fray Hernando
de Talavera, censured more than once. In contrast to this
love of display was the modesty and sobriety of domestic
life, as regards food and comfort in the home, which caused
an Italian traveller to remark that " the Spaniards were
lavish on the great feast days and lived poorly for all the
rest of the year."

VIII

POLITICAL AND SPIRITUAL SUPREMACY OF SPAIN IN ITS DECLINE

1517-1700

81. *National Interests*

FROM what has been said in the foregoing paragraphs it should be easy to determine what elements were advantageous in Spanish civilization at the beginning of the reign of Charles V, and what road the social activities of the State should take. As regards material things, the growing industries, so well protected by the Catholic monarchs, demanded, if not a protectionist policy, at least freedom from oppressive restrictions and the conservation of the economic forces of the country. The colonization of America demanded constant attention, directed not only towards the conquest of new territories, but to the furthering of the exploitation of agricultural and mineral wealth and to facilitating trade. Agriculture in the Peninsula also needed great encouragement, to bring under cultivation the great stretches of virgin soil, to increase the rural population and better its condition, and also to improve the condition of the land itself, and by canalization of the rivers to advance the means of communication. There was also great need to increase the population, already much diminished (the censuses of the 15th century give only from 7,900,000 to $9\frac{1}{2}$ millions under the Crown of Castille, which included the greater part of Spain) and which declined further after 1492, by the expulsion of the Jews—about 165,000—and the emigration of a good many Muslims. As regards the intellectual and moral life of the people, it was able to develope vigorously, in close contact with other cultivated peoples. Teaching establishments increased in number, especially primary schools for the use of the people.

Much of this programme had already been embarked upon (as we have seen) by the Catholic monarchs, especially in Castille. Its later development urgently required peace, a rigorous administration of the public finances, and a great breadth of view and close attention on the part of the monarchs, with regard to the problems of economics and education. Many of these conditions, unfortunately, were absent, especially from the end of the 16th century onwards. Hence it happened that in the short space of 200 years, in which reigned the successors of the Catholic monarchs, the House of Austria (so-called because Charles V was the son of the Austrian Archduke Philip the Fair), Spain's pre-eminence, after a short period of brilliance, rapidly declined.

82. *Imperialism and its Consequences.* As regards the hegemony of Spain at this time, it must be observed that then, as now, with all due respect to the value of social prosperity and the culture of the people, the conception of power and international importance depended generally on the military strength of the nations and the extent of the lands that they ruled. In this sense Spain was, at the beginning of the 16th century, the first nation in the world. Her king, Charles V, as well as being Holy Roman Emperor, held the greater part of the Italian Peninsula, several countries in the North-West of Europe (§ 69), some in Africa, almost the whole of America, and many islands (the Philippines, discovered in 1521, and others). A little later his son, Philip II, though he was not heir to the Imperial Crown of Germany, added new lands to Spain, among them, Portugal.

But this vast empire, on which it came to be said that the sun never set, brought in its train much inconvenience. First, it aroused the suspicions and envy of other States, who regarded with fear the spirit of domination of the kings of Spain. Difficulties and quarrels naturally arose, apart from the aggressive actions which emanated from the imperialistic ambitions, no less strong among the rulers of other nations than in Spain. To withstand these attacks and uphold the integrity of their possessions, our monarchs were forced into continuous warfare, which wasted much money and diverted numerous workers from agriculture and industry, though the chief military system of that time was to employ foreign mercenaries. Besides this, the sense of religious unity of the kings and the clergy produced, on the one hand, wars caused by their zeal to prevent the spreading of Protestantism, and, on the other, losses to the population of Spain through the expulsion of all the Moors in 1609, preceded by struggles and bloodshed in Andalucía and other parts. However, in this expulsion, as in the earlier expulsion of the Jews, historical exactitude obliges us to recognize that, added to the religious motive, there was a political motive—the problem of national ethnological unity (*cf.* the problem of foreign minorities to-day in certain new States of Europe and Asia), and by the dangers revealed by association with the African Muslims and the Turks. The desire to preserve orthodox purity in the Peninsula led to a lessening, and even an attempt to abolish, intellectual communication with other countries. Foreigners were regarded as suspect and the liberties of the native professors and writers were curtailed in matters concerning dogma or anything which might be suspected to be connected with dogma, although, strictly speaking, it was not so connected; the work of the Inquisition was thereby much increased. Finally, the religious ideal (in virtue of which the kings of Spain were regarded as commanders and genuine defenders of the Church)—Spain's traditional opposition to the Muslims—(who were now a real danger to Europe, since they had conquered much land in the East, with Constantinople as their capital, and other territories in Northern Africa) all obliged her to engage in a constant struggle, beneficial, doubtless, for all the European nations, but one which helped to lessen the national forces and increase the outlay of the treasury. In these struggles, which began with the African expeditions

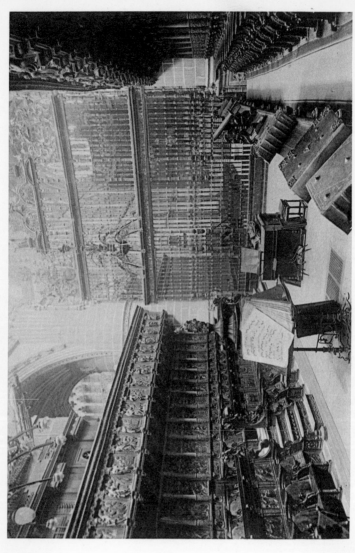

THE CHOIR: BURGOS CATHEDRAL.

of Cardinal Cisneros and characterized the anti-Turkish policy of Charles V and Philip II, Spanish ideals were represented, not only by the kings but also by the Spanish Popes, such as Calixtus III (§ 69) and Alexander II, steadfast preachers of the Crusade against the Turks.

The main results of the various facts mentioned were: the absorption of the State in military questions, the impoverishment of the country, the decline in the number of hands for farm-work, industry, and commerce, the forced abandonment of a policy of interior betterment, for the prosecution of which there was neither time nor money enough; the isolation of Spain, and finally her cultural decline. In the following paragraphs we shall give details of these results.

83. *The Downfall of Catholic Imperialism.* The early successors of the Catholic Monarchs (their grandson Charles V and especially their great-grandson, Philip II) tried to realize in full the ideals of the nation and the Empire. They personally directed policy and the foreign wars. Charles, with a ceaseless activity, went about his dominions and took part in the wars. Philip, from his study, entered into all negotiations, resolving them himself, and dictating or writing with his own hand even the details of the instructions that were sent to his subordinates. At the same time both kings managed to see to economic and cultural affairs. Charles made vain efforts to restrain the constant drainage which the wars imposed upon the treasury and the people, while Philip interested himself seriously in public works, libraries, the fine arts, and other aspects of intellectual life. The demands made upon them were too much for human strength, apart from the inevitable contradiction between the military needs and national prosperity, and it is not surprising that both broke down before them. Charles, though endowed with a robust physique, and an energetic mind, succumbed to fatigue and gave over the government when still young. Philip, less fiery, weaker physically, yet tenacious and unshakable in his self-abnegation, continued to struggle until his death. Nevertheless,

even in his greatest efforts (*i.e.*, to keep his dominions whole and to vanquish Protestantism) he saw the downfall of all his plans.   In fact, though during his reign he had acquired the Dukedom of Milan (1555), Portugal and its colonies (1580), certain territories in Africa, and great extensions in America, with which he increased the inheritance received from his father, yet from 1578 the Low Countries may be considered to have been freed, and in consequence of the repulses and defeats received during his various attacks on England, he lost his former military prestige and also, irremediably, all hope of vanquishing Protestantism, against which the Society of Jesus had roused the national religious feeling.   This Society, the most essential organ of the Catholic reaction, grew all the more vital in the face of the greater energy and power of the Protestant kings and peoples.   The founder of the Society was the Basque, Ignatius Loyola (St. Ignatius), who was succeeded by other Spaniards, among them Laynez and Borja (San Francisco Borgia), Duke of Gandía.

The political decadence, thus begun, was precipitated by Philip's successors, who were less zealous for good government than he, less intelligent, and given over to favourites or ministers who cared more for their own than for the public good, or else to confessors who made use of the powers of the confessional for political intrigues and also fomented religious fanaticism among the kings.   The last of these, Charles II, sickly, imbecile, and highly superstitious, believed himself to be possessed by the devil, and was the plaything of the ambitions of all who surrounded him.

As a result of all this, Spain had lost, by the end of the 17th century: the Low Countries, Portugal, Rousillon, part of Artois and Flanders, the Franche Comté, part of St. Domingo and the Island of Jamaica (Antilles).   Moreover, trade with America was constantly harassed by English, Dutch, and French pirates.   New powers arose in Europe with the fall of the great Spanish Empire: France, who benefited most, Holland, and England.   Protestantism triumphed in the two latter and in Germany, dividing Christendom into two hostile camps.

84. *Absolutism.* Just as the kings of the House of Austria continued the imperialistic and religious policy of the Catholic Monarchs, so also they followed their examples of centralization and absolutism, and indeed, reinforced them. As regards Castille, the abuses of Charles V gave rise to a revolt, called the revolt of the *Comunidades*, in whose programme were the following proposals: that the *Procuradores* or Deputies of the Cortes should receive no favours from the king; that the Cortes and the Royal Council should elect the regent of the kingdom and the tutors of the kings; that instead of *Corregidores* nominated by the Crown towns and villages should have *alcaldes* (mayors) elected by the citizens; that public goods should not be wasted, nor the old taxes increased; that the king should not make war without the consent of the Cortes, and that he should expound before them the costs and causes of such a war; finally, that the Cortes be convoked at fixed periods, or should meet automatically every three years. Before this the inhabitants of Segovia had hanged their *procurador* for having voted certain taxes in the Cortes against the recommendations of the citizens.

The great revolt of the *Comuneros* was promptly quelled. The nobility, who had supported it in principle, dissociated themselves from it. Castilian towns (Segovia, Toledo, Avila, and others), found themselves alone, and received aid from no other region. Those of Andalucía even formed a league against them, in favour of the Emperor. The rebels subdued, and their ringleaders, Padilla, Bravo, Maldonado, and the Bishop Acuña, put to death, royal absolutism found no further obstacles.

A little later, in the reign of Philip II, political agitation reached Aragon, though in a less severe form. Charles V had already thought of diminishing the *fueros* and liberties of Aragon, in so far as they opposed the absolute authority of the king. His son, as a punishment for a certain rising, led by the *Justicia Mayor* (1590), caused him to be hung, and

modified the prerogatives of that office (making it again
permanent, and at the king's pleasure), and those of the
Cortes (§ 67). Elsewhere there was no change. The tendency to unify and codify, which had begun in the 13th century (§ 67), was not followed by the absolute monarchs in
the direction that seemed to correspond to the political
direction that they represented. In the period with which
we are now concerned, there appeared no general code,
with the sole exception of the summaries of new laws. The
special laws of bygone kings continued; and also there
continued differences that had arisen through the variety
of laws in earlier centuries, through the various sources of
law that had formed them, and, above all, through differences of regional and local custom. The new general laws
which were substituted for these diversities (and which
made possible the action of a single political power on be-
half of all the Spanish territories) were concerned only
with certain points of public law. Another source of unification in the sphere of private law (marriage, family, etc.),
was the incorporation of national laws in the dispositions
of the Council of Trent, in the elaboration of which many
Spanish theologians took an active part.

On the other hand, from this time onwards the Cortes lost
all their power. They were formally convoked for the
recognition of a new king, the passing of statute laws, etc.,
and to vote new taxes. But the vote was no longer free.
At times they were suborned by the *procuradores*, at others
they were threatened by the army, and not rarely they
themselves bribed the ministers or favourites of the kings
to lower the taxes. The discontent roused by this conduct
was one of the chief causes of the revolt of Barcelona (1640),
put down two years later, without the town losing its
charter (*fueros*). Finally, a decree of 1665 put an end to
the principal function of the Cortes, as it transferred to the
Ayuntamientos (bodies of magistrates in the cities and towns)
the right to vote or authorize taxes to the king. The meet-
ings subsequent to this date were quite unimportant.

85. *Splendour, and Economic Misery.* The power of the

A PRIVATE HOUSE IN SARAGOSSA

(16th cent.)

Spanish State until the end of the reign of Philip II, the pains taken by him and by his father to promote internal prosperity (§ 83), and the influence of the new sources of wealth represented by the Indies, produced for a time a high degree of economic prosperity. This is attested by the public and private buildings of the 16th and part of the 17th centuries. These clearly show, even in thinly populated parts of Spain that later fell into decay, the well-being which they enjoyed at a certain period, and the wealth of the principal families. Later, however, political decadence and the growth of royal absolutism were accompanied by the bankruptcy of the exchequer and general misery of the population.

With the expulsion of the Moors and the continuous warfare, the population much decreased. This is confirmed by almost all the writers of the 17th century, though the lack of reliable statistics does not allow of our determining the numbers. The number of emigrants to America was also considerable. Moreover, a great number of the inhabitants of the Peninsula led a religious life, secluded in monasteries and therefore cut off from agricultural and industrial life. The Cortes of 1626 stated that there were then 9,088 monasteries, not counting the convents. Thus the fields were unpeopled and the factories empty. Production was much restricted, wages fell enormously, the cost of living rose, and there were various crises of famine. Since, from an impoverished population no great revenues could be extracted, the kings were in need of money at every step. They came to the extreme disgrace of making collections from house to house, and placing collecting boxes in the streets, to help the royal exchequer. In the case of many towns (*municipios*), independent through ancient charters, the Crown sold their *fueros* to the nobles to raise money. Almost all the public offices came to be given also for money. either for life or permanently (*oficios enajenados*). The army, which, as we have seen, consisted largely of foreign mercenaries, often revolted for lack of pay, refusing to fight, and plundering the towns. Those who were maimed in war crowded to the Court, begging money from the king and his ministers, and fighting among themselves for the *sopa* which the monasteries distributed free of charge. By the end of the 17th century, according to a contemporary writer, there were not more than 6,000 able-bodied soldiers in Spain, and thirteen ships of war. The government employed a foreign navy to keep at bay the pirates who harassed the coasts. The representative type of Spaniard of those days came to be the hero of the Picaresque novel (§ 78)—later to be found in Hispanophobe foreign literatures—that is to say, the generalization that the Spaniard was a more or less hungry man, who hid his misery behind his pride of race, as a *hidalgo*, or a man of gentle birth.

Only the monasteries, churches, and certain nobles enjoyed prosperity. With the former this was because of the enormous properties which had continued to accrue to them, and which could not be sold or divided. With the latter it was because of the entails, the permanence of family properties (which also might not be sold), in the hands of one of the sons, usually the eldest. The enormous revenues thus produced were badly administered and their owners squandered them at Court. It often happened that, owing to the nobles' neglect of their estates, they were permanently uncultivated. The public highways became full of bands of robbers, often very numerous and ferocious (*e.g.*, in Catalonia). The *Santa Hermandad* (§ 74), fallen from its former vigour, could do nothing against them.

With all this, a great part of the manual work, especially certain low occupations, despised by the populace themselves, was in the hands of slaves, acquired in wars against the Turks or Moors, or by purchase. They were sold publicly as goods, by deeds drawn up by notaries. On a certain occasion some 2,000 of these slaves were brought to Cadiz, and though many of them were baptized, they did not acquire full liberty, and continued to be employed as dock-hands, and in other ways, to the profit of their owners.

Yet it would be inaccurate to put down all the economic

VALENCIA: GALLERY AND CEILING OF THE " AUDIENCIA "
(16*th cent.*)

misery of Spain to the causes already indicated. Much of it was due to the erroneous economic ideas of the age and the equivocal system that arose from these ideas. The over-estimation of precious metals, the possession of which was supposed to indicate wealth, led to the consideration of other products as of secondary importance. The method of reckoning the prosperity of nations by the balance of commerce, supposing that the important thing was to sell much and buy little abroad, because in this way much gold entered the country and little left it, led to absurdities for which the general economy of the country suffered in the end. If the lands in America discovered and conquered by the Spaniards had been less abundant in gold, silver, and pearls, or if these things had been non-existent (as they were in the territories colonized by other European countries), Spanish economic life would undoubtedly have been different, and would have reacted sooner against the false economic ideas then current in the world, and which other countries also applied for a certain time.

Again, the cupidity of the European governments and of adventurers of all nations—the former more or less in league with the latter—kept the trade routes between America and Spain in a continual state of war, either against the militant navies of England, France, and Holland, or against pirates. This demanded constant vigilance and the mobilization of military forces to protect our ships. It produced the system of convoys of ships bearing precious metals and merchandise, guarded by ships of war, a system which we have seen reproduced during the war of 1914-1918, through the same needs of defence that originated and maintained it in the 16th and 17th centuries. In spite of all these precautions, pirates and warships of other nations often fell upon Spanish ships from America, so causing serious losses to the public exchequer and to private fortunes.

86. *The Classic Period of Spanish Colonization.* In the 16th century, or, more exactly, in the reigns of Charles V and Philip II, were completed the discovery, conquest, and

colonial organization of the countries of America and
Oceania, an enterprise begun in the foregoing period. This
does not mean that at the death of Philip II (1598) the
Spanish regime remained fixed and unalterable till the fall
of the House of Austria. On the contrary, during the 17th
century, in matters concerning important elements of
government and civil institutions there were constant and
vital actions and reactions. But the fundamental lines laid
down in the 16th century persisted. What followed was
simply complementary, a rectification of detail or the adoption of regional peculiarities, consequent on the special
conditions of the inhabitants or the way of life in a given
district.

The series of discoveries, apart from those made in the
reigns of the Catholic monarchs, by Columbus and his immediate successors (Amerigo Vespucci, Solís, Hojeda, Juan
de la Cosa, Pinzón, Ponce de León, Núñez de Balboa, etc.),
constitute one of the longest epics of achievement of the
human race, and one of the richest in heroic deeds and geographical results. There were voyages by sea, which followed the coasts of America, in the Atlantic and the Pacific,
crossing from the latter to Asia. There were expeditions
over land, starting from Chile and La Plata, penetrating
almost the whole continent, far inland, into what now belongs to certain Western States of North America. In their
marvellous exploits (setting on one side the technical
ability of the sailors) they put to the proof and defined
those human faculties which must chiefly be displayed in
such enterprises, if they are to achieve the ends that inspire
them. Without pretending by any means to exhaust the
list of names worthy of mention, the following may be
quoted. Most of them are Spaniards by birth and nationality, some few are foreigners in the paid service of the
Spanish Crown: Fernando de Soto, Legazpi, Urdaneta, El
Cano, Mendaña, Magellan, Yáñez Pinzón, Loaysa, López
Villalobos, Rodríguez Cabrillo, Núñez de Vaca, Hurtado
de Mendoza, Alvarado, the great Hernán Cortés, Garay,
Hernando de Soto, Coronado, Orellana, Alonso Camarco,

Mendoza, Ayolas, Cabeza de Vaca, Fernández de Quirós, Sánchez Vizcaíno, Sáez de Torres, Padre Salvatierra, Padre Kunt, and many others. To these we should add the leaders and members of scientific expeditions (botanical, zoological, etc.), such as Hernández (§ 88), and also those who were in fact conquerors, Pizarro, Almagro, Valdivia, etc. All this resulted in an extraordinary increase in the knowledge of geography, navigation, physical and natural sciences, linguistics and sociology, which had formed the basis of European culture before these expeditions.

Colonial government was arranged on the following principles: the existence in the capital of a directing idea and scientifically established plans; the organization of the State, which laid down general lines for political and administrative institutions, with a certain flexibility which allowed of modifications adapted to the conditions in each country. These institutions were modelled on those which existed in Spain and in other European countries under Spanish rule (viceroyalties, governorships, etc.), and, in spite of the privileges ceded to the organizers and leaders of certain expeditions of conquest (always with the good will of the State, which fixed the conditions), the power of the government from the capital always made itself felt (§ 75).

The government action in America was not only directed towards conquest, but towards colonization in the proper sense of the word, that is to say, the exploitation and improvement of the natural resources of the country. To this end the following measures were taken: emigrants were chosen for their abilities in various trades and professions; economic support was given to those who went out to establish themselves and exploit the land; seeds, unknown in America, were sent out, such as cotton, coffee, wheat, and many others, 170 in all; animals unknown there, such as horses, cattle, etc., were imported; a commercial policy was established in accordance with the economic ideas of the age (so general then, and still influential to-day), *i.e.*, the exploitation of the colony, mainly in favour of the capital.

But Spain was not so much concerned with the economic advantages of colonization as with the extension of her rule. She sought to civilize her new dominions, not only by an egotistic policy of favouring the white colonists, but also by helping on the Indians.   To this end she endowed them with all the means and institutions of learning that were employed in the metropolis itself, and that reflected the spirit of the age.   Sources of learning ranged from the clergy (especially missionaries) to the university, with the foundation of special schools for the natives.   Thus the white inhabitants of America (*Criollos* or Creoles) established a culture of their own.   They created a basis of wealth and well-being, which is revealed, amongst other things, by their houses, many of which are still to be seen in America.   Also the spiritual condition of the Indians was bettered, in so far as was possible, according to the programmes and the processes of education then known and applied.   The educational and cultural work done by the missionaries deserves special mention in this connection. Though their essentially religious aims tended to limit the scope of their labours amongst the natives to conversion, this did not prevent their extending their work to the instruction in trades: farmers, herdsmen, or industrialists. They were also able to prevent ignorant people from abusing the Indians, and to better their condition in many ways.

87. *Culminating Period of Culture*.   A curious phenomenon (which is noticeable nevertheless, in almost all nations) is that the 16th and much of the 17th centuries, so disastrous in the realm of politics and economics, were illustrious in the cultivation of the sciences and letters.   Universities and colleges continued to be established in great numbers, many of them being very beautiful as buildings.   There was an attempt to make primary schools general and education compulsory, under pain of banishment (municipal ordinances of Madrid, 1512; Mondoñedo 1542, and other laws); meanwhile, on the other hand, establishments such as the *Escuelas Pias*, due to the Aragonese Calasanz (later, San José de Calasanz), provided for the teaching of the poorer

Photo, Arxiv Mas.

A LECTURE AT THE UNIVERSITY OF SALAMANCA

(1614)

classes. The mayor of a town (*alcalde*) was expected to be able to read and write; the kings, ministers, and nobles patronized the professors, poets, painters, architects, musicians, and other artists; and it was generally held that " no one could call himself a *caballero* who was not a man of letters."

It is true that, by the end of the 16th century, signs of decadence were already perceptible in this desire for culture. The number of Spanish students at foreign universities diminished notably, and this indifference was clinched by an order of Philip II, forbidding them to study outside of Spain, except in Coimbra, Bologna, and Rome. His aim was to prevent Spanish university degrees from deteriorating, and Spanish students from being contaminated by the anti-Catholic ideas of other countries.

As regards its first object, Philip II's order effected nothing, for the general apathy included culture, and the routine into which the universities had fallen, and finally their own plethora, lack of suppleness, and quarrels amongst themselves, brought about the ruin of many of them. Thus by the end of this period, even in so famous a university as that of Salamanca, the number of students had dropped from 7,800 to 2,076 about the year 1700.

As regards the lack of communication with the rest of Europe, and the fall in intellectual production consequent upon the order of Philip II alone, it should be known that this order was not so absolute as has been supposed. This is proved by the fact that Spanish men of science had relations with foreign scholars other than with those of Rome and Bologna, sanctioned by the king, and also by the translations of Spanish literary and scientific books that were produced after this date. Nor was the decline in intellectual productivity so serious as might be supposed, seeing that many of the principal products of the Spanish genius —works of experimental sciences, of observation and of invention—date from the reign of Philip II, and his successors in the first part of the 17th century.

The suspicion which gave rise to the above-mentioned

order acted chiefly in the realm of philosophy and theology. Also, along with other causes, it produced the regulation and excessive fiscalization of academic life, causing it to lose its former liberties, subjecting books to a rigorous censorship, and monopolizing the printing of elementary textbooks. At the same time the furious zeal of the Inquisition paralysed instruction by interfering with the professors on the slightest suspicion of heresy, whether justifiable or false. This happened to Fray Luis de León, professor of Salamanca, who was twice tried; to Mariana, the historian; to Nebrija; to " el Brocense "; Arias Montano, and other humanists.

Nevertheless, as has been said already, the splendour of culture grew, at least in literature, and the arts, until well on in the 17th century, so that our decadence in this respect was gradual, and limited to a fairly short period, at least as regards certain branches of spiritual activity, which were revived extensively in the 18th century (§ 100). To the 16th and 17th centuries belong the majority of the best writers, artists, and men of science which Spain has produced up to the present day. Owing to a character which is eminently positive on the one hand and eminently idealistic on the other (especially in the realm of religion and the arts), a character which seems to define the Spanish spirit, the studies most cultivated, apart from theology and Catholic mysticism, were: law, political science, political economy, cosmography, and the practical application of mathematics, physics, mineralogy, geography (in the form of expeditions of discovery, and the studies promoted by these), natural history, history, lyric poetry, the Picaresque novel, the theatre, and the fine arts, especially painting. Pure philosophy was less important, by reason of the small number of its devotees, rather than to any inferiority of the works actually produced, which were often excellent. Outstanding among them was the Valencian, Luis Vives (1492-1540), whose learning spread through various European countries, and Fox Morcillo, author of the most scientific attempt to reconcile the systems of Plato and Aristotle. On the other hand, theology flourished in an extraordinary way, and to it belong writers who made their names in special applications of it, such as law. One fact must be mentioned, which is characteristic of the period and symptomatic of the Castilian supremacy in the national life of Spain and of the spiritual harvest it bore—this is that the vast majority of the cultivators of the sciences, letters, and arts, and especially the most eminent of these, were inhabitants of the ancient territories of the Crown of Castille, and many of them were from the centre thereof.

88. *Scientific Progress*. The main practical results of this great cultural movement in the realms of physical and natural sciences were as follows: the notable work of Fernando Columbus (Colón), Pedro Esquivel, López de Velasco and others, in the geographical and geodetical description of the Peninsula; similar undertakings in America by Ovando, Santa Cruz and, in general, by the technical officials of the *Casa de Contratación*; the plans for the canalization of the principal rivers (already begun in the time of the Catholic monarchs) and for opening a canal in the isthmus of Panama; and the construction of reservoirs, irrigation canals, and other hydraulic devices; the invention of the compass by Felipe Guillén (1525); that of the instrument known as the *nonius* by Pedro Juan Núñez; the correction of the Gregorian calendar by Pedro Chacón and others; the invention of the first metal bilge-pumps, due to Diego Rivero; the perfecting of naval construction, in which our engineers and shipbuilders were famous; the correction of the ballistic theories then prevalent in Europe —due to Jerónimo Múñoz; the construction of telescopes, for which the Spaniard Rogete was famous; the initiation of the study of the power of steam, undertaken by Juan Escribano and Juan Bautista Porta; the studies in algebra and geometry of Núñez, Juan de Herrera, Ciruelo, Ortega, Muñoz, and others; the improvement of cartography and studies of cosmography (maritime currents, the use of instruments of navigation, magnetism, etc.), upon which many pilots and employees of the *Casa de Contratación* were

engaged; anatomical discoveries on the human body, especially those connected with the circulation of the blood (seventy-three years earlier than Harvey), in which the physician Miguel Servet made his name, and which were cultivated by other men in the clinics of our hospitals and in the practical classes of some of our universities (*e.g.*, that of Valencia); the work in ophthalmology of Daza de Valdés, with his invention of spectacles; the researches of Guibernat on crural hernia; the establishment of model hospitals for epidemics, such as that in Seville (early 17th century); scientific expeditions to America, such as that organized in 1570 under the direction of Francisco Hernández, for the study of the natural history, geography, and customs of New Spain and Peru; and the monumental works in botany, zoology, and pharmacology of the above-mentioned Hernández, and of Fragoso, Acosta, Oviedo, Cobo, and Monardes; works on mineralogy and mining by Carrillo Lasso and Alonso Barba; the improvement of metallurgical methods for the exploitation of metals, especially precious metals, in which Pedro Fernández de Velasco excelled, introducing the system of amalgamation adapted to the peculiar mining conditions of Potosí; the discovery of a great number of new species of plants and animals of America. The above-mentioned Dr. Hernández alone catalogued, described, and painted more than 14,000 vegetable species in the 15 volumes in which he recorded his voyage. Only part of them, without the plates, were published in Mexico in 1615. Among new plants discovered was the potato, which Parmentier first brought to Europe; and the age saw the beginning of collections, botanical gardens, and many other experiments.

At the same time, Spanish cultivators of the moral and political sciences, our historians (especially all the chroniclers of the Indies) and our theologians instituted the study of sociology and penal anthropology, forwarding those great principles that characterize the modern schools and systems of remedial imprisonment, and correcting the terrible defects of the older prisons, in the criticism of which

UNIVERSITY LIBRARY, SALAMANCA

Cerdán de Tallada, Chaves and Sandoval distinguished themselves. They laid the foundations of public international law and colonial law, which have since been adopted by legists all over the world, developing the ideas of Francisco de Vitoria and others; they investigated the basis of natural law, along with Suárez and the said Vitoria, whose books are consulted to-day with profit. Vives and Padre Mariana analyzed profoundly the institutions of civil law, coming to very radical conclusions on the question of property; they gave a powerful impetus to economic studies, investigated with great ardour the problems of political science, especially as regards the sovereignty of the people, the naturalness of the monarchic institution, and the conditions which should unite these two principles. The criticism and science of history were renewed, with a most ample conception of its plan and relations, by the work of Páez de Castro, Ambrosio de Morales, Zurita and many others; linguistic studies were established, with numerous vocabularies and grammars of American languages. They created studies in American archaeology and sociology, in which were pre-eminent various of the chroniclers of the Indies and certain scientists, such as Hernández himself in his *Antiquedades de la Nueva España*. The science of education was further investigated, in the works of Vives, Ponce of León, Juan de Castro, Ramírez de Carrión, Bonet and Simón Abril; in philosophy seeds were sown and foundations laid on which later the great German and French reformers were to base their systems; finally, one of the most profound and original manifestations of mysticism was created, in which Santa Teresa de Jesús and San Juan de la Cruz were the most outstanding figures.

89. *Literature, and Spanish Influences Abroad.* The finest creations of the Spanish genius, and those which have had the greatest influence on the world at large, are in the realm of literature. The novel, which began so brilliantly with *La Celestina* (§ 78), developed characteristics and a perfection unique in history, whether in the genre known as Picaresque, with Mateo Alemán, Espinel, Delicado, Que-

vedo and many others, or in satirical and idealistic narrative, in which the great Cervantes immortalized the name
of *Don Quixote*. At the same time the secular stage, developing with marvellous rapidity, created immortal works,
embodying both religious subjects (*autos sacramentales*) and
popular and Picaresque manners (*entremeses*) and adventures
("comedies of cloak and sword"), and historical and philosophical themes, thanks to the genius of Lope, Calderón,
Tirso, Alarcón, Moreto, and various others.

The contrast offered by the two literary genres just cited
(the novel and the theatre), is a new proof of the wealth of
inspiration and of perception of life, real and ideal, which
characterized the spirit of Spanish writers, and which will
continue to characterize it throughout our literary production, in its times of fecundity. The Picaresque novel
portrays, with vigorous and spontaneous realism, in which
artificial technique plays little part, a certain section of
Spanish society and manners. This section was so typical
of that age and so small numerically that it would be a profound error to consider it as an expression of the whole
of Spanish life, or even of the most important aspect thereof
in those centuries. In opposition to this, the theatre reflects, alongside the vulgar elements of society, the noble
side of the national soul, its great ideals and virtues, such as
its preoccupation in the highest problems of philosophy,
theology, law, politics, social relations, and human passions;
and it treats of all these subjects, save perhaps the last, with
a breadth of view, and an emotional intensity that was surpassed in no contemporary drama. The real and ideal
picture of Spanish society which our drama of the 16th and
17th centuries offers serves to temper and correct the impression of that society which might have been deduced
from the Picaresque novel.

The case of Cervantes is unique, and expresses the union
of these two tendencies in a sublime wholeness of vision,
which is both national and universal, in which the imperfections of contemporary reality and the long, if not eternal,
imperfections of man's estate, are understood, explained

BOOK BOUND IN CÓRDOBA LEATHER
(*University Library, Salamanca*)

and forgiven with gentle irony, by the light of an ideal of the bettering of souls and manners. If this ideal did not always triumph, the author thought it deserved to triumph, and therefore that it should be sought and ensued continually.

Lyric poetry, though inspired, as in the 15th century, by Latin and Italian models, rivalled these in the work of Boscán, Garcilaso, Herrera, the Argensolas, Rioja, Góngora, Quevedo, Fr. Luis de León, San Juan de la Cruz, Santa Teresa de Jesús, etc. At the same time, returning to traditional models, a new series of *romances* (ballads) came to birth (imitating the earlier ones, but inferior to them), both those called *romances moriscos*, and those based on ancient epic, which was revitalized by new themes or rejuvenated by those which had been handed down in the *Crónica General de España* (published in 1541). When this new kind of *romance* was cultivated, from the end of the 16th century, by good poets such as Lope de Vega, Góngora, and Quevedo it acquired great literary value; and because of this, and because these *romances* were so widely read, they have long been confused with the popular *romances* of the Middle Ages (§ 53). In the 17th century this genre decayed much, and Castilian prose, definitely perfected, acquired accents of inimitable majesty and harmony, with Pérez de Oliva, Hurtado de Mendoza, Juan de Valdés, Santa Teresa Mariana, Guevara, Luis de Granada. It became woven into a sober closeness of texture, admirable in its power of contrast, by Gracián, Melo, and many others.

Castilian, at the time when it was perfecting itself in literature and was fixing its grammatical forms, spread over the world, being spoken and learned in all parts. Spanish writings (scientific, and particularly political and ethical) and also Spanish mystics and authors of books of devotion were read and translated everywhere, or served as a basis for imitations, adaptations, and new literary currents. In Italy (to whose literature Spanish writers owed more than to that of any other country), it began to be the fashion in the 16th and on into the 17th century to translate the works

of Castilian authors, poets and novelists (both books of
chivalry, of the type of *Amadis* and of Picaresque tales,
starting from *La Celestina*), dramatists and moralists, mystics,
pedagogues, and even political writers: Vives, Torquemada,
Guevara, Antonio Pérez, Saavedra Fajardo, Gracián,
Santa Teresa, Luis de Granada, and other illustrious names.
From Italy the knowledge of our literature spread to France,
England, and Germany, apart from that which was disseminated from the Netherlands, where our occupation left
a profound impression.   In all these countries the same
authors were translated and imitated as in Italy.   Especially well known were the political moralists and the novelists and dramatists, who had great influence on the French,
English, Dutch, and German drama of the 17th century.
In the same way, Spanish heretics, that is to say, those who
came into contact with Protestant ideals and with the religious crises of Europe, abjured or modified their Catholic
ideas.   When they were obliged to fly from Spain, they published their work in other countries and influenced to no
small extent the thought of their adopted countries, being
admired as much for their genius as for the style of their
writings which were at times extremely beautiful.   This
happened, for example, to the brothers Valdés in Italy, and
to Cipriano de Valera and Antonio del Corro in England.

This vogue for Spanish writers still lasted when, at the
end of the 17th century, the political decadence of Spain,
both at home and abroad, was manifest.   At a time when
the enemies of the power of Spain were increasing their
attacks, both by force of arms and by pamphlets and books,
often full of slanderous accusations, the Spanish spirit, already weakened by other causes, faltered and gave way in
its pursuit of culture and in its intellectual output, which
for two centuries had been so admirable.

90. *The Plastic Arts.*   Progress in the plastic arts was
made along similar lines.   At the contact of Italian influences, architecture and sculpture turned their back on
older styles and allowed themselves to be dominated by the
classic reaction.   They forgot Gothic art, and in the first

half of the 16th century developed the *Plateresque* style, always including more and more Roman elements; and they developed also a pure Renaissance style, characterized by the round arch and groined vaulting, decorative medallions, columns, etc., on the façades and within, in imitation of ancient Roman buildings. Examples of buildings of this type are Granada Cathedral (Plateresque) and the monastery of San Marcos at León (partly Plateresque and partly Renaissance). In the second half of the 16th century the Romanistic reaction was exaggerated, and acquired great severity and a strength that was, above all, massive. Ornamentation disappeared or became very sober, and freely copied late Roman models. The most famous example of this type is the monastery of El Escorial, the work of Juan de Herrera. Finally, in the second half of the 17th century, the classic forms degenerated, the regularity of the lines was broken, their movement was violated; and ornamentation returned, heavy, often involved, vulgar, and out of keeping with the rest of the building. Nevertheless, when this style was employed by great artists, it produced fine work, worthy to be admired and preserved, which modern critics have again begun to value highly. Some of these consider this as the most national crystallization of art, and a truly native product, in which Oriental and mediæval influences were based on classical forms. Examples of it are: the portal of the *Hospicio* at Madrid and that of the Palace of San Telmo of Seville. This style, a degeneration of former styles, is called in Spain *Churrigueresco*, from the name of the architect Churriguera, who most distinguished himself in it. It is a form of *baroque*.

In painting arose the Spanish school proper, brought up in the double current of Flemish and Italian influences (and, within these, in a rich variety of schools and personal genius), and enriched by the perpetual presence in Spain of foreign artists, and by journeys to Italy and elsewhere, made by many Spaniards.

Modern historians of painting distinguish two periods in

the process of formation which was characteristic of this epoch. The first, which included the 16th and part of the 17th centuries, is characterized by the overwhelming influence of the schools of Rome and Florence, which crushed out temporarily the native Spanish style. In it are perceptible reminiscences of technical processes of the Gothic type (§ 61). The principal national painters of this time are: in Valencia, Macip and his son Juan de Juanes; in Andalucía, Luis de Vargas, Pedro de Villegas, Céspedes, Mohedano and Pacheco (father-in-law of Velázquez); in Castille, Fernández Navarrete (" el Mudo "—the dumb), Sánchez Coello and Pantoja de la Cruz, and Luis de Morales, a native of Estremadura, called " the Divine," because of the religious subjects of his paintings. Naturally each one of these painters had a tendency and character of his own, within the general characteristics of the period, which corresponded to the various influences that were at work upon the Spanish genius. Thus, in spite of the impulse of the already-mentioned Italian schools, the Spanish note is to the fore in Villegas and also in Mohedano and Navarrete, both painters of still life, and the second, an animal painter. Reminiscences of Gothic art are visible especially in the work of Morales. Finally, in that of Navarrete, Sánchez Coello and Pantoja (the two latter, notable portrait painters) are noticeable the various Italian styles already mentioned (including that of Titian), and of the Dutch style, represented at that time by Antonio Moro, who lived in Spain for a long time, and formed a school.

To this same first period belongs El Greco, a Greek by nationality, but a painter who was profoundly influenced by Spain in many of his conceptions. Along with a strange and powerful personality, and his disconcerting technique, El Greco reveals Venetian influences (he was a direct pupil of Titian), and archaic (Gothic) tendencies, which are contradictory, and which differentiate him sharply from his Italian contemporaries. El Greco influenced Spanish painters (among them, Velázquez) by these Venetian traits in his art, by his own Gothicism (in which he opposed

EL GRECO : THE DAY OF PENTECOST

(Prado Museum, Madrid)

the then triumphant Italianism), by his intense mysticism, which accorded with the Spanish spirit of that time, by his intimate assimilation of the Spanish type and Spanish psychology of the epoch, which are revealed by his portraits, his landscapes of Toledo, and by that grandiose composition, " El Entierro del Conde de Orgaz." His mysticism found its culminating point in his various and admirable presentations of St. Francis of Assisi.

The second period, which occupied most of the 17th century, is characterized by the triumph of the Spanish genius proper, which grew up vigorously during a reaction against the Roman and Florentine influences and those which took their place, either of Northern Italian origin (Venetian school) or Flemish (Rubens and Van Dyck). This is the glorious period of Velázquez, Murillo, Zurbarán, Ribera, Huguet, Bermejo, Berruguete, Ribalta, José Leonardo, Valdés Leal and certain others who, while each contributed the note of his own personality, conformed to the psychological condition of Spanish invention and methods. They produced in a short space of time a great number of masterpieces, which, in spite of the individuality of each painter, give in the mass the impression of a truly national manner, distinct from that of their foreign contemporaries, including those who most influenced them.

After this great effort, *i.e.*, at the end of the 17th century, Spanish painting declined. Its last great representative was in the time of Charles II, Claudio Coello, whose masterpieces are portraits, but in his picture of " La Sagrada Forma " (Sacristy of the Escorial), he well expresses the decadent period in which he lived. This decadence was, properly speaking, artistic, but it coincided with the decline of the spirit of Spain.

A new movement, and one of great splendour and originality, also began in sculpture in the 16th and 17th centuries. The work was done chiefly in wood and clay (especially in Andalucía) and occasionally in stone and marble. It usually took the form of altar-pieces, choir stalls, and processional images. In sculpture, far more than in painting, one sees the reaction of the Spanish spirit against the Italian and French schools, whose influence made itself felt then, not only through the fame of the great schools and artists, certain of whom came to Spain (Fancelli, Torrigiano, Indaco, Vigarní, Juan de Juni, Joli, León Leoni), but also because certain works were definitely ordered and sent from Italy, such as the sepulchres of the *Adelantado Mayôr* (Governor) of Toledo, and his wife (Cartuja de las Cuevas, in Seville), that of the Bishop of Avila (San Juan de la Penitencia, Toledo), and that of Ramón de Cardona (Bellpuig).

The most notable Spanish sculptors of this time are: Bartolomé Ordóñez, Zarza (tomb of Alonso Carrillo, Toledo); Alonso Berruguete (one of whose works is the sepulchre of Cardinal Tavera); Ancheta, Forment (*Retablos* of Saragossa and Huesca); Morlanes el Mozo, Diego de Siloé, and, above all, Gregorio Hernández; Montanés, Juan de Mesa (author of various figures of Christ, among them, perhaps, that of the *Gran Poder* of Seville), and Pedro Roldán (all three of them from Seville); Alonso Cano, who first worked in Seville (the great *retablo* of Lebrija), and later in Granada (" The Conception," " Adam and Eve," " The Guardian Angel "), and his disciples Pedro de Mena and José de Mora, who came at the end of the 17th century.

Many of these artists (among those who worked in wood) cultivated the polychrome genre, which was very characteristic of Spain, both at this period and in the Middle Ages. What is known as *Estofado* was produced by the paint being put on over a coat of burnished gold, which covered the bare plaster.

The industrial arts (goldsmiths' work, pottery, panelled ceilings, ironwork, etc.), continued for some time in the traditions of the foregoing period, with natural variations of form and style. This is seen in the reliquaries and processional crosses, which ceased to be Gothic and became Renaissance; in the ceilings, which abandoned the Mudéjar style; in the tiles, which imitated classic designs, etc. Furniture-making was much influenced by sculpture and pro-

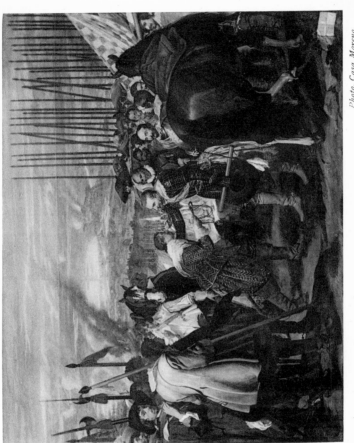

VELAZQUEZ : THE SURRENDER OF BREDA

(Prado Museum, Madrid)

duced, amongst other things, the famous *bargueños*, which had formerly been Gothic in style. Embroidery, especially on ecclesiastical vestments, produced work of great artistic value, just as it had done in earlier periods.

As was natural, all the Spanish arts, from architecture (especially Baroque and within it the Andalucían style) and painting, to the industrial and domestic arts, reached the Indies and produced there occasionally local works of art (sometimes, it is now thought, influenced by native elements). There was also a transplanting of works of art from the Peninsula. Spanish artists went there, and had much influence on the spirit of the Creoles. Churches, public buildings for political or administrative purposes (palaces of the Viceroys, Mints, etc.), and private houses still exist in almost all places reached by our dominion. They show the splendour and breadth of the Spanish influence in the colonies. Disciples of Murillo in painting and of the Toledan and Sevillian schools in architecture (Alonso Rodríguez, Becerra, Vespara, and others) went to America, and not only created there notable works—the cathedrals of Lima, Mexico, Havana, Bogotá, churches in San Francisco and Santo Domingo (Quito), Puebla (Mexico), etc., and many public and private palaces. They also created a tradition which has lately begun to interest other countries. Then, too, our engineers (Antonelli, and others) introduced there the most progressive methods of the age, as regards public buildings, civil and military, and constructed grandiose, and at times exemplary works. This whole chapter of Spanish art is as yet very little known, but it is already beginning to be studied technically, and from written records.

91. *Music.* Music developed in an original manner—continuing the expressive style that had originated at an earlier period (§ 74), and combining the influence of popular airs with religious sentiment and excellent technique. Morales, Cabezón, Guerrero, Ramos de Pareja, Salinas, and above all Victoria, not only shone in Spain, but went to Italy and made an indubitable impression on the musical

reform that was entered upon by the musicians of the Pontifical Court.

Along with this religious tendency, which included the compositions intended for the religious drama, profane music developed, sometimes for the theatre (incidental music to the works of Lope, Calderón, and others), at others in popular songs. These two branches of music were sometimes practised by one composer. In the composition of popular songs, some examples of which are already found under the Catholic monarchs, many composers (Luis Milán, Valderrábano, Pisador, Fuenllana, as well as those already cited) based their work on the *romances* which, under this form, gained fresh ground in all classes, both in the towns and country. *Cancioneros* (song books) began to be formed in the 16th century, so as to collect the words of these very Spanish songs. The first of these is the *Cancionero de Romances* of Martin Nucio, printed at Antwerp. This was followed by those of Saragossa (1550), Timoneda and others. Again, the work of Salinas deserves special mention, from the snatches of song quoted in *De Musica Libri Septem* (Salamanca, 1577), as do the lute-books of Milán, Valderrábano and Pisador (composers already cited), the songbook of Claudio de Sablonara (17th century), that found not many years ago at Upsala, the unpublished collection of the Biblioteca Colombina at Seville, which, like that published in 1890 by Barbieri, contains compositions of the end of the 15th and of the 16th centuries.

At the time when Spain was producing this Pleiad of composers, foreign musicians came to Spain, among them, Frenchmen, who worked chiefly in Catalonia. Juan Brudieu seems to stand out amongst them. He worked at Urgell and wrote a collection of Madrigals for performance in the open air, and a Mass for the Dead, for four voices.

The most common musical instrument in Spain up to the end of the 16th century was the guitar-shaped *vihuela* in its two forms: *vihuela de mano*, plucked by the hand, and *vihuelo de arco*, played with a bow. Later, the former was replaced by the guitar proper. The literature on the *vihuela*, both instruction-books and musical compositions, is characteristic of the period, in that it produced a notable school of *vihuelistas*. Amongst these are the Valencian, Luis Milán, author of the earliest known treatise on this instrument (1535), Narvaez of Granada, Mudarra of Seville, and the above-mentioned Pisador, Fuenllana, etc. Songs for the *vihuela* began at this time to form a sort of overture and *entr'acte* in theatrical performances, apart from the theatre-music proper, written to works of our dramatists, from which a form of opera developed (the score of one has been found, whose libretto was written by Calderón), and the Spanish *zarzuelas* (a kind of dramatic performance), as has already been indicated.

One of these forms was called the *cuatro de empezar*, and was sung by four voices. Others were the *jácaras mesadas*, the *entremeses*, the *mojiganga*, the *bailes*, the *tonadas*, etc., which developed so characteristically in the 18th century.

IX

THE REVIVAL IN THE EIGHTEENTH CENTURY
(1701-1808)

92. *Political Ideal of the Bourbons*

WITH the accession to the throne of Spain of the Duke of Anjou, Philip V, the dynasty changed and a French family began to reign, bringing with it many new ideas and influences, contrary to those of the House of Austria. Though the four Bourbons who ruled Spain from the beginning of the 18th to the beginning of the 19th centuries differed amongst themselves in many traits of character and tendencies, one can say that the political activity of all of them had points in common, more marked in one direction or the other, according to the times. They almost all showed great zeal for internal problems affecting the intimate life of the nation or of the State; the reconstruction of national wealth and of the public revenue; the increase of the population and of agriculture; the renaissance of traditional industries and of mercantile relations, and the spreading of culture, with a markedly popular and professional sentiment. But at the same time, the imperialistic tradition, complicated by international compromises, derived from the relationship between the kings and the ruling family of France, led them on to new military enterprises, necessitating enormous efforts and great expenditure, thanks to which the policy of regeneration was seriously impeded. We shall examine separately the direction and consequences of both movements.

93. *The New Imperialism.* The first wars of Philip V were not caused by his desires for aggrandizement, but were provoked by the opposition on the part of England and of the Holy Roman Emperor to his accession to the throne.

GOYA : LA PRADERA DE SAN ISIDRO

(*Prado Museum, Madrid*)

Attacked in its Italian dominions, in America and in the Peninsula itself, Spain was obliged to fight energetically against the invaders, and finally come to an agreement with them through peace treaties (1713-1714). Spain lost Gibraltar, the Southern Netherlands, Luxembourg, Milan, Naples, and part of Tuscany, Sicily, Sardinia, and Menorca. The last two were recovered later, but Sardinia was lost again and definitively. Austria, England, and the Princes of Savoy acquired what was lost.

Soon the spirit of domination, represented by the second wife of Philip V, Isabella Farnese, involved Spain in new wars, for the recovery of her Italian territories. By gigantic efforts the army and navy were reorganized, and came to be as important as they had been in the 16th century, or at any rate, to inspire great uneasiness in enemy countries. The final result was the establishment of a kingdom of Naples and Sicily, for the Infante Don Carlos, son of Isabella, but this kingdom was to be separate from Spain. In the reign of Charles III, two wars against the English (one of them in favour of the independence of the English colonies in North America), led to no definite result, since part of our colonies were in turn lost and regained. Menorca was recovered in compensation, and the islands of Fernando Poo and Annobón were acquired through a treaty with Portugal, which also put an end to the questions of boundaries in South America. Finally, and as a result of the wars with the French Republic, and of alliances with Napoleon, the following possessions were lost in 1808: San Domingo, Luisiana, the territories of the Mississipi and Trinidad. Through other causes Oran was lost in 1791. One century of Bourbon rule had thus brought about the disappearance of Spanish rule in all European countries and also, in part, in America and Africa, and the loss of Gibraltar to the English. Thus the imperialistic policy was defeated and the internal decadence of the Spanish State was aggravated, apart from the heavy damage done to the life-forces of the country.

94. *Internal Policy.* In spite of their sense of responsibility

and their good feeling towards the people, which was manifest in various ways, the Bourbons were frankly absolutist and had even a stronger feeling for centralization than
had the House of Austria. This is apparent in the following
facts: abolition of the *fueros*, or special political laws, of
Aragon, Catalonia, Valencia and Mallorca, so destroying the autonomy of these regions (which, as a matter of
fact, was already more apparent than real, except as regards
taxation); abolition of the special civil laws of Valencia
and Mallorca, making them uniform with Castille; consolidation of the royal power in every sense, particularly in
its relations with the Church, which resulted in a renewal,
with fresh force and vigour, of the royalist system employed
by Ferdinand and Isabella, Charles V, and Philip II.

In this point the struggle took on vast proportions,
nourished as it was by the anti-clerical feeling of the age,
and by the resentment that had been caused by the intrusion
of ecclesiastical organizations and personages into civil life.
The results of this struggle were: that royal permission had
to be obtained for the publication of any Papal Bull in
Spain; the lessening of the tribute money which was paid
to the Curia Romana, which had reached large sums; the
modification of certain ecclesiastical tribunals in Spain;
the recognition of royal patronage, that is to say, the right
of the monarchy to nominate to certain offices and bene-
fices in the Spanish churches; the restriction of the judicial
competency of the Inquisition and of the *tribunal de Cruzada*
in non-religious matters; the suppression of the immunity
of the clergy (which gave them the privilege of not being
tried by the ordinary courts) in cases of tumults, riots, and
failure in the respect that was due to civil magistrates; a
plan to put back into circulation the vast possessions that
had accumulated to the churches and monasteries, and the
expulsion of the Jesuits for political reasons.

Although many of these measures had considerable consequences in social life, their main effect was to strengthen
the power of the monarchy, as represented by the State.
Certain ministers of the kings were important factors in this

work of secularizing the political life. Such were Macanaz, Patiño, Ensenada, Wall, Aranda, Floridablanca, Campomanes, Roda, Azara, and Jovellanos. They had almost all risen from the middle classes, representing the apogee of this class and of the *jurisconsultos* or *golillas*. They were passionate imperialists, though much influenced by liberal tendencies, which were already appearing in French and English literature and were much read in Spain. The only really democratic move in political matters was the reform of the *Ayuntamientos*, in the reign of Charles III. This gave the popular elements the right to hold positions in them, and reduced the exclusiveness of the ruling classes, which had taken possession of all public offices.

95. *Philanthropy*. But if monarchic absolutism continued to hold sway, and even increased, in this sphere, in others which did not affect the government, the kings and ministers took a real interest in the fate of the people. Among the cultured classes in those days there was a certain widely diffused sense of humanity, of love for the poor and the outcast, for one's neighbour in general—what is known as philanthropy. This led them to regard social works with interest and to procure better economic conditions for those less favoured by fortune, and to see to their education. The application of this feeling to the activities of the government was called enlightened despotism, and its formula came to be "all for the people, without the people." It reflected itself finally in social and economic reforms, the spread of culture.

This tendency originated in certain English and French philosophers (Locke, Montesquieu, Voltaire, Rousseau, etc.), whose works, widely disseminated, enjoyed a very definite influence in most parts of Europe. The monarchs themselves not only read them, but often sought the friendship of these authors, and kept up an active correspondence with them. The change of dynasty in Spain led to the re-establishment of the old intellectual relations with the rest of Europe. The exaggerated fear of endangering Spanish institutions, or of being contaminated by anti-

M

Catholic ideas—that fear which had led to the restriction of all communications with Europe at the end of the 16th century (§ 87)—disappeared to a great extent. The constant alliance with France, whose kings were also Bourbons, and the new wars with Italy, renewed Spanish intercourse with these two countries. Many nobles were educated in French colleges, receiving the influence of the reigning ideas, and certain of them kept up a correspondence with Voltaire, Rousseau, and other writers. Thus a great thirst for reform was awakened in the upper classes, in imitation of the philanthropic rulers of France, Germany, Russia, and other countries. Only at the end of the 18th century, in 1792, did the government try to interfere with this intercourse with France, for political reasons, that is to say, to avoid the spread of revolutionary ideas. As a matter of fact, very radical groups had already revealed themselves in Spain, producing the humanitarian ideals already cited. In Salamanca, Gerona, Vergara, and other places they published periodicals that were very liberal in tendency, in opposition to the absolutist ideas generally held by the middle and lower classes. An external and practical expression of these tendencies was the desire, in 1789, to restore the old Cortes, with greater legislative power and a more liberal spirit than they had had of old. Furthermore, the first republican conspiracies appeared. The government tried to remedy all this by forbidding the entrance of certain books, leaflets, periodicals, etc., to Spain. But the seed had taken root, and very promptly, as we shall see, it gave proof of great vitality (§ 102). One must add, so as to show more clearly the complexity of the foreign influences that were then at work on the Spanish spirit, that alongside the French, the influences of Englishmen (economic, aesthetic, and literary), and of certain Germans were of appreciable importance, as is demonstrated by the numerous translations of the books of these countries.

Along with other things, these foreign influences produced a lessening of the old religious intolerance, at least in the cultivated classes. Yet the masses continued to be intolerant, and the Inquisition held certain much talked of trials such as that of the Minister Macanaz, the reformer Olavide, etc. But the sentiment of the ruling classes, without ceasing to be religious, was opposed to persecutions of this character, or at least showed a certain repugnance for them. Certain of the most important legislative reforms realized at this period, especially in Penal Law, seem to have been inspired by these humane ideals. Among them are: the interesting *Ordenanza de presidios de los Arsenales* (1804), which instituted, at a much earlier date, a regime analogous to the famous Crofton reforms, with a classification of prisoners, the dividing of them into groups of twenty-five, the construction of compulsory baths for them and protection of the prisoners. Then, in 1807, there were the general Prison Regulations, by which were established vocational training of the prisoners, physical drill, good-conduct certificates, the system of rewards and even the education of difficult, but not criminal, children, on the principle of reformatories. There were other reforms, on the same lines; the first of them seems to have been the order of 1791, demanding that children and adults should not be imprisoned together. This same spirit was seen in the organizing of a home and school for foundlings in Seville (1723), by Brother Toribio, under the protection of members of the Royal Family. In this home, training in the workshops was given to its inmates.

96. *Economic Recovery.* Both kings and ministers realized the necessity of restoring the economic life of the country. They began with the Exchequer, regulating taxes, administration and expenditure, so as to avoid waste and dishonesty in the employment of public revenue. The originator of this reform was a Frenchman, Orry, minister of Philip V, but he was assisted in a great measure by Spaniards, such as Patiño and others, in the time of Ferdinand VI and Charles III. By this means the debt was much reduced, and the revenue reached a sum of 12,500,000 dollars in 1762. But for the frequent wars, the Exchequer would have achieved great prosperity. At the end of the 18th

century, during the reign of Charles IV, these figures diminished sadly. The State Debt at his accession to the throne was 2,000 millions; on his abdication in 1808 it was 7,000 millions. In 1801 it was 4,108,052,771 reals.

But the prosperity of the Exchequer depended on that of the country, and so the kings and ministries tried to stimulate commerce and agriculture and increase the population, which was much diminished by war, poverty, and other causes already indicated (§ 85). To this end they encouraged an influx of people from other countries, so as to populate definite districts, and, in general, bettered the living conditions of the people, as we shall see. The result of these measures was that in the last years of the 18th century the number of the inhabitants of Spain had risen to 10,541,221, 168,248 of whom were ecclesiastics and 31,981 were workmen. More than 50,000 of the clergy were regular clergy, friars, and monks. According to other data, this number rose to 92,727, scattered over 2,051 monasteries and 1,075 convents. This reduced considerably the number of useful inhabitants.

The kings also managed to suppress vagrancy, in which many people lived. They ordered that those fit for military service should be taken into the army (*levas*), and the rest should be housed in special establishments. Severe laws were passed against the gipsies.

At the same time they effected the restoration of certain national industries, such as textiles and silks. Other industries were officially created, such as mining, pottery, salt, cloth, clock-making, tanned leather, linen, etc., in Almadén, Linares, San Ildefonso, Moncloa, Talavera, Alcora, Valdepeñas, Valencia, Avila, Madrid, Seville, Galicia, Asturias, and other places. Experts, foremen and workmen were brought from Germany, England, and other countries, and workshops and technical schools were set up. Officials were given rank, by means of social distinctions; privileges were given to industrialists and merchants; mercantile relations with America were facilitated, the duty was taken off wheat; the commercial exploitation of certain

of the colonies was advanced by the constitution of companies such as that of the Philippines; the roads were improved (339 leagues of high road and 605 bridges were
built between 1749 and 1800). Rivers were improved by
the digging of canals (Castille canal, Huescar canal, and the
Imperial or Pignatelli canal); reservoirs were made (Val del
Infierno, Puentes); dockyards for the building of ships were
inaugurated; arsenals for the making of arms (Oviedo,
Trubia, Ferrol, etc.); and the first official bank was
founded—the San Fernando.

97. *Internal Colonization.* But what was chiefly insisted
upon was the improvement of agriculture and the cultivation of still unexploited land. For this was to improve the
condition of the labouring classes, who were poor and
ignorant, subject to the great landowners, and *dead hands*
(*manos muertas*), or living laboriously on small holdings. Up
to this time it had been thought that the wealth of nations depended upon coinage and the possession of precious
metals (§ 85). Now the most influential men of science
affirmed that the basis of economic prosperity was agriculture, and accordingly the governments of every country
hastened to encourage the cultivation of the fields. The
effect of these measures was a series of colonizations of
the interior of Spain (Andalucía, Extremadura, Alicante,
Murcia, etc.). They were promoted by the State, either
through the distribution of uncultivated public lands, free
or for a nominal rent, or of marsh lands, which were
drained and put under cultivation. Colonization on a
grand scale took place in Sierra Morena, German labourers
being introduced, and settlements of them being formed,
such as La Carolina. Near Orihuela, the settlements of San
Felipe, Dolores, etc., grew up in the same way. On Crown
Lands and at Aranjuez fruit growing and horticulture grew
up, with families of Valencian workers, and gardens, of the
type of Versailles (very different from the local gardens of
the South and East), were made by French gardeners. The
same thing happened in La Granja.

At the same time certain privileges of the Mesta, authorizing the enclosure of private property, were revoked. Also, since the general tendency of the epoch was against the liquidation (*i.e.*, de-entailing) of property, even in the towns where it was to the profit of all the neighbours (as communal ground), various laws were passed, directed towards the repartition of arable lands, belonging to the towns, between labourers and poor day-workers, and the *Economic Society of the Friends of the Country* opened a competition, to which four memoranda were submitted, in order to study the national agrarian problem. The most illustrious representative of the ideas for agricultural reform was the minister Jovellanos, who summarized them in his famous *Informe De la Ley Agraria*. Nevertheless, the dominant tendency of earlier ministers and the method adopted in the time of Ferdinand VI and Charles III were not individualistic, as was that of Jovellanos, but was a communal enjoyment of the fruits of the land according to the old Spanish customs. On the other hand, Jovellanos was original enough to set himself in harmony with the exclusivist doctrines of the epoch, in order to defend the need for industrial direction, but with an agricultural basis.

This democratic character, which has already been noted, is found in other institutions then created, such as the banks for lending money to industry, the suburban committees, etc. Yet, in spite of all these measures, the general condition of the lower classes continued to be wretched. A proof of this is that the monasteries continued to distribute soup, the *Sopa de las Conventos*, through which a great part of the urban proletariat was fed.

98. *Colonization and the Governmental Regime in America*. Administrative reforms spread also to colonial territories. Strictly speaking, not all these changes and innovations can be attributed to the same spirit that brought about the reforms in Spain. Part of them were, doubtless, due to a determination to cut short the corruption, abuses, and negligences in the government of these countries, and to regulate the functions of the Colonial Exchequer and the profits from taxation. Part also were the natural out-

come of the change in Europe of economic ideas on production and commerce (§ 96), which gained in repute from
day to day. Part also was due to the development of
colonization itself, which demanded new offices and organs
of government, and to the result produced by two centuries of emigration, and the exploitation of the natural
wealth of these lands.

To this last factor was due the creation of new Viceroyalties (*virreinatos*); New Granada in 1718, which was
given part of Tierra Firme (Central America), and the
regions of Santa Fé de Bogotá and Quito; that of La Plata,
1777, with, roughly, almost all the land that now forms
the republics of Argentine, Uruguay, Paraguay, and Bolivia.
At the same time the following became *Capitanías Generales*:
Caracas (Venezuela), Chile, Puerto Rico and Luisiana.
Yet one can see that the fundamental basis of organization
of the 16th century suffered no formal modification. At the
end of the 18th century, however, a new organism was
superimposed—the *Intendencias* and *Subdelegaciones*. The
first legislation on this matter was in 1782, and after going
through various stages it was published finally in 1803. The
Intendentes possessed jurisdiction over matters of justice,
police, finance (this highly developed), and war, so that
they could intervene in almost all departments of government which had formerly been in the hands of the viceroys,
governors, *audiencias*, etc. The *Subdelegados*, in their turn,
came to replace the *Corregidores* and *Alcaldes Mayores*.

Before the introduction of this innovation, *Visitadores* had
been established throughout America. These officials were
ordered to inspect public administration, give a reckoning
of its defects and put into force remedies for them. The
work of these functionaries had good results, and at
times the best of them were chosen as governors of other
districts. Thus high government officials became more
specialized and more able, to the betterment of the land
they administered. There set in a period of good government, known as the " period of the good viceroys." Pre-
eminent amongst them were: Vertiz, Ceballos, Arredondo,

Amat, Manso, Buccarelli, Gálvez, Azanza, O'Higgins, and the Marqués de Croix.

At the same time emigration was encouraged by new methods, and suitable colonists were established in America, a policy which is illustrated by the introduction of Basques and Frenchmen by Captain-General Manso. Abuses in the *repartimientos* and *encomiendas* were rectified, and this institution was finally abolished in favour of the ideas of Las Casas (§ 76), although it was not always possible to suppress the extra-legal abuses of certain landlords. The Secretaryship (*Secretaría*) of the Indies was created (1714), with certain functions which used to belong to the *Consejo*, *Cajas Reales* and *Depositaría* of the Indies. A regular service of couriers was established from 1764; the *Casa de Contratación* of Seville was suppressed and transferred to Cadiz in 1777, and some of its functions were transferred to the Consulates, which increased in number in America. Great public works were carried out in the various colonies—aqueducts, high roads, breakwaters, canals, ports, public buildings, etc. Plots of ground were transferred to the Indians, so as to give them an economic basis. In general, the administration was made more orderly and moral. Various archives of the colonial epoch bear witness to the zeal and technical perfection of the bureaucracy then in power.

For the economic and commercial exploitation of the colonies the system of companies was inaugurated, a system new to Spain, where it had never developed spontaneously. Thus were created the *Real Guipuzcoana de Caracas* and those of Havana, Barcelona, Ezcaray, Burgos, and the Philippines, some of which had good results in production and trade. Also the system of private independent voyages was substituted for that of convoys (§ 85), first by means of special permission (1735-1778) and then as a general rule (1778). The commerical monopoly of the Port of Seville was replaced by the liberty of direct trade with America, first at the Catalan ports (1765 *et seq.*), and then from thirteen ports, scattered throughout the Peninsula, and, from 1789, with all colonial territories. In 1774 free

inter-colonial commerce, hitherto restricted, was authorized, and other similar measures were taken.

The results of all these efforts were seen in the increase
in public revenue, commerce, and cultivation, and in the
economic well-being of the colonial population and the
improvement of certain exploitations. These things are
attested by various foreign travellers in the 18th century,
especially by Humboldt (§ 100). His eulogies, concrete,
and based upon personal observation, are the best proof of
the success of Spanish colonization at the end of our epoch
of colonial domination.

A spiritual improvement corresponds to this improvement in the administrative and economic spheres. Ad-
vances in the applied sciences and speculative philosophy
will be considered later (§ 100). At this point we must
only mention the establishment of new centres of instruction, especially in the sciences, the publication of scientific
reviews, and the activities of men of science sent to America.
Apart from documentary records, all this is attested personally by travellers of the period.

Further, there was the missionary colonization of Upper
California, carried out by the Franciscans, with Brother
Junipero Serra, the Mallorcan, as its principal organizer
and agent. Modern Californians have erected two statues,
as a sign of recognition and gratitude for his goodness, his
humane treatment of the Indians, and the zeal with which
he furthered the exploitation and economic development
of the country. In this State there are preserved various
churches and other buildings, which perpetuate the Spanish names and memories of these missions.

Unfortunately, the last years of the century (reign of
Charles IV), reveal the abandonment of the administrative,
financial, and social measures which had formerly produced
such beneficial results. Thus various sorts of abuses came
into being again, and were met with propaganda of independence, the natural product of the political ideas of the
age, ideas which various European governments and the
United States of North America fomented, with a view to

depriving Spain of the economic profit of such extensive and rich territories.

99. *Public Instruction and Culture.* The kings, ministers, and private people also took great interest in public education. This was one of the outstanding products of the philanthropy of the nobility and middle classes. It was not unusual to see nobles, such as the Count Fernán Núñez, founding primary schools for both sexes on his estates; planning " a house of education for poor orphan girls, in which they should be brought up to be good mothers of families, not being required to take the veil, wear monastic dress, or do anything appertaining to the education of nuns." Such enlightened noblemen even wrote treatises on education.

This movement was chiefly stimulated by the influence of foreign pedagogues, Rousseau and Pestalozzi. Rousseau's influence was the earlier, the more general, and the longer lived. That of Pestalozzi is reflected in the founding at the end of the 18th and the beginning of the 19th centuries, of primary schools based on his special system of instruction (in Tarragona, at the instigation of Swiss officers, and in Santander by the creation of the *Sociedad Cantábrica*), and of a *Real Instituto Militar Pestalozziano* (an official creation) which functioned for a bare three years (1806-1808).

The main reforms, apart from these, were: the formation of primary schools, subsidized by the Crown; the charitable organizations, the Women's Leagues, the Economic Societies, religious Corporations, etc., the increase in the number of free schools (by the example of the *Escuelas Pías*), and a tendency to secularize them; the establishment of academies or seminaries for teachers (Madrid, Santander), and of pensions; the extension of technical schools for the education of the artisans (schools of drawing, arithmetic, geometry, trade, looms, workshops for embroideries in silk, gold- and silversmiths' work, artificial flowers, etc.).

What would now be called secondary education was furthered by the *Seminario de Nobles*, that of Vergara, the Institute of Gijón, founded by Jovellanos, the reform of the studies in San Isidro, Madrid, which was directed by the Jesuits until their expulsion, and by various other means. The universities, which had so declined in every sense, were not so easily reformed, because of the great resistance they showed towards any innovation. Various plans of reform were made, but most of them broke down, although certain new studies were introduced (Spanish law, public law, political economy, natural law, and certain sciences), and some of the existing studies were improved (dissection was brought in again in medicine, an experimental character was given to various studies, etc.). At the same time, learning began to be centralized; royal commissions of inspectors were nominated, and certain faculties of the rectors and principal members of the universities were curtailed. But the most fruitful measure taken in higher and professional education was the creation of new bodies, outside the universities, which really succeeded in renewing culture. Such were the academies of linguistic studies (*Academia de la Lengua*), history, fine arts, medicine, letters (in Barcelona and Seville), various academies of law and jurisprudence, and others; the *Estudios Reales de Madrid* (Royal Society of Madrid, dedicated to the experimental sciences and directed by Professor Fernández Solano, with its accompanying laboratories, with physical and astronomical instruments), the chemical laboratory; the schools of mathematics (Barcelona), veterinary surgery, road engineering, artillery; the school of commerce of Barcelona, with chairs of physics, and chemistry, libraries and laboratories; the *Colegio de Guardias Marinas*; the Royal School of Medicine, schools of army and navy surgeons, and schools for deaf-mutes; the museum of instruments and machines in the Retiro; the zoological gardens of Sanlúcar, and the botanical gardens of Madrid, Pamplona, Saragossa, Barcelona, Valencia, Cadiz, Orotava, and Manila; the National Library, the Observatory of San Fernando, the Museum of Natural Sciences, the Hydrographic Museum, and the Ordnance Survey; the many chairs of science founded by private individuals in Valencia, Seville, Cadiz, Ferrol,

Avila, etc.   There were also abundant scholarships to
enable professors and students to travel abroad.   Finally,
various important geographical and scientific expeditions
were sent to America and other places, and certain foreign
experts, such as Humboldt, were patronized, the French
expedition of 1735, which aimed at the measurement of
certain of the degrees at the Meridian, in which Spanish
scientists took part; the expedition of the Frenchman,
Dombey, that of the pupil of Linnaeus, Pedro Loefling, and
others.

Women helped much in this great work of renewing
culture, especially the women of the aristocracy.   They
created academies, certain of which formed part of those
already mentioned, founded by the kings.   They established primary schools and helped forward the spreading
of knowledge in every way.   But the highest, most conscientious and most untiring representatives of the movement
(intimately connected with the improvement of economic
life), were the Economic Societies of the Friends of the
Country (*Sociedades Económicas de Amigos del País*).   Founded
by private enterprise, welcomed, patronized, and disseminated by the government, they united all those who
were open to new ideas and inspired by a desire for the
regeneration of their country.   To their initiative were due:
the creation of schools of artisans, the holding of literary
and scientific discussions; investigations of an industrial
and agricultural nature, etc.   Their chief preoccupation
was popular education and the progress of agriculture and
the national industries.

At the same time, as a new result of culture, there arose
various periodicals and reviews, historical, literary or
encyclopaedic, imitations of those which were being published with great enthusiasm in England and France.   In
them questions of the day were discussed, new books were
announced, and the scientific progress in Spain and other
countries was reported.   Unpublished documents were
reproduced, descriptions of cities, statistics, reviews of the
theatres were given, and the prejudices and errors of the

populace were combated. In this last field Padre Jerónimo Feijoo especially distinguished himself, with his *Theatro Crítico*, in which he exposed all the fanaticism and narrowness of judgment of the masses and of those who refused to follow the new scientific currents. To this same end contributed many of the foreign professors and savants who taught in the new university chairs, or travelled throughout Spain, studying it in great detail. Such were Bowles, Briant, Tournell, Casiri, Godin, Proust, Humboldt, Herrgen, and others.

100. *Effects of the Reforms and the Impulse given to Culture.* The result of all these influences was a renaissance of various branches of learning, especially of the natural and physico-chemical sciences. This renaissance bore fruit, however, rather in stimulating the germs of culture which, under the decadence of the end of the 17th century, had almost perished in Spain, than by any new creative product of the reforms themselves, whether they were carried out by officials or by private enterprise. One cannot otherwise explain the fact that the efforts of the State brought forward immediately, or in a short space of time, a great number of men prepared to bring these ideas to fruition, men who represent the scientific history of Spain in the 18th century. The formation of such men is always a great task, and a task which takes a long time to give results. The phenomenon of scientific activity which is patent even before the great stimulus given by the ministers of Charles III (1759-1788), and those of Ferdinand VI (1746-1759), indicates that what really happened is that the men of science found, in this patronage of the State and in the thirst for culture suddenly exhibited by the aristocracy and by a great part of the middle classes, a medium and the necessary material help to enable them to bear all the fruit they were capable of bearing, after the preceding years of indifference and neglect, which had paralysed their output.

By this means work was then conceived which gave fame and scientific authority (not necessarily preserved in the memories of the generations that immediately succeeded them), to the following Spaniards: Jorge Juan and Antonio de Ulloa, commissioned to measure the quadrant of the meridian, which serves as a basis of the metre; to Rodríguez y González, author of works of the same nature in 1802-1803; and later on, to other work of the same kind, in collaboration with Chaix and the French physicists, Biot and Arago; to Tosca, Cerdá, Eximeno, Randon, Tofiño, Ciscar, López, Antillón, and other mathematical professors and writers; to Salvá, author of the first essays in electric telegraphy (1796); to the physicists and chemists Fernández Lozano, Munárriz, Del Río, Lanz, Betencourt, Luzurriaga, Araluja, Carbonell, González Bueno, Elhuyar, the above-mentioned Rodríguez, and González de Gutiérrez, organizers of experimental investigations of this nature, authors of important discoveries and of mechanical theories, such as that of the machines of Lanz y Betencourt; Espinosa, director of the Depósito (*hidrográfico*), to Virgili, Gimbernat, Martín Martínez, Piquer y Ruiz de Luzurriaga, physicians and surgeons, educational reformers (§ 99) experimental and theoretical scientists, and many others. Great stimulus was also given to voyages of discovery by sea and land, and to studies of geography, cartography, geodesy, astronomy, which already in the 16th and 17th centuries had lent glory and authority to Spanish men of science (§ 88). The most notable names in this period of the 18th century are: Malaespina, Churruca, Fidalgo, Maldonado, Antillón, Moreno de Escandón, Alzate, Pérez, Cañizares, Quadra, Constanzó, Mascaró, López de Bonilla, Oteiza, Quiroga, Ulloa, León y García, Bauzá, Salamanca, and many others. Certain of these, and others, distinguished themselves in studies, observations and discoveries in physical chemistry, such as Del Río, discoverer of vanadium; Abad, who determined the altitudes of certain mountains; Pineda, Mocino, Riaño and this same Del Río, explorers and scientific investigators of American volcanoes; Ezeta, Quadra, Fidalgo, Quimper, etc., who examined expeditions in search of the N.W. passage, among

them others who took up again investigations on the opening of an inter-oceanic canal.

At the same time Spanish naturalists, very numerous and
many of them famous (as was recognized by their foreign
contemporaries, Linnaeus and Humboldt, enriched the
study of the fauna, flora, and geology of the Peninsula,
America, and the Philippines, with a constant stream of
works in which were discovered and studied new species of
plants and animals, and which made illustrious names for
Cavanilles, Mutis, Quer, Pavón, Jiménez Gil, Cornide,
Gómez, Ortega, Sessé, Mociño, Azara, Tafalla, Pulgar,
Cuellas, Jumilla, Molinas, Pombo, Unanúe, Bálmez-Zea,
Lozano, Montenegro, Lastarria, Née, Boldo, Asso, Ruiz,
and many others. The above-mentioned Gómez Ortega,
published also, at the order of Charles III, three of the
botanical volumes of the colossal work that Dr. Hernández
had written at the end of the 16th century (§ 88), the entire
manuscript of which, with the engravings, was kept in the
Escorial until 1671, and was lost in the fire of that year.
Gómez Ortega's partial edition (like the earlier one made
by Fr. Francisco Jiménez in 1615), could be undertaken,
thanks to the unillustrated copy of the text, which Dr.
Hernández himself took the precaution to leave in Mexico.
At this time also a Spanish friar discovered in the bed of
the River Luxan (La Plata) the skeleton of a megatherium,
which he sent to Madrid (1788).

The stimulus of the official centres and the intellectual
production of the specialists was not limited to the exact
and experimental sciences. The same thing happened in
the study of economics and jurisprudence and, above all,
in history. Some of the most brilliant historical investigators Spain has ever known belong to this period: Padre
Flórez, Capmany, Burriel, Mayáns, Pérez Bayer, Casiri,
Jordán and de Asso, Cortés, Campomanes, Llorente,
Lardizábal, Sempere, Masdeu, Martínez Marina, Muñoz
(investigator of American history and author of a history
of this continent, of which only the first volume was published), Finestras (first compiler and commentator of the

Latin inscriptions found in Catalonia), Mondéjar and others. Expelled Spanish Jesuits, who had taken refuge in Italy, did good work both in history and literature, whilst archaeological expeditions were carried out in America and important remains of Aztec civilization were discovered and studied, music, and Inca remains, various private and public collections of which already existed in certain of our colonies. The two main works produced by these studies (apart from that done by Humboldt, through the generosity of the Spanish authorities and specialists) were: the twenty volumes on Mexican antiquities by the Italian Boturini, a naturalized Spaniard (this work was seen by Humboldt; all that remains of it are the *Idea de una Historia general de la Septentrional America*, printed in Madrid in 1746, and the first volume of the *History* itself in manuscript), and the *Descripción de las Reales expediciones de antiguos monumentos*, with its collection of corresponding engravings, written by the officials commissioned to carry out the expeditions made in 1805, 1806, and 1807 by Captain Guillermo Dupaix, and the professor of drawing and architecture, Luciano Castañeda. Besides these, there were other historiographic works about America, which, without being on the level of the classic works of the 16th century, contained valuable information on the matter of which they treat.

In Spain the new points which characterize the abundant and varied historiographical production are: on the one hand, the publication of documents, monuments, and bibliography (*España Sagrada, Semanario erudito, Medallas de las colonias municipios y pueblos antiguos de España, Alfabeto de letras desconocidas*; bibliographies, such as that of the works and manuscripts of the *Escorial*, that of Aragonese writers, that of the writers of the reign of Charles III, the *Económico-político* of Sempere, the sacred and secular *Crítica* of Father Miguel de San José, etc.); on the other hand, general histories, such as the *Economía política de Aragón* of Asso; that of the ancient legislation of León and Castille, of Martínez Marina; that of the navy, commerce and arts of Barcelona, by Capmany; that of Spanish poetry and poets,

by Padre Sarmiento, the literary history of the PP. Mohed-
anos, etc. In this same group may be found works of such
force, and such copious data as the *Memorias sobre los Frutos,
fábricas y minas de España*, by Larruga. They also founded
centres of historical studies, such as the Royal Academy of
History (Madrid), the centre of historical studies of Andalucía (Seville), and others. Hervas, founder of comparative philology, was the most distinguished specialist in
philological studies.

The *Historia Crítica de España y de la cultura española*, by
Masdeu, deserves separate mention. In it the author incorporated in Spanish historiography a new conception,
which was realized simultaneously by Voltaire and Velly
in France, and by Fergusson, Robertson, and Gibbon in
England. Masdeu broke the narrow frame of pure political
history, which had already been overstepped by our
chroniclers of the Indies of the 15th century (§ 88). Whilst
being a historian of culture, Masdeu is one of the Spaniards
who, with most erudition and serenity of judgment reacted against contemporary Hispanophobia in France
and Italy.

101. *General Culture of the People.* Had this force, produced in higher and professional circles, been exercised
with equal intensity in the general culture of the masses,
Spain would indubitably have been one of the most advanced States in Europe, with regard to popular education
at the end of the 18th century. But it was morally impossible
that this should have been so, partly because the majority
of men of those days, especially the ruling classes, lacked
any conception of the importance to a country, socially and
economically, of the general instruction and education of
the masses. In previous centuries, the complete illiteracy
of the great majority of the inhabitants, had been no
obstacle to the extensive intellectual attainments which
were so specially characteristic of the 16th and much
of the 17th centuries (§§ 87-91). This fact was not disposed
to awaken in the men of the 18th century (narrow intel-
lectualists, all of them), the question of general education.

N

Added to this, the anti-democratic sentiment of the age
(§ 94), led them to mistrust an excessive spread of instruction, a mistrust which had equal effects on private life, as
can be seen in various comedies of manners of the end of
the 18th century.   Therefore the new democratic tendency
of culture was limited to technical instruction, that is to
say, it had a purely utilitarian and economic aim, although
there is evidence of a higher purpose in the law of the Cortes
of Navarre, 1780, concerning compulsory education.

On the other hand, the conception of popular schooling,
of its educative aim and the breadth of its programme, was
a new thing in the world, both in theory and in fact.
Rousseau's *Emile* had been published in 1762. The books
of Pestalozzi, and especially the example of the schools
created by him, are of a later date (1781-1805 and onwards),
and, in spite of their profound social significance, they
drew attention to methods used elsewhere, rather than being put into immediate practice in Spain (§ 94). But what
was lacking quite as much as this, and in a social sense
perhaps more than this, was a general distribution of
schools, and an ample programme of instruction and education. Both things had been barely initiated in Europe.
They made a beginning also in Spain, but were not advanced enough to be compared with the renaissance of
higher and specialized culture. As regards the programme
in particular, it is enough to say that the only things expected of a teacher in the primary schools were the ap-
proval of his Bishop as to his knowledge of Christian
doctrine, a certificate of good conduct and *limpieza de
sangre* (*i.e.*, having no Jewish or Moorish blood), and an
examination in the arts of reading, writing, and arithmetic.
The *Colegio académico del noble arte de primeras letras*, a sort of
normal school, founded in 1780, reduced its principles to
" promoting to the highest degree, in the youth of the whole
kingdom, a complete education in the *rudiments of the Catholic Faith*, in the *rules of good workmanship*, in the *exercise of the
virtues* and in the *noble art of reading, writing, and arithmetic.*"
Although one must recognize the educative, apart from the

purely instructive, value of this programme, it is indubitable that the actual instruction it contained was very
slender. And though it was broadened later on, through
the initiative of Godoy, with the addition of drawing,
geometry, natural history, and applied physics, these novelties were of short duration. In any case, popular schools
were too few in number to produce the general culture of
the masses at this date. Thus the period came to an end
with the same disproportion between the cultured minority
and the ignorant majority, which comprised not only the
working class but much of the middle classes as well. This
disproportion in the 18th century, and those which preceded it, did not profoundly affect the life of the country,
because of the non-dependence of the intellectual production upon the state of culture of the masses, who themselves
had no voice in the public life of the nation. Yet very soon,
at the revision of the political institutions of the country, the
illiteracy of its masses was to have a very grave effect upon
its destinies.

On the other hand, this cultured minority itself was to
come upon obstacles which show that other ideas and other
feelings were uppermost in the minds of the directing elements. Over and over again enterprises such as that of the
Pestalozzi Institute enjoyed only an ephemeral existence,
and the labours of many of our men of science were coun-
tered by bureaucratic zeal and questions of bureaucratic
etiquette. Their collections and manuscripts, once they
came to Spain, were put into archives and forgotten, instead of being made use of promptly and efficiently for the
increase of common knowledge. All these are facts which
show how the well-meaning efforts of certain kings, many
ministers, and no few illustrious men, worked without the
co-operation of general interest, and were often rendered
useless, or at any rate far less beneficial than the excellence
of the idea might have led one to expect.

102. *French Influences on Literature and the Spanish Reaction
to them.* If in the sciences and in the general arrangement
of life French influence was useful, as has already been said

(§ 92), it was not so in literature and the arts. In these the taste of the French men of letters and critics, academic, cold and formal, clipped the wings of Spanish inspiration, which was original and free. Thus there came about amongst cultured people a revulsion against the great authors of the 16th and 17th centuries, especially in the theatre, though the works of Lope, Calderón, and other authors were still played, and greatly applauded by the mass of the population. This break with the native tradition and the excessive formalism and intellectuality of French rhetoric brought about the fact that none of the many good writers of the 18th century strove to follow up the glories of their predecessors. The Picaresque novel ceased to be cultivated at all. So did religious drama and the plays of cloak and sword (*capa y espada*). Furthermore, the literary language became full of gallicisms.

The taste of the learned favoured didactic literature: fables, comedies with a moral thesis, in which the thesis dominates the literary element, scientific poems, investigations in literary history, and books of rhetoric and of poetry were written. Many writers distinguished themselves in these genres (some of them have already been mentioned in another connection) such as Padre Sarmiento, Padre Isla (translator of *Gil Blas*, and critic of bad pupit-oratory in his *Fray Gerundio de Campazas*), Arteaga, the Mohedano Fathers, the Abbé Lampillas, Forner, Cadalso, Iriarte, Samaniego, Padre Andrés, Garcia de la Huerta, and others.

Yet the ascendancy of French taste did not destroy the traditional Spanish spirit. Among the erudite themselves this spirit had been revived by the polemics of the day between Hispanophiles and Hispanophobes, and it produced many defences of our classical literature. In the literary production of the epoch, and especially in the theatre and its more popular forms, this spirit is also revealed. Its most characteristic, and, from the literary standpoint, most valuable representative was Ramón de la Cruz, author of farces of a markedly realistic nature. Breaking away entirely from the French school, and often combating the

SANTIAGO DE COMPOSTELA
(Baroque towers and cloister)

influence of the spirit of French " snobbery " (*snobismo*), he described the customs of the lower quarters of Madrid.

In other forms of polite literature (poetry, drama, high comedy, etc.), there shone certain original authors, whose personalities fought so well against the tyranny of the French mode that they produced noteworthy work and, at times, work of indisputable beauty. Such were: the two Moratíns, Meléndez Valdés, González (imitator of Fr. Luis de León), and Quintana. But, on the whole, literature was afflicted with vulgarity and bad taste.

At the same time, and as a sort of compensation for this general deterioration of our classical literary tradition, certain great foreign writers revealed to the new generation, in their respective countries, the beauties of our theatre, our novel, and our popular epic poetry (this last, as represented by the modern tales of the 16th and 17th centuries, and not in their original form). The names of Calderón and Cervantes as authors, and of the Cid and Don Rodrigo as personages, become popular once more; and the men who exalted them, and who translated and made known the old Spanish masterpieces were, to mention only the most illustrious: Lessing, Goethe, Schlegel, Southey, Fielding, Herder, Metastasio, etc.

103. *The Plastic Arts and Music.* In architecture *baroque* continued to hold sway, represented by Ribera (designer of the Puente de Toledo and the Church of San Sebastian in Madrid, and other buildings), by Donoso and Duque Cornejo. A classical reaction came about later, born in Italy, patronized in France, and brought to Spain through the influence of Italian and French architects and professors (Bonnavia, Carlier, and others). The main representatives of this style are Ventura Rodríguez (1717-1783) and Juan de Villanueva (1739-1811). Examples of this new classicism are: the Madrid churches of Les Salesas, San Justo y Pastor, San Marcos, the Incarnation (interior decoration), the Royal Palace, the Puerta de Alcalá, the present-day Ministry of Finance, the Prado Museum, the Astronomical Observatory, the Casa de Infantes, the

Cathedral of the *Pilar* at Saragossa, the Cathedral of Málaga, the Casa Lonja of Barcelona, and other buildings.

The great impulse given to the construction of public buildings in the reigns of Ferdinand VI and Charles III, favoured the development of architecture and sculpture. This latter, *baroque* being outworn, came to be influenced chiefly by the Neopolitan school, whose representative in Spain is Salcillo (1727-1777), maker of religious images, certain of which deserve to be counted as the most perfect products of our sculpture up to that date. Classical French influences were also at work in Spain, through French artists, brought in by the Bourbon kings, and by Spanish artists brought up in this style. Such are: Juan Pascual Mena, author of the fountain of Neptune, Madrid; Francisco Guliérrez, who made the fountain of the Cibéles, and Manuel Alvarez, to whom we owe the fountain of the Four Seasons, Madrid, with the statue of Apollo which crowns it.

The *Baroque*, and later the neoclassic tendencies of the principal arts, always elegant and decorative, were reflected also in the furniture and appointments of the houses, and in the gardens. This is seen in the furniture of the Palace of El Pardo and the Casita del Principe (couches, cornucopias, tables with incrustations of bronze or of gilt carved wood); also in the gardens of La Granja and Aranjuez, etc.

Dress was radically changed by the introduction of short knee breeches, coats, coloured waistcoats, shirts with collars, frilled fronts and embroidered or laced cuffs, cloaks, etc., for the men, and for the women, short, very full skirts, close-fitting shoes, bodices with a great tucker, all very brilliant in colouring, and made of silk in the wealthy classes. Curled and powdered wigs also came into fashion, plaited for the men, and three-cornered hats or complicated horn combs for the women. A variation of the old uncocked hat, with a broad brim that hid the face, designed by a minister, the famous Squilache, gave rise to a popular riot. Along with these modes of dress there existed others in the lower classes, which either imitated those of the fashionable world, or perpetuated traditional types of

DOOR OF THE BAROQUE PALACE OF THE MARQUÉS DE DOS AGUAS

(Valencia)

costume. An interesting album has been made of them, taken from the life, the sketches of Juan de la Cruz Cano.

Painting fell into great decay; French and Italian influences were paramount in it too, in the decadent style, represented at the end of the foregoing century by Lucás Jordán and his imitators (§ 90), and continued by Bayeu, Maella, and others in the 18th century. At the end of the century a very original painter, Francisco Goya, renewed the ancient glories of our classical school, although in quite a distinct genre. He had been brought up in the decadent tradition, but was an extremely vigorous and original personality. In conformity with the high Spanish tradition, his work is characterized by the colour, expressiveness, and realism of the scenes and people, and by a humane intention, seen in his more personal creations (drawings, engravings, etc.). Like Velázquez, Goya was also an admirable portrait painter. Another notable painter was López, friend and comrade of Goya, of whom he has left a fine portrait. Other works of López are the portraits of the family of Charles IV (1802) and decorative panels on the outside of churches and palaces.

The weaving and embroidery of tapestries was also revived, thanks to the establishment of a *Real Fábrica de Tapices* (1721), for which Goya designed many cartoons. Tapestry was the characteristic decoration for our walls, along with silk and damask, of which there was a famous factory at Talavera. At the same time, pottery was revived (Retiro, Alcora, Talavera), and produced either native models or imitations of English and French china of the epoch.

The outstanding influence in music was the Italian opera; an Italian company performed for the first time in Madrid in 1703. This influence increased later, through the presence at court of musicians such as Scotti and Farinelli, who enjoyed high favour there. The most illustrious cultivators of this school were the Valencian Vicente Martín (1754-1806), whose operas were performed with much applause in Italy, Austria, and Russia, and Manuel

Vicente García, master of the choir at Seville, and founder of a large family of famous singers. In 1799, doubtless as a check to this foreign fashion, there was a royal order, forbidding the representation, singing, or dancing of any piece not written in Castilian and not performed by Spanish, or naturalized Spanish, actors and actresses.

The Spanish musical tradition in its popular form took refuge in minor theatrical productions, such as *sainetes* (farces), although examples are also found of operas in the old Spanish mode of the 17th century (§ 91), such as those written by Zamora, and Cañizares, with music by Durón and Literes, and those of Ramón de la Cruz, whose chief musical contemporary was Rodríguez de Hita. At the same time the *Tonadilla* (songs with choruses), which, in the foregoing period had played only a secondary rôle, as *entr'acte*, etc. (§ 91), developed and overpassed its original limits, making itself independent of the farces, and forming short *zarzuelitas* or *pasillos*, comic or satirical. The forms taken by the *tonadilla* in the 18th century are: solos and songs for two, three, four, or many voices, which already carry a certain argument and a certain amount of action. Choruses were sometimes introduced into them, and, later on, traditional songs and dances, such as the *jácaras*, *danzas primas*, *seguidillas*, *tiranas*, *jotas*, etc. The chief writers for this genre were Guerrero, Misón, Laserna, Plá, Esteve, and García, who, despite their Spanish sentiments, often introduced purely Italian elements into their work.

As regards erudite, non-theatrical music, it underwent, both in its religious and profane manifestations, an interesting modification, in regard to the forms into which it had crystallized in the 17th century. The main representatives of these new doctrines were the Catalan, P. Antonio Soler (pupil of Domenico Scarlatti), author of notable chamber and church music, and of a very important treatise on technique, called *Llave de la Modulación* (key of modulation, 1762); the Valencian Jesuit, P. Eximeno, author of *De los Orígenes y reglas de la Música* (1774), where, for the first time, " popular taste " in music is spoken of, and the Aragonese, P. Arteaga, whose *Historia de las Revoluciones de la Opera Italiana* (1783) shows how Italian opera was the precursor of lyrical drama as it was conceived and executed (especially by Wagner) later on in the next century. His *Investigaciones filosóficas sobre la belleza Ideal* (1789), is one of the most original books on aesthetics of that century.

At the same time the great foreign composers of the epoch (Haydn, Bach, etc.), who were well-known in Spain, showed their appreciation of the good musical tradition in Spain, as did also the foreign writers of that day (§ 102). A curious example of this is to be met with in Handel's *Cantata Spagnuola* to Spanish words, written for a solo voice, with the accompaniment of guitar and bass.

X

THE NINETEENTH AND BEGINNING OF THE TWENTIETH CENTURIES
(1808-1914)

104. *New Political and Social Programme*

THE Napoleonic invasion of Spain and the absence of the kings, who were prisoners in France from 1808-1814, produced a peculiar political situation which had very important consequences. Without any central government to direct it, and suspicious of the higher authorities, who were dominated by French influences, the nation took upon itself the initiation of the *War of Independence* and the direction of public affairs. In this way it was possible for the political and social aspirations which had been suppressed by the absolutism of the foregoing regime to come to the fore, publicly and without reservation. In accordance with a natural tendency the various regions of Spain constituted themselves as centres of activity, with governing *Juntas* (councils). They aspired to reinstate the old Cortes, as a general organism, which should represent them all and which should respect the needs and desires of the nation in the absence of the king. Thus there met at Cadiz (1809-1813) an Assembly made up of four classes of deputies: those from the cities, who had voted in the earlier Cortes; those from the newly constituted *Juntas Provinciales*; deputies from the people—every 50,000 souls choosing their representative, and from America, one from every 100,000 white inhabitants.

Many of them, especially the deputies from the *Juntas*, introduced a reformative spirit (already expressed in the petitions of the *Juntas*), in which the humanitarian and liberal programme of the 18th century found expression,

SPANISH FAN, SHOWING OCCUPATIONS OF THE EARLY 19TH CENT.

as well as the recent influences of the French Revolution.
It must be noted that many of these reformers were priests,
e.g., Ruiz del Padrón, Muñoz Torrero, and others.

The Cortes having been constituted as sovereign in legislative functions, they began their tasks on the basis of the
fourfold oath of the deputies, who bound themselves to
maintain the Catholic religion, the national integrity, loyalty
to the laws, and proclaimed Ferdinand VII as King. In
successive decrees and resolutions, which formed the major
part of the so-called Constitution of 1812, they developed
the new liberal programme, whose fundamental points
were: the sovereignty of the nation in conjunction with
that of the king; a constitutional monarchy; separation
of the power of the State; the inviolability of the deputies,
who were not allowed to occupy public offices; equality of
rights between Spaniards and Americans; the abolition of
abusive rights over the Indians; political liberty of the
press, though the old censorship with regard to religious
questions was maintained; the submission of the king to
the Cortes as regards his marriage and international agree-
ments contracted while he was in captivity; the abolition
of torture; the regulation of a national budget, which imposed taxes also on the clergy to meet the costs of war; the
abolition of feudal jurisdiction where it still existed, and of
seignorial and vassalage rights; the initiation of the liberation of the negro slaves; and the abolition of corporal
punishment and imprisonment for baptized Indians; the
recognition of intangible individual rights (civil liberty,
property, fitness for public offices, equality in the sight of
the law, etc.); the reformability of the Constitution; the
responsibility of the King's ministers; the establishment of
elective *Ayuntamientos* (town councils); national militia and
a permanent army; great development of public education; abolition of the tribunal of the Inquisition, religious
offences being handed over to the tribunals of the bishops,
as they had been before the establishment of the Inquisition
(§ 71); limitation of the number of religious communities;
the division of uncultivated and common lands between the

poor and those who had served in the army; the suppression
of corporal punishment in schools; a plan for a single direct
contribution to the budget, and many other innovations
made in a similar spirit.

105. *The Reaction against the New Programme.* Although
all these measures were approved of by the great majority
of the deputies, they really only represented the opinion of
enlightened people, influenced by the reformative spirit of
the age. They had many opponents, headed by the king,
who saw with disgust the annulment of his absolute rights.
All those social classes and groups whose old privileges were
disappearing in the face of judicial equality (especially
many of the clergy) stirred up public opinion against political and social reform. The masses, indifferent because they
knew nothing of these new ideals, willingly allowed themselves to be persuaded of the value of tradition rather than
of innovation. Thus, on the return to Spain of Ferdinand
VII, it was possible to abolish entirely the work of the Cortes
of Cadiz. Moreover, the reaction went further than this.
Not only were the liberals persecuted to death, the decrees
given in the absence of the king declared void, the Inquisition re-established (the principle was proclaimed that the
years between 1808-1813 were to be considered never to
have happened), but further, the absolutist principle was
extreme, and the country went back to a state of greater
restriction than it had known in the 18th century. To
these political measures were added others of a religious or
cultural nature. Thus the Jesuits were again admitted,
monasteries and convents increased in number, the universities and theatres were closed, the publication of any papers
other than the official *Gaceta* was forbidden, and all propaganda for the material or moral betterment of the country
was prevented. The Exchequer became disorganized,
public wealth diminished, the number of government
officials grew inordinately, and once more the people were
hungry and the army was miserable and unpaid.

Such liberals as could escape persecution fled to France
and England. Contact with more advanced civilizations,

the sight of people better governed, a desire for revenge and the bitterness of exile, not only confirmed their beliefs, but accentuated them, arousing the longing to see them once more applied in their own country.

These two irreconcilable tendencies defined inevitably the course of the national history during almost the whole of the 19th century. The problem consisted in deciding what ideas and what men should govern the nation, whether liberals or reactionaries. The struggle of necessity entered upon the political ground, so that power might be won to limit absolutism, and so that the aspiration of the reformists and of the oppressed people, might be realized. Both parties were obdurate. The resistance of the reaction, which was always strenuous, consisted in not conceding the least point to the *Doceañistas* (a name given to the partisans of the Constitution of 1812). The cruelty of the persecution of these latter, and the hatred that reigned in both parties, made of the period between 1814 and 1833 (date of the death of Ferdinand VII) an endless series of conspiracies, risings, and plots, by one party or the other, which engrossed the attention and the resources of the whole country. The short Liberal Government, from 1820-1823, entered once more upon legislative reforms (the division of the land into provinces—those that exist to-day; a basic law for the navy, public beneficence, fixed rates of custom duties, the Penal Code, a new plan of education. All this inflamed men's minds more and more and brought about, with the help of a French army of occupation, a re-action in 1824, severer than that of 1814, and a new emigration to France and England.

The end of Ferdinand VII's reign (1832), saw a less rigorous political regime, thanks to his fourth wife, María Cristina, who was obliged to rely upon the liberals to defend the succession of her daughter, Isabella II. She granted an amnesty to the exiles, protection, once more, to the universities, and adopted other means, through force of necessity. The reactionary programme was defended in its entirety by Don Carlos, son of Ferdinand VII, who aspired to the Crown. Thus the *Carlist party* came into being.

The struggle thenceforward was twofold, against Carlism, fought out in civil wars, and against the Crown itself, fought out in the Government, in order to insure the acceptance of liberal reforms, a thing which the reactionaries managed to avoid as long as possible, by means of various subterfuges.

The main spirit of the monarchic policy was to compromise between absolutism and the sovereignty of the people, thus constituting what was called *doctrinarismo*. The essentially conservative inclinations of the doctrinaires, and certain abuses of power, along with other causes, brought about a renewal of conspiracies and banishments, until a final and exaggerated reaction led to the revolution of 1868.

106. *The Revolution and its Consequences.* During all this time the liberal party had changed much. Already in 1820 a part of it (the *Exaltados*) considered as insufficient the policy of 1812, and aimed at more radical reforms, and the same thing happened in the Cortes of 1837, which voted a new constitution.

The progressive current manifested itself in a special way in the Cortes of 1854, in which also a republican tendency publicly declared itself. It was not widespread, but it grew steadily from that time onward. In 1868 it was already important, as was also the radical tendency among the monarchists. The Constitution of 1869 reflects these new ideals, along with those of 1812. It granted full national sovereignty, universal suffrage, a declaration of the rights of individuals, division of independent powers among themselves, reformability of the Constitution, liberty of religious worship, secularization of civil life. The revolutionary governments, especially those of the republican period (1873), stressed this radical feeling in other laws and in their project for a new constitution.

During the republic the federalist doctrine took a special direction. It was preached in Spain by Pi y Margall, and its basis was absolute autonomy in the separate regions of Spain, which were to be linked only in a completely voluntary pact, for the creation of a central government, charged with matters that are considered to be of common interest to them all. This tendency, to the principle of which most of the republicans subscribed, was modified very soon by many of them. This produced a schism, and a new, though short, civil war. The federalists have continued as a party until now, and their principles are represented in part by the Regionalists of to-day (*Catalanismo*, aiming at an independent Catalonia, and *Bizkaitarrismo* at an independent Basque province, etc.). They are chiefly concerned with autonomy, and entirely opposed in general to republican federalism and to liberal radicalism (§ 108).

The Bourbon restoration of 1874 produced a violent reaction in the first years, rooting out the liberal conquests of 1869. Yet in the constitution of 1876 the footprints of revolution are visible. Although somewhat vague in many of its terms, leaving ample room for many very diverse interpretations, it recognized, in a more or less attenuated form, certain liberal principles. More reactionary than the constitution itself were the first governments of Alfonso XII. In 1881 this feeling began to be righted, with the appearance of a "fusionist" party (headed by Praxedes M. Sagasta). Thanks to its policy and to that of the republicans (to Emilio Castelar more definitely than to any one else), various other points of the programme of 1869 were reincorporated in laws: universal suffrage, the jury, freedom of the press, etc.

Yet much was needed (both in legislation and in the interpretation of the laws and the practice of government) to accomplish the revolutionary ideals, including those of 1812; and thanks to this disagreement, there continued to be both radical and conservative groups within the monarchist parties, as well as Republican and Carlist groups (this latter, much reduced, and partly reformed). They all agreed in aspiring to change the regime, in order to establish their respective programmes, which were entirely opposed to one another.

In 1879 a socialist labour party was constituted, the *partido socialista obrero*. This aspired to give effect to all the petitions of the manual workers. Part of their programme was upheld also by certain groups of the republican party. In 1888 the "General Union of Workers" was formed (*Unión general de trabajadores*), and in 1889 it made its headquarters in Madrid, under the presidency of Pablo Iglesias, who was, until his death, the spiritual director of Spanish socialism.

From the same mass of workers arose later various branches of socialism, such as anarchism, syndicalism, and communism, which counted among their proselytes certain intellectuals who introduced new problems of ideology and practice, the discussion of which are still among the burning questions of the day.

A final political phenomenon of this period reveals a change in the ideals of the country, or rather, in that section of it which took part or directed political struggles. This was the break in the unity of the old parties, both in those which governed and in those which never had the chance to govern. The outstanding effect of this in the last years of the period, and still more in those which followed it, was to render very difficult the constitution of parliamentary majorities, and more difficult still the stability of the governments. Thus arose one of the gravest problems of the parliamentary system. The legislative task of the Cortes was made almost useless and often enough the government was obliged, in order not to raise questions which might oblige them to resign, to carry on an uneventful policy, with no characteristic programme and, in the main, without those traditional differences which had formed the demarcation between liberalism and those parties more or less opposed to it. Thus began the crisis, not only of the parliamentary system, but also of the entire liberal regime. This crisis was later to grow more acute. At the same time, in the general masses of the country there appeared a grow-

ing scepticism towards politics and politicians, and a very
marked tendency to dissociate from them all those departments of national life which could live independently of
the political and administrative sphere. This scepticism
as to the functions of citizenship, was held by a great
number of people, who believed their participation in the
government to be useless, and it has helped to aggravate
the conflict which in 1914 and successive years has remained without solution.

107. *Juridical Unification.* Another characteristic of the
19th century was the continuation, and the almost complete accomplishment of the centralizing and unifying ideal
of the monarchy (§§ 84-94). The aim was to make the
regional and municipal government entirely dependent
upon the central offices, so that the *fueros* and judicial
idiosyncrasies should disappear and the same laws be
applied to all Spanish people.

At the beginning of the century many of the old differen-
tiations and privileges, both in public and private law, still
existed, in spite of the many common laws dictated by the
kings. Navarre and the Basque provinces still retained
their *fueros* intact; Aragon, Catalonia, and the Balearic
Isles retained their civil *fueros*, as well as certain clauses
in the administrative sphere. In Castille there ruled at the
same time, though more in appearance than in reality,
very diverse sources of legislation, such as the *Fuero Juzgo*,
Fuero Real, the *Partidas*, etc., and local peculiarities were also
recognized. There remained traces of seignorial jurisdiction in many points and, moreover, certain social classes, the
clergy, the army, merchants, etc., possessed tribunals of
their own, which judged their cases independently of the
common courts. In the same way, in the application of the
penal code and also in the payment of taxes, differences
were made, according to the class of the delinquent. All
the efforts of the 19th century, and especially of the liberal
party, were directed against such particularism. At different times from 1812 onwards, special class jurisdiction
was abolished, as were also the political and administrative

rights of Navarre and the Basque provinces, and exemption from contributing to the national exchequer. The legislative diversity of Castille disappeared with the publication of Codes and laws, with regard to commerce, the penal code, waters and waterways, mines, mortgages, notaries, hunting and fishing laws, compulsory military service, civil rights, etc. These were obligatory throughout Spain, except for the civil code of 1888. This held force in Catalonia, Biscay, Aragon, Navarre, and the Balearic Isles, only as supplementary, and in cases where it did not conflict with the special laws of these regions. No special court remained, save the penal courts of the army and navy, which had their own codes. The clergy were subject to the same laws as other citizens.

At the same time the old territorial divisions were suppressed. These had been fixed by various kings, or had come into being through the peculiarities of geographical or historical regions. They were substituted by the now existing forty-nine provinces, plus the two insular provinces, with a unified regime, largely dependent on the central government.

As regards civil or private law, the 19th century strengthened the individualist tendency, with the aim of breaking the barriers which opposed the liberty of each individual. In conformity with this aim, the *desamortización* of church property was brought about—all real estate that had been in the hands of the churches, monasteries, and municipalities were taken over by the State as national property (*bienes nacionales*), and sold by public auction, in exchange for certain indemnities. This was why, from the middle of the century onwards, the State took upon itself to pay the expenses of the cult and the priesthood (*Culto y Clero*). Similarly, legislation tended to suppress the communal possessions of the *vecinos*, and, generally speaking, all forms of collective property. They abolished entails (*mayorazgo*) and compulsory guilds, declaring that labour and the grouping of workmen were free, and in fact, trying to realize the absolute ideal of the liberty of each individual. Later on another tendency arose that was opposed to this.   It grew much stronger towards the end of the period, and necessitated the rectification of individualism in many of its tenets, and the restoration of certain of the old institutions which had been abolished.   The socialists, many liberals, and certain conservatives sympathized with this tendency, though with very different aims in their various doctrines. At the same time they studied and made an inventory of the many juridical customs which still existed in almost every sphere of the law.   This was not only a labour of scholarship, but had the practical aim of saving from oblivion all such elements as were useful to the social and economic life of our people and incorporating these in our legislation.   The originator and chief cultivator of this movement was the jurist Joaquín Costa, whom we shall mention later on in another connection.

The labour-laws also contributed to mitigate the rigour of absolute individualism.   They were begun in the time of the republic, patronized later by Cánovas del Castillo, and developed still later both by the conservative party and by the most radical elements in the liberal party, with their tendency to protect the labour of the manual workers, to better their condition, to find a peaceful solution for their quarrels with their employers, and to reform and sanction certain of the principles of the new economic feeling.   So as to help forward these proposals and to prepare with due investigation the plans for this legislation, an *Instituto de Reformas Sociales* was founded in 1903, with representatives from both workmen and employers.   From it have issued the chief initiatives towards these reforms, and the most important texts, as well as works on statistics, and the necessary information about the state of economic problems of the present day.

108. *The Reaction against Unification.* Yet the unremitting labour devoted to the juridical unification of Spain did not result in the elimination of laws that had grown up by custom, the existence of which had often been proved, and is recognized even by official reports.   These pecu-

liarities of custom exist even in civil law (in spite of the code), under the form of district, or local, variations in the region of common or unified legislation. The great mass of legal custom which formed the positive bases of our social life (especially in rural districts), and which were expressed even in the forms of the enjoyment of landed property, demonstrate the inefficacy of abstract principles when they strive to impose a theoretical unity in contradiction to the natural tendencies of a particular group.

This experimental manifestation and the natural love of a region, in which a legislation of its own had survived, for certain juridical institutions (*legislación foral*), produced a movement in favour of the maintenance of these modifications and for the so-called " civil liberty " or juridical autonomy. Its chief definer and defender was the jurist Joaquín Costa, and its most numerous and radical nucleus was formed in Catalonia.

Independently of this technical aspect there arose in Spain at the end of the 19th century, the question of the integral autonomy of those regions which in the past centuries had formed, in a greater or lesser degree, sovereign states or districts, united to a monarchy, but retaining completely, or in part, their *fueros* and privileges. The region in which public opinion held most profoundly and solidly to this aspiration was Catalonia. Here the programme of restoring the old national character touched upon every factor, from the political and administrative regime to the language and literature. Similar tendencies were found in the Basque Provinces, especially in Biscay, though here they were less intense and less widespread. In Galicia, too, there were manifestations of a similar feeling, though it was less political in aim.

In Catalonia and the Basque Provinces this programme produced political parties, first *regionalistas* and then *Catalanistas* in Catalonia, *Bizcaitarra* or *Bizkaitarra* in the Basque Provinces. The Catalanists, becoming more powerful, and with a growing parliamentary minority, played a more and more important and influential rôle in Spanish policy, in the last years of the period covered by this chapter. They were in open conflict with the government itself, which resisted any concession, as it suspected the excessive autonomy to which the extremist groups in Catalonia and the Basque Provinces aspired, an autonomy which bordered upon independence. Yet at the end of 1913 Catalanism realized its first triumph with the royal decree which authorized the constitution of provincial *Mancomunidades*. This rendered possible the establishment of the *Mancomunidad Catalana* in April 1914, with a wide margin of autonomy.

The final result of these conflicts, and one of transcendent historical importance for Spain, was the conversion of the particular autonomist problem of certain regions into a general autonomist problem, which covered all parts of the country and aimed at remodelling the political texture of Spain. Some wished to change the earlier centralization, some into a semi-federal combination, others demanded internal differentiation in the administrative and partly in the political order. The predominant political opinions ran along these lines when the outbreak of war in 1914 brought about disturbances and general disorientation of the processes of the ideals and political institutions in many countries.

109. *The End of the Spanish Dominion in America.* Although naturally linked to the history of the mother country, the colonial history of Spain in the 19th century forms a separate chapter, and its final consequences brought the century to a close with events that had widespread political repercussion.

In spite of the loss or cession of Florida, the territories of the Mississippi, Santo Domingo, and Trinidad, already mentioned, Spain still had under her dominion in 1808 a large portion of American territory: the South West of the present United States (California, Texas, etc.); Mexico, all Central America, and all South America except Brazil, and certain small possessions of European powers (Guiana). In Oceania there were the Philippines, Marianas, Carolinas and Palaos—all Spanish colonies.

Spain had put as much interest into the progress and education of its American as of its Peninsula subjects, save for the restrictions imposed for political reasons at the end of the 18th century.   And, as always happens in colonies that are advancing in power, an anti-Spanish party had been forming in America, or at least a party imbued with suspicion and unfriendly feelings towards Spain.   It was made up of the descendants of the colonists and *Mestizos*; their attitude was caused both by the spirit common to colonial and mixed races, and even more by frequent mistakes, abuses, and anachronisms on the part of the Spanish authorities and clergy.   A similar state of mind had already manifested itself in the 18th century.   Certain of the ministers of the Bourbons pointed out the danger, and even suggested remedies for it, in a change of regime for the colonies. Something indeed had been done, but not as much as was necessary (§ 95).

The example of the old English colonies, which in 1783 emancipated themselves and formed the nucleus of what are now the United States, inspired the Spanish-American separatists, swelling their ranks and quickening the spirit of independence.   In 1809 there were already premature attempts in Caracas, Quito, and Upper Peru.   In 1810 took place the first insurrectionary movement in Venezuela, followed very soon in Buenos Aires, New Granada, Chile, Quito, and Mexico.   Yet at the Cortes of Cadiz, American deputies were received from all the *virreinatos* and other governmental units, and emancipation would perhaps have been avoided with the more flexible attitude of the Spanish liberals.   These had, in fact, begun by declaring that the Spanish Dominions in the Indies should not be considered as trade depots or colonies, but as " an essential and integral part of the Spanish monarchy," which ought to be governed in exactly the same way as the Peninsula;   they were to be called *provincias ultramarinas*, and the absolute legal equality of Spaniards and Americans was to be declared.   But in the application of this doctrine to the convocation and constitution of the Cortes, all who were not white and free ("descendants of Spaniards on both sides"), were excluded from citizenship and from electoral rights. Also an unequal proportion of representatives between the Spanish and American regions was established. The American delegates opposed these differences, and their disputes with the Spaniards "led to much friction and wounded susceptibilities. . . . The Spaniards resented the accusation of being illiberal, and the Americans were aggrieved because they considered themselves slighted in the domain of fact and the sphere of action."

The revolt continued in South America, directed in the Northern part by Bolívar; by Belgrano and Artigas at first, and later by San Martín, in the region of La Plata and Chile (in collaboration with O'Higgins); by Hidalgo and Morelos in Mexico. Of these regions the following had achieved *de facto* independence by 1813: Buenos Aires, Uruguay, Paraguay, Chile, and a great part of New Granada. The government of the first Bourbon reaction (1814) revived the struggle, applying terrorist measures in certain of the territories still dominated by Spanish troops and Spanish partisans. But this only excited the hatred of the Americans. The energy of the rebels, and the lack of Spanish troops (because those who had been prepared to proceed to America revolted with Riego and Quiroga in 1820), brought about a definitive Spanish defeat, followed by the independence of the whole of South America in 1824. The same thing had happened a little earlier in Mexico (1821), Venezuela (1821), Ecuador (1823), and Guatemala (1821). After this Spain only retained in the New World the Antilles (Cuba and Puerto Rico), and her Oceanic possessions. In the space of a few years we lost more than 300,000 square leagues of country, with about 12,000,000 inhabitants, whites, negroes, half-castes and, above all, Indians (6,000,000 alone). From our emancipated continental colonies arose the new republican States of Argentina, Uruguay, Paraguay, Chile, Peru, Bolivia, New Granada (later Columbia), Ecuador, Venezuela, the United Provinces of South America (later divided into the five Central American republics), and Mexico. They all carry on our civilization and speak our language.

The Spanish governments refused for some years, and from various motives, to recognize these States, thus maintaining the lack of communication with them, begun by the struggle for independence. The official recognition of Mexico began in 1836, on the basis of a resolution of the Spanish Cortes (Law of 4th December), which authorized the government to " conclude treaties of peace and amity with the new states of Spanish America on the basis of our recognition of their independence." But there were still some conflicts, among them the war between Peru and Chile in 1864-1866.

At the end of the 19th century the cordiality of relationship between Spain and her former colonies was fully established. At the conference and congresses in Madrid, held to celebrate the fourth centenary of the discovery of America, delegates from all the Spanish-American countries were present. The demonstrations were enthusiastic, and marked the beginning of a movement that is known as *Hispano-Americanismo*, which thenceforward has become more and more emphasized and concrete in its programme.

110. *Policy in the Antilles.* The possessions or colonies that remained to Spain after 1824 were still very important. The Oceanic (or as some call them Asiatico-oceanic) possessions covered more than 14,640 square kilometers, with 700,000 inhabitants (in 1818), and Puerto Rico, less than 10,000 square kilometers, and 100,000 inhabitants. The attention of the mother country and of commercial exploitation were centred mainly on the Antilles, whose population and wealth grew very rapidly. Thus the inhabitants of Havana, who in 1800 had numbered only 60,000, had increased in 1900 to 236,000; Santiago (Cuba), grew from 20,000 to 43,000; Matanzas from 7,000 to 36,000, etc. Along with this, the last census from Cuba shows 1½ million inhabitants, and from Porto Rico, more than 800,000, many of whom are Spaniards or the descendants of Spaniards.

But in both islands the same desire for independence arose as in the continental territories, desires strengthened by the excitement of the 1810-1824 risings in South America, Mexico, and the Central region. As regards Cuba and Puerto Rico, two other factors complicated the problem: the negro slave population, a constant element of agitation; and the ambitions of the North American Republic, which aspired very early to the possession of the Antilles, and attempted it repeatedly, by means of purchase or intervention, whilst at the same time they favoured conspiracies and landings in Cuba on the part of the partisans of independence. The Spanish governors either did not see the full gravity of the danger, or were powerless to avert it. At the same time they did not succeed in calming the separatist spirit by means of political or administrative reforms, in spite of the good intentions of certain governors and of Cánovas del Castillo, who was colonial minister in 1865. The example of what had happened in the continental colonies availed nothing. Spain continued to haggle over the rights of the *Antillanos*, suspicious of any liberal movement, and employing forceful methods as the situation became graver. The separatist party grew, notwithstanding, and finally promoted a war in Cuba which, beginning in 1868 (the Revolt of Jara), did not end until the Peace of Zanjón in 1878.

The revolutionary Spanish governments (1868-1873) modified the old policy to a certain extent. They restored to Puerto Rico the right of electing deputies (1869); they abolished many measures taken against the revolutionaries and suspects in Cuba, which had led to grave abuses; they limited the excessive powers of the Captains-General, and in points of emigration, colonization, courts of justice, etc., they dictated measures calculated to benefit the colonies. But this reformist feeling broke itself against the enormous power of those who were intransigent. These were very numerous, and were represented in Cuba mainly by the armed volunteers, who imposed their will repeatedly on the Captains-General. By such acts as the death of the rebel leader Arango, and the shooting of certain Havana students accused of being separatist conspirators, the home government further strengthened the fears and hatreds which caused a constant state of war.

111. *Autonomism and the Reforms.* The Peace of Zanjón forced upon the Spanish governors an effective change of policy. Many Cubans put great faith in this, for, while desiring liberty for their country, they desired also peace, and did not wish to break completely with Spain. The natural and wise thing to do would have been to found an autonomous regime which, whilst maintaining the dependent relations between Spain and the two islands, should give the latter a certain latitude in the direction and administration of their interests. This feeling, which was shared in Spain by many republicans and by certain monarchists, was represented by the so-called autonomist party, whose first manifestos date from 1872, though the party was not formally constituted until 1879, after a programme-manifesto (August 1878). But the die-hards, who continued to be numerous both in Spain and in the Antilles, fought strongly against autonomy, labelling its defenders as buccaneers in disguise and bad patriots. The main doctrine consisted in considering Cuba and Puerto Rico not as colonies, but as ultra-marine provinces, which should not be assimilated but should be granted special laws. Thus, when in 1878 the municipal law was applied to Cuba, they were granted the right of electing deputies, but the vote was more restricted there than it was in Spain; the same thing happened in Puerto Rico, which, since the revolution, had enjoyed universal suffrage. In the same way (*i.e.*, with reservations), the Spanish penal code was applied in 1879; the mortgage laws (*legislación hipotecaria*), in 1880; the Constitution of 1876 in 1881; the law of *Enjuiciamiento* (preparation of law-suit for judgment), in 1885; the commercial code in 1886, etc. Such methods were not sufficient. The desire for autonomy grew ever stronger, and in the Cortes this was pointed out by the colonial deputies, without their gaining a hearing, or even having

justice done to their intentions. In 1882 the law of mercantile relations between Spain and Cuba, although it made certain general concessions, increased the discontent in the Greater Antilles. In 1893 hopes were revived by a plan for political and administrative reforms of an autonomist nature, presented by Antonio Maura; but it was rejected and the very inadequate law which was substituted for it in 1895 was hardly put into force.

As regards negro slavery, a very prompt and efficacious remedy was found. Abolitionist tendencies had appeared in the Cortes of Cadiz (§ 104), and were repeated in those of 1854-1855 by Orense, Rivero, Castelar, and other democrats. In 1865 they culminated in the formation of an Abolitionist Society, whose aims met with a great deal of opposition, but which won over public opinion year by year. In 1868 the negro slave trade, *i.e.*, the introduction of new slaves, was definitely suppressed. In 1870 a law prepared the liberation of those which existed and another, in 1872 (despite the keen opposition of the slavers), freed the negro slaves of Puerto Rico. By the Peace of Zanjón, the liberty of all rebel negroes was equally recognized. Justice and logic demanded that those slaves who had always been faithful should get an equal concession. Yet the law referring to this was not passed until 1880, and it decreed that these faithful slaves should remain in servitude for another eight years. Finally, in 1886, this date was advanced and their liberation was made effective.

112. *The Colonial Disaster.* The warning given by the inadequate reforms of 1895, together with complaints against Spanish administration and the little zeal for anything connected with increasing the culture or wealth of the country, encouraged the separatists, and war broke out again with the revolt of Baire (1895), a war that was encouraged by a great body of opinion in the United States. Many Spanish politicians then advocated anew that autonomy should be granted, as a honourable compromise. But the majority of them, represented in this case by the leader of the Conservative party, Cánovas del

Castillo, shut themselves in complete obduracy, favoured the doctrine of " war against war," and demanded that the rebels should submit before any reforms were granted. This attitude increased the revolt in Cuba, though some of the Autonomists remained loyal to Spain. Puerto Rico stood aloof from the war, as it had done on the previous occasion.

But the United States considered that the time had come for a decisive step in their policy, and precipitated the *dénouement*. They advanced as reasons for their entry into the dispute: its protracted nature; the military methods of General Weyler (stern repression, concentration camps, etc.); the blowing up of the cruiser " Maine," anchored in the Havana harbour (unjustly attributed to the Span- iards), and the need to protect the lives and properties of the North Americans resident in Cuba or interested in pro- duction and commerce there. Although none of these reasons had a basis of proven fact, still less a valid juridical justification in international law, they exerted pressure of an undoubted importance. Thanks to this, and to the consciousness, already clear among certain liberals, that reforms alone could cut short the rebellion, the reforms of 25th November 1897 were produced and applied in January 1898. These were of a very markedly autonom- ous nature. But the remedy came too late. And the United States neither expected that this would have any effect, nor facilitated the application of the law, to which the separ- atists also opposed all sorts of difficulties. It is impossible to say whether it would have taken root in the islands and reduced the strife. There was by then not time enough for the experiment to bear fruit.

In face of the exaggerated pretensions of the United States' Government, entirely unacceptable to Spain, war broke out between the two countries in April 1898. The result was unfavourable to us (whose economic and military means were vastly inferior to those of the North American Republic), in spite of the heroic sacrifice of our navy at Santiago de Cuba and Cavite, and of that part of our army which took the field.

The war ended with the Treaty of Paris on 10th December 1898, by which Cuba and Puerto Rico passed into the hands of the United States. The same happened with the Philippines, whose inhabitants had revolted against Spain in 1896, and which were also acquired by the United States in 1898.

In this way Spain lost the last of her Oceanic and American colonial power.

113. *The Moroccan Question.* The old-standing possession of cities and territories on the North Coast of Morocco, and the strategic importance of this zone on account of the neighbouring maritime zone of Andalucía, were facts which caused Spain to give particular attention to the future of that Muslim empire, which was in complete decay at the end of the 19th century. Save for the episode of 1859, commonly called the " War of Africa," an artificial and romantic revival of a feeling characteristic of certain moments of the Spanish Reconquest, neither in public opinion nor in the political opinions of any of the governments had there been any desire for expansion in Morocco. The loss of the Antilles and the Philippines had even further constricted any national desire for foreign exploits. But Spain was obliged to abandon her former indifference owing to the colonial policy of other European states, especially France; to the great advance made by that country in establishing a preponderant influence in North Africa in the last years of the century, and to the impossibility, which became more and more obvious, that the Moroccan Empire should retain its independence in the face of its interior anarchy. A first French proposal in 1902 to divide that Empire with Spain was rejected by the Spanish government. But a secret agreement between France and England, in 1904, opened the question directly for us, by reason of a clause by which France engaged herself to come to an understanding, " taking into consideration the interests of Spain, resulting from her geographical position and her territorial possessions on the Mediterranean coasts."

There was no doubt a political possibility of Spain's refusing to participate in the division of Morocco, though this participation was an implicit result of the Anglo-French agreement of 1904 and of others signed by France, which combined in securing and guaranteeing to Spain the integrity and the strategic value of her old coastal possessions (Melilla, Ceuta, etc.). The Spanish government believed, however, that national security and national interests demanded something further, and it signed a treaty with France, by which it accepted a zone in North Morocco, that is to say, one contiguous with the Spanish coastal possessions.

A sudden intervention in the Moroccan question on the part of William II of Germany (1905), made an international conference necessary. This was held in Algeciras in 1906, and resulted in an Act in which the signatory states confided to Spain and France the guardianship and policy of Morocco. Soon afterwards native revolts began in the Spanish and French zones. Of the former those round Melilla in 1909 were especially serious and cost Spain considerable losses of men. This led at last to a new treaty with France in 1912, in which the Spanish zone of influence in Morocco was officially established, bordering on the French protectorate in the South, and covering almost the same territory as under the pact of 1904. But the consolidation of their zone, and the development and political penetration which the various Spanish governments have deemed necessary, began a new period of more or less continuous warfare against the natives, which was still going on in 1914.

114. *Economics*. The War of Independence, the great political upheavals from 1814-1833, the civil strife that followed on that year, combined with frequent risings and revolutions and the loss of political influence abroad, were not things calculated to inspire the country or the governments to develop the enterprises of the 18th century in industry and commerce. Nor did they help the country to make advantageous terms in its economic relations with the

rest of the world. But the problem of the distribution of land, in relation not only to the economic state of the working classes, but also, and principally, to the necessity of cultivating a much larger area than is cultivated at present, was still unsolved in 1914, and stated in the same terms as before.

The first effect of the War of Independence was a paralysis of all enterprise in areas covered by the war. During the struggle (and not always through military necessity) many factories were destroyed, either by the French troops or by our English allies, and agriculture suffered enormously. We have already seen what harm the reactions of 1814 and 1824 did to the country. And, as if the internal disturbances were not enough, trade received a new and heavy blow with the emancipation of the continental American colonies.

In the last years of Ferdinand VII, certain ministers, more well-meaning than the majority, had already tried to promote a renaissance of economic life, regularizing the Exchequer and founding institutions that should favour mercantile and industrial progress, such as the *Colegio de Comercio*, and the *Dirección general de Obras Públicas*. These attempts did not take root, however, until after the death of that king, and especially until the end of the civil war (1839). This last fact, along with the *desamortización* of church property realized by the decrees of Mendizábal (1836), confirmed and amplified by later laws, produced a new desire for industrial and commercial negotiations, land cultivation, and building. In some places, groups of small proprietors were formed, amongst whom was subdivided the former accumulated property, and in others, great fortunes were made and invested in capitalist enterprises.

At the same time the State interested itself in the development of auxiliary means of commercial life on a larger scale than hitherto, helping forward public works. In 1834 the School of Road Engineers, which had been founded in the end of the 18th century, was reopened. High roads,

which in 1807 measured only 706 leagues, were considerably
increased and some important roads, such as the Cabrillas
Road, were constructed. In 1839 the first modern light-
house was constructed in Santander, followed by others,
until in 1856 there were forty completed and nineteen
under construction. Great works of canalization were
undertaken or planned on the Guadalquivir, Tagus, Ebro,
Alcocer, Lozoya, etc., and steamship lines were started
(1854, from Málaga to Cadiz). Railways were constructed
(begun already in 1828, though not put into practical use),
especially from 1851 onwards, and still more after the dis-
establishment of 1855 (in 1854 the line from Madrid to
Aranjuez, in 1858 that from Madrid to Alicante, and later
that to Toledo and Andalucía, and, above all, that to
Barcelona). The telegraph came into general use (first
signal, then electric telegraphy), and gas-light was introduced. When all these innovations are compared with what
had existed at the beginning of the century, they represent
an enormous progress. But when one considers the enormous advance made by other nations in these matters, and
the special attention demanded for them by our peculiar
geographical conditions (§ 5), the results were, doubtless,
much below our national needs, even taking into account
all that was done in the last third of the 19th century. This
deficiency showed itself acutely in regard to the lines of
communication as well as in what concerned their full
development so as to link up the districts and localities
which chiefly required to be in close contact, or to have
ways of transport for their natural products. But more acute
even than this was the problem of changing the hydrographic conditions of many regions, where the lack or
irregularity of rain and the scarcity (so natural to the configuration of our soil and its slopes), of permanent water
supplies, endangered agricultural enterprise at every step,
or made it impossible. In order to meet this last, and very
vital, need, there arose the so-called " hydraulic policy," at
the end of the 19th century, begun, and consistently urged
by Joaquín Costa (§§ 119 and 124). Although this question

ISABELLA II LAYING THE FIRST STONE OF THE BARCELONA HARBOUR-WORKS
(1860)

has been taken up by the government for some time, thanks to the co-operation of certain ministers, and though certain irrigation schemes have been drawn up and put into practice, there was still a great deficiency in this department in 1914.

At the same time the textile industries were revived in Catalonia, and the exploitation of minerals in many parts of Spain. Commerce, like the public revenues, was submitted to heavy burdens on account of the terrible weight of taxes levied on the country through the wars and the work of centralization. From 1850-1860 the imports amounted to 279,500,000 pesetas, and the exports to 237,000,025 pesetas. In the ten subsequent years both were doubled, and from 1870-1880 exports increased from $312\frac{1}{2}$ million pesetas to more than 507 millions. In 1913 the total of our commerce was 2,351,455,500 pesetas, the imports being 1,223,100,000 and the exports 1,078,300,000. The receipts of the Treasury were 175 millions in 1820, and grew until in 1883 they were 800 millions, and in 1913, 1,505,228,712.

After the revolution of 1868 there was a marked development in economic life which, despite certain crises, has continued until the present day, and was increased by such things as the transfer to Spain since 1898 of capital that had formerly been employed in America. This growth was expressed in the following developments: the birth of industries entirely new to Spain and the improvement of certain traditional industries; the investment of capital (much of it from abroad), in productive undertakings; the circulation of wealth and the betterment of conditions of life in all classes, compared with what it had been formerly. According to the calculations of an economist, the national wealth of Spain in 1894 was from 65,000 to 66,000 millions, somewhat higher than the computed wealth of Italy (50,000 millions). By 1914 the figure was much higher, but it still remains much lower than it might be.

The population had also increased. In 1860 it was 15,668,531. In 1877 it was 16,731,570. In 1887 it was

P

17,560,352, an increase which equalled that of Italy and much exceeded that of Ireland, Austria, Greece, France, and the twenty principal German states. This increase was in spite of the heavy and growing immigration to America from the North and North-Western regions, and to Africa from the South and South-East. Later it rose to 19,995,446 in 1910, a figure which certain authors consider to be too low. The four most densely populated provinces are Biscay, Barcelona, Pontevedra, and Guipúzcoa. The least in this respect is Cuenca. The richest and most industrial regions are Biscay, Catalonia, and Asturias. Valencia, Murcia, and part of Catalonia and Andalucía are very important from the point of view of agricultural products.

Nevertheless, Spain still produces little in comparison with its needs, and too little for its commerce to be flourishing. It buys more than it sells, and its future depends upon changing this proportion or on depending less on the foreigner, exporting more of its natural and characteristic products of every kind (mineral, agricultural, stock-breeding, etc.), and producing more manufactured goods within the Peninsula itself. Whether or no these were the fundamental and most profound causes of the general economic situation in 1914, it was certain and evident, in spite of all the progress made up to that date (which was considerable), that Spain produced, as we have said before, much less than her rich natural resources would have led one to expect, and produced it at a higher price than did the majority of foreign countries. The result of this is that the mean cost of living is still very much higher here than in almost all the normal European countries, and a great deal higher than it should be if the national economy were well organized.

115. *Education.* The War of Independence made education impossible in many places, or at any rate disturbed it profoundly. Most of the University students hurried off to fight the invaders. And though the French government of Joseph Bonaparte on the one hand, and the Cortes of 1812 on the other, managed to push forward public instruction,

creating new schools and drawing up plans of education, all this took little root.

The reaction of 1814, with its narrow and suspicious outlook, furthered the decline of education. The only progressive movement was the foundation, in 1818, of the society which introduced the Lancasterian system into our schools. And though the liberal movement of 1821 attacked the problem anew, instituting, in the regulation of the 29th June, the incorporation of all teaching establishments in the State, the new reaction of 1824 brought this plan to the ground and even went so far as to cause to be issued a Royal order that all foreign books introduced to Spain, and all those printed in Spain between 1820 and 1823, should be called in. A rigorous watch was kept on the Customs to prevent the entry of suspect literature. Later, in 1830, Ferdinand VII ordered the universities to be closed. The only educational institutions founded under Ferdinand VII were the Prado Museum, the College of Surgery in Madrid (Colegio de San Carlos), with the scheme of surgical instruction of 1827, the work of Professor Castello, and the Conservatoire of Music and Declamation (1830).

The liberal revival was begun by Maria Christina, who brought back to the country many of the liberals who had emigrated in 1813 and other years. The first consequence of this was the increased penetration into our life and thought of all the influences (political, literary, economic, etc.), which these men had encountered in England, France, Germany, and other countries, and of the natural reaction and spiritual fertility which they had experienced during their exile. This was a factor which should not be forgotten, as it explains, to a large extent, the changes of direction and organization which have been gradually effected since then, by such means as were possible, in the face of the opposition of other groups of society. In public education, the first of the changes was the reopening of the universities, and a wide series of reforms and new institutions, beginning with primary education.

This was announced in the decree of August 1834, and was probably inspired by the teacher Pablo Montesino. Its most important result was the inauguration of the Central Normal School for Teachers (*Escuela Normal Central de Maestros*). On the suppression of the regular religious orders, by the decree of 1835, those dedicated to teaching were exempted. In 1838 a society for propagating and bettering the education of the people was founded in Madrid. Its chief aim was to create schools for little children, a project to which Montesino had already given thought. In 1843 medical studies were reformed and a special faculty of surgery, medicine, and pharmacy was instituted, thanks to the influence of the famous writer and professor, Mata, who held the first chair of medical jurisprudence. In 1845 the energy of the first Marqués de Pidal and of the writer Gil de Zárate laid the basis of the general modern organization of education. The universities were incorporated in the State, their autonomy and their academic dress were suppressed, as was also the faculty of theology. A faculty of philosophy was created (including the sciences), as were also the institutes of secondary education. In 1846 the Astronomical Observatory was founded; in 1847 the Academy of Sciences (*Academia de Ciencias*), and in 1856 the *Escuela de Diplomática*. On the basis of the collections of books from the suppressed monasteries, public provincial libraries were formed, while at the same time the archives of historical documents were augmented and put in order. Finally, in 1857, the Minister, Claudio Moyano, availing himself of the ideals and aspirations of the little group of men who at that time were interested in the problems of education, passed the general law of public instruction. This is still considered to be in force, although almost all its articles have been amended, as was proper, considering the passage of time and the change in the people's needs and tendencies. Thanks to this law, however, and to the regulations of 1859, a whole series of establishments concerned with public education have been made uniform in their establishment and confirmed in their existence:

primary schools, normal schools, institutions of secondary education, university faculties, and special schools (engineering, veterinary, etc.). The financial support of higher education was entrusted to the State, that of secondary education to the provinces, and that of primary education to the municipalities.

116. *Defects of Instruction and Education.* From 1859 to 1914 there were numerous reforms in public education. But the majority of them broke down through lack of proper foundation or were incompletely carried out. The interest of the ruling classes in popular education and scientific culture was more apparent than real, save in a few exceptional cases. This is fully proved by the figures of the estimates, in which public education is almost always allotted a sum lower than the return which it yields to the Treasury, and insufficient to insure good organization. It is proved also by the neglect with which the municipalities treated their duties in this respect, which resulted, for many years, in the shameful fact that an enormous debt was owing to the masters in primary schools, who were more than once reduced to asking alms, in order to supply their most pressing needs. The situation of the teaching profession began to improve when it was made a State employment, as regards salary and the creation of situations, *i.e.*, of schools or departments of schools. But the municipalities continued to be held responsible for the school buildings and the houses of the teachers, and, as a general rule, they went on being as negligent as before in the fulfilment of these obligations.

Before 1903 the minimum salary was not more than 200 pesetas (£8) a year. In 1903 it was raised to 500 pesetas (£20), and in 1911 to 1,000, while the maximum was raised to 4,000 and the intermediary stages were improved. This improvement continued, more or less rapidly, until 1914, especially in the direction of assuring to all the teachers of the lower grades their minimum salary, and in raising the intermediate salaries. At the same time, salaries and their augmentation were declared personal, thus avoiding the necessity of transferring a master in order to better his category. In this they were not only aiming at bettering the economic conditions of the teaching profession, and giving it dignity, but, above all, they wished to attract a better class of persons to the profession, offering them a future which might draw people of intellectual and moral attainments, who hitherto had sought more remunerative professions. At the same time a determined effort was made in the direction of reform in the preparation of the school teachers themselves. It took the form of specialized courses given to the professors in Normal Schools, and was held in what was known as the *Escuela Superior de Magisterio*. This institution had been preceded by another whose aims were similar though its methods were different —the *Museo Pedagógico Nacional*, founded in 1882—which opened a library (the *Biblioteca Central Pedagógica*) and arranged holiday courses and summer colonies (*Colonias escolares de vacaciones*) together with other institutions for the benefit of education. The body of primary school inspectors was also reformed and amplified in 1913, and inspectors for girls' schools were appointed for the first time. In 1912 the first circulating libraries for both teachers and pupils were established.

The other fundamental problem of primary education lay in increasing the number of schools, so as to make them proportionate to the needs of the growing school-population of Spain, and also so as to make useful that system of compulsory education, which, as we have already said (§ 99), had been instituted by the Cortes of Navarre in 1780-1781, and which had later been repeated by our national legislation of the 19th century. Moreover, the criterion adopted in 1857 to decide the quota of schools in each locality was based upon the total number of inhabitants, and had not the same denominator in every case. It was, therefore, expedient to replace it by the criterion of the number of inhabitants of school age, and at the same time, to adjust the denominator of this to the experience of modern educational practice as regards the maximum number of pupils that each master can teach efficiently.

In 1908 the total number of government schools was 24,861, whereas it ought to have been 34,366, even upon the basis of the above-mentioned and insufficient calculation according to the law of 1857. The deficit would have been even greater had one adopted the criterion of actual educational experience, for, on the basis of the criterion of 1857, every one of these 34,366 schools was obliged to educate about 122 children, an impossible thing for one single master, whether he taught the school as a whole or in sections. Since 1911 many new schools have been founded, that are either taught as a whole or in classes; but still, in 1914, their number was insignificant, in comparison with our real needs, in spite of the valuable contribution made in certain regions by the patriotism and love of education of emigrants in America, and, in very exceptional cases, by certain municipalities. To these one can only add the pious and enthusiastic movement of the professor of the University of Granada, D. Andrés Manjón, whose institutions in that city have begun to spread throughout the Peninsula.

The results of the backwardness of primary education are as follows: the lack of a solid foundation in the other grades of education, not only through the influence of an uncultivated average of citizens, but also through the deficiencies of the schools; a considerable disproportion between the ignorance of the immense majority of the Spanish people and the culture of a small minority, who, through fortunate personal conditions, contact with foreign countries, etc., continue to develop according to the modern type and give the appearance of an effective and general incorporation of contemporary civilization. It should be noted that, even if the correctness of the relation (§ 99) between the general culture of a country and its scientific and literary production continues to exist, yet the incorporation of the masses of that country in a democratic regime, and its influence on the resolution of many national questions, has changed the basic elements of the problem, and has made it doubly desirable that the general mean of culture should be as high as possible, whatever the express relationship of illiteracy and spiritual creation may have continued to be. On the other hand one must note, as a fact which is important in view of analogous movements in other countries of Europe, the complete ease with which women have gained entrance to all educational establishments, secondary, university, and professional, without any co-educational problem arising as a consequence, so that the mixed staff in all the centres of learning in the State has arisen as a natural and usual thing.

The general political tendency since 1859 has been, on the one hand, for the State to take upon itself the responsibility for public education, and on the other, for the public to proclaim and support the principle of " liberty of instruction " (*libertad de enseñanza*). This principle affects both the foundation of schools, colleges, universities, etc., and the power of the pupil to choose his master, while the latter has the right to complete doctrinal independence. Yet, in spite of this principle, education has continued to be mainly in the hands of the State, which has the sole power of granting university degrees after the examinations, and other tests practised in official establishments, have been duly passed.

It must be added that, generally speaking, the problems of secondary education in the period of which we are speaking (both university and technical education) were as great as those of primary education, except as regards the number of universities, which, instead of being inadequate, was considered excessive by a section of public opinion.

As regards scientific studies, which are usually considered to fall within the sphere of university education, the two chief innovations of the period were the creation of travelling studentships for pupils and professors, which began to function in the universities in 1901, and the *Junta para ampliación de estudios e investigaciones científicas*, a committee for widening the scope of all studies and investigations carried out scientifically (1907) This is a most important organization, which has under its control a large number of the above-mentioned studentships, and has also created specialized centres of investigation in different subjects, including philology, the exact and applied sciences, and has provided opportunities for scientific experiment and research. A large proportion of the teaching staff is connected with the universities. The *Junta* was mainly responsible for the foundation of the *Residencia de Estudiantes*, in some ways a modern form of the ancient university colleges of Spain [but the first college to be founded there on the lines of a hostel at Oxford or Cambridge].

117. *Science*. Having dealt mainly up to now with the intellectual minority, of which mention has been made (§ 116), we will consider its chief tendencies and its influence during the 19th century.

Those studies called by antonomasia *scientific* (the mathematical and natural sciences, etc.), which had been started by the ministers of Ferdinand VI and Charles III (§ 100), and were almost completely paralysed at the beginning of the 19th century, were the latest to be revived, and then only in a very half-hearted way, compared with other studies. Owing to the special conditions and problems of life in Spain from 1808 till the end of the century, other orders of culture (law, philosophy, history, etc.), had received greater consideration, both from Spanish thinkers, and from the government itself, while experimental science and mathematics were neglected. Thus (although, as we have seen, attempts had been made ever since 1834 to bring about a renaissance of the teaching of these subjects) this kind of culture made very scanty progress, until the beginning of the 20th century, and that through the efforts of a small minority. Although certain individuals stood out, the product of entirely personal conditions, self-taught or educated abroad, no really Spanish school was formed, except in the natural sciences, particularly botany; investigations of this sort did not arouse the necessary appreciation, nor did the government lend them such support as was required for their proper development.

Thus it happened that in the series of great scientific discoveries and innovations that have made the history of science illustrious in the 19th century, the contribution of the Spaniards was very small, compared with that of men of science of other countries. The following deserve mention, either in this field, or in the promulgation and application of science, and in the practice of teaching: the mathematical work of Rodríguez González (1770-1824), and Chaix, products of the 18th century (§ 100); Lucio del Valle, Lista, Vallejo, Zorraquín, Pérez del Rivero, Alemany, Sánchez Cerquero, Eulogio Jiménez, Coello and others, publicists, engineers, and professors, certain of whom undertook scientific journeys through America and Africa (Rio de Oro, Muni), which were of great scientific interest, as was also that of the famous Catalan traveller, Badia, at the beginning of the 18th century. He is best known by his Arabic name of Sidi Aben el Abassi, and he travelled through various parts of Northern Africa and Western Asia, Arabia, etc. There was also General Ibáñez, whose authority on questions of geodesy was, and continues to be, recognized throughout Europe; Cecilio Pujazón, Director of the Observatory of San Fernando, whose astronomical and mathematical work was highly thought of by foreign specialists; of Elhuyar (1757-1833), experimental chemist and the discoverer of new bodies; of Torres Muñoz, Luna, Rioz, Bonet, Sáenz Díez, Camps, Calderón (Laureano), Gogorza and the meteorologist Arcimis, etc. One should also mention the discoveries, cataloguing, and studies of the naturalists La Gasca (d. 1839), Rodríguez, Donato García, Rojas Clemente (d. 1827), Cavanilles, Fontán, Boutelou, Laguna, Puga, Casiano del Prado (founder of the geology and pre-history of the Iberians), Mallada, Loscos, Pérez Arcas (creator of the Spanish Society of Natural History), Colmeiro, Jiménez de la Espada (to whom is due the knowledge of many new American species), Botella, Quiroga, Vilanova, Calderón (Salvador), Macpherson (father of modern Spanish mineralogy and geology), Paz y Membiela, Amor, Isern, Martínez y Sáenz, Almagro, Lázaro, Machado, Fernández de Castro (president of the Commission for the Geological Map of Spain, created in 1873), Castellarnau, Vidal, Boscá, Graells, González de Linares, Reyes Prosper, and others; the anthropological and biological work of Dr. Velasco and of Olóriz, Cazurro, Simarro, Achucarro; the geographical work of Coello, Gómez Arteche, Torres Campos D'Almonte, and others; the beginnings of submarine navigation, due to Monturiol y Peral; the invention of the laryngoscope by the Spaniard García, son of the Spanish musician, the friend of Rossini (§ 123); that of stenography by the Valencian, Francisco Martí (1827), the technical skill and scientific enthusiasm of doctors and surgeons such as Seoane, Castelló, Argumosa, the Marqués de San Gregorio, Sánchex Toca, Isern, Asuero, Monlau, Méndez Alvaro, Mata, Velasco, Nieto y Serrano, Gutiérrez, Rubio, Cardenal, González Encinas, Barraquer, etc., and, finally, the discoveries contributed to chemical science by Orfila (1787-1853), the founder of toxology; he did all his work in France and was naturalized there, but he was a Mallorcan by birth, studied in Valencia and Barcelona, and, with a grant from the Junta de Comercio of the latter city, he went to Paris, where he completed his scientific education and developed his excellent abilities.

118. *Philosophical and Juridical Studies.* As we have seen, these were what were chiefly cultivated in the 19th century.

The tradition of the old Spanish school of philosophy had been broken by the great decadence of scholasticism in the 18th century (well illustrated by Feijoo), and because the original direction of certain Spanish thinkers of the 16th and 17th centuries had been forgotten. Another cause was the spread of the new ideas of the French Encyclopaedists (§ 95), which did not bear any really scientific fruit here.

In the middle of the century the Catalan priest, Jaime Balmes (1810-1847) attempted to restore Catholic philosophy, reanimating its traditional forms with new elements. Through his books, *Filosofía elemental y fundamental, El Criterio,* and *El Protestantismo comparado con el Catolicismo,* he aroused general interest in these questions which none of his direct followers could maintain.

His effort was not entirely lost, however, apart from the intrinsic value of his publications. It found new birth, on the one hand, in works that were properly speaking philosophic, akin to St. Thomas Aquinas in sentiment, which had a great influence on teaching, especially on that of the clergy, and whose greatest representative was Cardinal Fr. Ceferino González (1831-1894); and, on the other hand, in a campaign of vindication of classical Spanish philosophy, begun already by Balmes, and taken up with great vigour by Laverde Ruiz and Menéndez y Pelayo in 1876. The result of this movement was to enrich the current of ideas and to give it roots in the national tradition. Somewhat later there were added to these influences, in the direction of the restoration of studies in Catholic philosophy, the influence produced by a general renaissance of the ideas of St. Thomas Aquinas in Europe, especially in the direction represented by Cardinal Mercier, of whom certain Spaniards were direct disciples.

A tendency opposed to that which we have just noted, and one which, through an exaggeration of the religious sense, fell almost into heterodoxy, was the so-called *traditionalist* movement, represented by Donoso Cortés, a man of letters rather than a philosopher, and much inferior to Balmes. This tendency was short-lived and without importance.

Some years after the death of Balmes a new philosophic tendency came to have influence in Spain. It was entirely unconnected with dogmatism or in any sense with the confessional, but was inspired by the contemporary German schools, particularly that of Krause. The originator of the tendency was the Spanish thinker Julián Sanz del Río (1817-1869), who, after a scientific journey abroad (commissioned by the moderate minister Gómez de la Serna, in order to study the German philosophic systems), held for many years a chair in the University of Madrid. All the liberal youth soon gathered there, and from it there issued,

later on, many of the great figures of the revolution of
1868.

The influence of Sanz del Río was not based on the
doctrine of Krause. He did not propose to teach a definite
system, but to exercise thought in free investigation, submitting it to the most severe logical discipline, whose only
aim was to discover the truth. In this sense the teaching
of such a master exercised considerable influence on the
generations of the second half of the 19th century, and
without it one could not explain many of the phenomena
of the scientific history of Spain at this time. In many minds
(adverse, by reason of their liberal feelings, to the way in
which such studies were generally practised at that time in
Spain), it aroused enthusiasm for philosophic investigations.
It provoked, even among its opponents, a renaissance of
philosophical study; and, in general, it directed the younger
generation towards the study of the culture of Germany
and other European countries, thus bringing about the
knowledge of many authors and books, which have been
the basis of the education of several generations.

Krausism, as this tendency was called, did not perpetuate
itself as a school of philosophy. The metaphysical side of
its influence, represented for a time by various professors
(Tapia, Quevedo, Canalejas, Arés, Castro, Sama, Salmerón,
Giner de los Ríos, etc.) disappeared. This was due partly
to its contact with Positivism, which reached Spain some
years later, and partly because the Spanish spirit seems to
have been more attracted by particular philosophic questions, especially such as have reference to practical life.
Thus the two realms in which Krausist influence was con-
solidated were jurisprudence and pedagogy. In the first,
a wide and brilliant Spanish tradition, notable exponents
have already been signalled, such as Pacheco, Pérez Hernández, Arrazola, Cortina, García Goyena, Alcalá Galiano,
Donoso Cortés, Gutiérrez, etc. The translation of the
Philosophy of Justice, by Ahrens (1841), by Navarro Zamorano and the lectures of Sanz del Río, definitely submitted legal studies to the Krausist influence, in a more or

less modified form. This inspired the formation of a school which, after being influenced by Ahrens, Röder, and others of a similar tendency, came to have certain original characteristics. Vestiges of this current are still seen in those jurists of the end of the 19th century who were hostile to it, or who, without going as far as this, maintained a certain independence of doctrine. Among these were Manuel Silvela, Alonso Martínez, La Serna, Montalbán, Comas, Pérez Pujol, Sánchez Román, Durán y Bas, Santamaría, Doña Concepción Arenal, and others. The main representatives of what may be called the Krausist tendency, penetrated as it was by Positivist influences and even more by the historic sense of Savigny, were Giner de los Ríos, Azcárate, and Costa. To it were also added the influences of the modern German and Austrian juridical schools, in which the new generations have been educated.

From this complex juridical culture arose many innovations that were incorporated in the movement of codification (§ 107), and which have sometimes deposited in modern legislation interesting novelties which give it a special value, and at other times continue the tradition of earlier reforms. This was the case in the school of the Barcelona *presidio*, founded in 1820 by the initiative of Antonio Puig, and in that which, apart from applying the principles of the Ordinance of 1804 and the *Reglamento* of 1807 (§ 95), tried the Monitor System, which has later become famous in the United States of America. The sphere of penitentiary reform was widely influenced by the noble and profound spirit of Doña Concepción Arenal, who also showed herself to be a pacifist in the modern sense in her book on International Law and in her *Cuadros de la Guerra*.

The creation by Fernando de Castro of the Association for Women's Education (*Asociación para la enseñanza de la mujer*, 1869), continued later by Manuel Ruiz de Quevedo, and others, was followed by the foundation in 1876 of the *Institución libre de enseñanza* (Free Institute of Education), the nucleus of which was always made up of pupils of Sanz del Río, as was that of the Association. The *Institución Libre de*

Enseñanza instigated the putting into practice of other fundamental tendencies implied in Sanz del Río's lectures, that
is to say, pedagogy, the study of questions referring to the
organization, direction, and methods of teaching and education. For a long time after this the members of the Association and of the *Institución Libre* (especially the latter)
have represented the special cultivation of this branch of
anthropological science (*i.e.*, pedagogy), which, thanks to
its development, has won over little by little the co-operation and interest of thinkers and politicians in other spheres.
The leader in this characteristic product of modern Spanish
thought, and its chief representative was Francisco Giner
de los Ríos (1839-1915) whose personality inspired and
maintained most of the new currents in education that
appeared in our country from 1881 until his death.

Apart from the Krausist movement, other less important influences had made their way in Spain. Such were
Hegelian philosophy, both in metaphysics and in political
science; the doctrine of Bentham in law; the so-called
Scottish philosophy both in its pure and in its French forms,
which was particularly developed in Barcelona, where it
was begun by Martí de Eixalá and developed by the great
personality of Professor Llorens (1820-1872), whose teaching is springing to life again to-day with great force and
originality, and did not fail to influence in their time so
independent a spirit as that of Menéndez y Pelayo;
the Neocartesianism and the theories of Cousin, and later,
in the modern German schools, both in a neo-Krausist
and other directions (Schopenhauer, Nietzsche, etc.).
Various professors and publicists distinguished themselves
in the cultivation and spreading of these various philo-
sophies such as Contero, Alvarez de los Corrales, Huidobro,
Fabié, Ribero, Moreno Nieto, Castelar, Azcárate, Martín
Mateos, García Luna, Arnau, Vidart, Perojo, and others
(apart from those already mentioned). The influence of
French and Italian Positivism deserves special mention, as
does also the historical school of Savigny, which finally
came to be combined with, and, in no small measure, as-

similated by the original Krausist tendency, as has already
been mentioned in regard to juridical philosophy in particular. The most original representative of this fusion of
influences, and one who vitalized them by the vigour of
his own thought was Nicolás Salmerón, whose doctrines,
through never having been set down in books, have been
almost completely lost.

119. *Economics.* Whilst the main character of Spanish
life during almost the whole of the 19th century paid attention to the study of law and political science (subjects intimately related with the general preoccupation of the time),
it also held to the old economic tradition, which had given
rise to *arbitrism* during the time of decadence (§ 85), and
which, in the 18th century, had awakened with great
vigour the impulse towards ministerial reforms and the
activities of the *Sociedades Económicas de Amigos del País* (§ 99).

In the 19th century the direction of these studies was
governed by two main currents. Firstly, the science itself
was much influenced by the great social movements abroad,
which were preparing the formation of the socialist party in
Spain; secondly, the financial problem had become crucial
through the reconstruction of the public Exchequer and the
conflict between liberal ideas and those of the old regime.

This second current had already been foreshadowed and
represented since the last years of Ferdinand VII by certain
ministers, and later on by Mendizábal, Mon, and others;
it acquired great force in the preparatory years just before
the Revolution of 1868, with the formation of the *Sociedad
libre de Economía política* (in which were gathered all the
energetic liberal individualists), and of its offspring, the
Asociación para la reforma de los aranceles. In this there soon
came to the fore such men as Alcalá Galiano, Francisco de
P. Canalejas, Carballo, Gabriel Rodríguez, Bona, Pastor,
Sanromá, Castelar, Azcárate and others, and it provoked
the persistent fight between the *librecambistas* (Free Traders),
and *proteccionistas*, which continued during all the revolutionary period; the former gained the advantage, since the
liberals were given over almost to a man to the free trade

doctrine, which was applied to the legislation, especially during the republic, through the ministerial activities of Pedregal and de Figuerola. The protectionist school, which had been upheld before the revolution by Morquecho, Menéndez de Luarca, Güell y Renté and others, enjoyed preponderance after the Bourbon restoration, thanks, above all, to the influence of Cánovas del Castillo and of the Catalan and Basque economists.

Outside this conflict between tariff doctrines, the chief aim of all those concerned with economics was more or less pure individualism. To it, apart from those already mentioned, belong La Sagra, Colmeiro (historian of Spanish political economy), Valle Santoro, Espinosa, Paso, Pastor, Oliván, Madrazo, Aller, Beraza, Carreras y González, Figuerola, and others. From the movement arose Flórez Estrada, an economist with a European reputation, who later upheld collectivist theories, being the originator in this century of the socialistic reaction. Without going so far as this, Pi y Margall circulated ideas in this strain later on; he maintained them during the whole of his political life, together with others that were markedly individualistic. Krausism, for its own part, helped to modify the old economic orthodoxy, introducing into it more social and organic ideas, expressed in the works of Giner de los Ríos, in the later works of Azcárate, in the speeches of Salmerón and, above all, in the books of Costa, especially in those on *Derecho consuetudinario*, and that on *El Colectivismo agrario en España*. Other influences from French and German writers and revolutionaries helped forward this same end, and found expression in the *Cortes Constituyentes* of 1869, through the channel of certain radical deputies.

The last years of the 19th century were characterized by two main things: first, by the very definite advance of socialist tendencies, not only of Marxist theories in the working classes, but also, *latu sensu*, among the intellectuals; and secondly, by the greater attention paid by statesmen to financial problems, with a reaction against the feelings that led to the earlier, purely political, struggles, and obedient to the necessity of reorganizing the Exchequer and raising national credit. In this complex field, especially in the first part, *i.e.*, that which refers to the social question, the economist Adolfo A. Buylla distinguished himself particularly, as did Professor Piemas in the domain of financial studies. Since Mendizábal (1790-1853), Camacho and Villaverde have stood out in matters concerning the national exchequer.

120. *Historiography and its National Tendencies*. Besides the social and political sciences, examined in the foregoing paragraphs, the chief intellectual advance made in this century was in history. Spain responded to this, not only because of the progress made by other nations, but also through the national tradition, which was very strong in this respect. Really the impulse had already begun in the 18th century, both in critical investigation and in the writing of history of a rigorously scientific nature (§ 100). Historical criticism continued its production, especially in literary and juridico-social history, through such eminent men as Martínez Marina (1754-1833), Llorente, Gallardo, Lista, Clemencín, Sempere, Pidal, Navarrete, La Canal, Bofarull, Quadrado, Ferrer del Río, González, Yanguas, Gayangos, Milá, Aribau, Amador de los Ríos, Caballero, Godoy, Gonzalo Morón, Torres Amat and others; whilst, enthusiasm for archaeology being aroused, the study and appreciation of ancient monuments and of the life of other days was renewed, chiefly through the work of Piferrer, Parcerisa, Quadrado, Pí, Madrazo, Caveda, and other writers and artists. The cultivation of historical studies was particularly keen after the Revolution of 1868, with the publication of unpublished documents and of specialized historical reviews, the organization of libraries, archives, and archaeological museums, and the reform of university teaching. To this period, in which modern French and German methods had an increasing influence, belong Muñoz y Romero, Milá y Fontanals, Jiménez de la Espada, Fernández Guerra, Pérez Pujol, Hinojosa, Costa, Fernández Duro, Fita, Bofarull, Lafuente, Zarco del Valle, Sánchez Rayón,

Riaño, Fuensanta del Valle, Valmar, Rada, Saavedra, Codera, Rubió y Ors, Balari, Becker, Vives, Herrera, Gaspar, Zobel, Catalina (J.), Rodríguez Villa, Serrano Morales, Paz y Melia, and many others.

Menéndez y Pelayo deserves special mention; he is the historian of our literature, of our philosophy, Catholic and non-Catholic, of our science and, in a great part, of our mediaeval and modern society, and the restorer of methods and traditions which have strongly influenced his contemporaries. Bonilla y San Martín was his disciple and, in part, his continuer, especially in the literary and philosophical history of Spain. In scientific history this movement was followed up by Fernández Vallín, Luanco, Calderón, Colmeiro, Chiarbone, Mallaina, Rua Figueroa, Reyes Prosper, Morejón, Comenge (L.), and others.

In the middle of the 19th century the critical direction of these studies was disturbed by an incidental preponderance of the literary conception of historical composition, along with the influence of the political and religious struggles of the epoch. Hence arose many historiographical works which are pure rhetoric, and which contained a preconceived idea, either political, religious, or in some other sphere. At the same time, the preponderance of questions of internal policy maintained the classic historiographical sense of external history, in spite of the example of our Chroniclers of the Indies (§ 88), the lead given by Masdeu at the end of the 18th century, and the doctrines of method of various Spanish writers since the 16th century. To this order belong the works of Lafuente, Toreno, Castelar, Ferrer del Río, and others. But a change to the opposite direction began to take place already in 1840, with the appearance of compendiums or manuals of the *Historia de la civilización española* (Tapia y Morón), although this effort seems to have been lost for some years. In 1891 there arose a restoration of what may be called integral historiography, in the sense of method; and since then, in growing numbers, researches and books of general history, Spanish or universal, including text books, are written in this direction.

As regards special researches, and histories dealing particularly with one definite branch of human activity, the two spheres which have been most extensively and most profoundly exploited, and which have contributed the greatest innovations, are literature and the plastic arts. Next in importance to these were the histories of philosophy, the sciences, and the Spanish colonization in America. In conjunction with this, the whole scientific movement was directed towards illuminating national history and vindicating, or bringing back to memory certain of its manifestations which had been most distorted or lost by earlier historians, most of them foreigners. Thus this science took on a definitely national character, both in the usual meaning of the word, referring to the whole of Spain, and in its particular application to the regions in which the sentiment of their own individuality and of their times of historical independence was reviving (§ 108). These things explain the scantiness of studies of foreign or general history in our historiography.

Similarly, this development at the end of the 19th century produced a development in sociological studies which, in its mainly historical or descriptive direction, contributed to the same end as history, properly speaking. The title of pioneers and cultivators of this genre belongs to Sales y Ferré and Azcárate.

121. *Literary History.* In the various literary genres, both of creation and criticism, in prose and verse, the work of the 19th century was brilliant. Two periods are to be remarked in it: one with the predominance of neo-classic French influence, whose greatest cultivators in poetry are Quintana (one of the most inspired poets of the century), and Gallego, and the other, in which French romanticism triumphed. Its way had been prepared by the influence of certain German and English romantics (Byron, Scott), and its position was strengthened by the re-vindication of the old Castilian theatre, which had never at any time ceased to have certain partisans (§ 102). This tendency was followed in its various genres by Martínez de la Rosa, the Duque de

Rivas, Lista, Espronceda, Larra, Arolas, Pastor Díaz, Zorrilla (the most popular, though not the best, of the romantic poets), Tassara, García Gutiérrez, Hartzenbusch, Bretón de los Herreros, Gertrudis Gómez Avellaneda, Bécquer, Gil y Carrasco, Fernández y González, Sanz, Ruiz Aguilera, etc. Its highest manifestations were lyric poetry and the theatre (*Don Alvaro, Los Amantes de Teruel, El Trovador, Don Juan Tenorio*, etc.).

The effervescence of romanticism passed, and our writers renewed their taste for a more intimate contact with our classic authors and with those of other countries. This, together with the influence of new European currents, produced a third period, better balanced, in which, while traces of romanticism remained, our traditional realism gained ground on the one hand, and on the other, a classical restraint or the ideal basis of poetry. This tendency was already foreshadowed by poets such as Cabanyes (1808-1833), novelists such as Fernán Caballero (1796-1877), and narrators of national customs such as Mesonero Romanos (1803-1882), Estébanez Calderón (1799-1867), Somoza (1781-1852), and, in part, the above-mentioned Larra (*Fígaro*); but its heyday is, of course, much more modern, and is represented by the names of Ventura de la Vega, Ayala, Tamayo, Echegaray, Feliú y Codina, Galdós, Dicenta in the theatre; Querol, Campoamor, Llorente, Bartrina, Manuel del Palacio, Núñez de Arce, Balart, Reina, Gabriel y Galán and others in poetry; Alarcón, Galdós, Alas, Pereda, Valera, Pardo Bazán, Escalante, Ganivet, etc., in fiction.

The doctrinal and technical progenitors of these writers were very varied, and one may say that, apart from the intrinsic originality of each one of them, they have represented (either separately or in different moments in the literary development of each one of them) the various influences which divided the literature of the time. These comprise classicism (particularly Spanish classicism), and the neo-romantics; English realism; the naturalism of Zola and his followers; the social and ethical sense of the

Russian, Scandinavian, and German writers; the French theatre, etc. Of all these currents, those which left the deepest impression on the period that we are discussing are: naturalism as regards fiction, and the theatre; neo-romanticism, much interfused with the old Spanish mode of the " Comedies of Cloak and Sword," the taste of the French theatre, and the Russian and Scandinavian innovations, which also influenced the novel.

In this genre the work which can be considered as most characteristic of our spirit are: the *National novel*, begun in conformity with contemporary foreign models (Walter Scott in the first place), by Gil y Carrasco, Villoslada y Larra, and imbued with vigorous personality and truly Spanish feeling by Pérez Galdós in his *Episodios Nacionales*, and later (restricted to certain social classes and certain representative localities), in his *Novelas contemporáneas*; and the *Regional Novel*, which brought to notice the psychological and picturesque peculiarities of certain districts, such as la Montaña of Santander, Asturias, Galicia, Castille, Andalucía, Catalonia, etc.

In poetry the most important influence in the last years of the period was that of the Nicaraguan poet, Rubén Darío (*d.* 1916), who lived in Spain for a long time (since 1892), and whose technical audacities in metre and in other elements of versification, as well as in imagery, profoundly shook the traditional forms of Castilian verse, and determined certain of the characteristics which have since then stamped the originality of our poets.

The 19th century also saw the restoration of regional literatures in other dialects than Castilian, especially Catalan, whose characteristic organ was the *Juegos Florales* (*Jochs Florals*: 1859). This renaissance numbered among its representatives men of great worth, chief among whom are: in Catalonia and Mallorca, Rubió y Ors, Aguiló, Soler (*Pitarra*), Balaguer, Aribau, Masferrer, Briz, Blanch, Bofarull, Milá, Maspóns, Ixart, and above all, Verdaguer (the greatest Spanish epic poet of the 19th century, and notable also for his lyrics), Guimerá, Costa y Llovera,

Alcover and Maragall (an admirable poet and prose writer, both in the Catalan and Castilian languages). The outstanding names in Valencian were: Baldoví, Escalante, Llombart, Iranzo y Llorente; in Galician Rosalía de Castro, Pintos, Añón, Camino, Pondal, Pérez Ballesteros, Fernández Morales, Lamas Carvajal, Losada, Barcia, Saco, Posada. The most important of all these regional movements was in Catalonia.

122. *The Press and the Ateneo.* Two important factors in the intellectual life of Spain in the 19th and beginning of the 20th centuries were the Press and the *Ateneo* of Madrid.

The growth of newspapers—on the basis of the 18th century, though these were mainly literary—coincides with the liberal periods of 1810 and 1820, and with the years after 1833. In the two former, the political and polemic press acquired great development, and in this the following men distinguished themselves: Gallardo Villanueva, Sánchez Barbero, Padre Lacanal, Quintana, Gallego, Lagasca, Antillón, Alvarez Guerra, Mejía, Morales, Estala, Miñano, García Suelto, San Miguel, Pidal, and others. After 1833, and especially after the Peace of Vergara, not only did the number of political journals increase, but literary, and illustrated encyclopaedic reviews were begun, especially interesting for studying the advance of Spanish culture. The principal types of these were the *Museo de las Familias* (1839), *No me olvides, El Artista*, and *Las Novedades*, the first journal of culture, founded by Fernández de los Ríos. The most notable publicists of this period (before 1868), are: Larra (*Fígaro*), Bretón, Alcalá Galiano, Bergues de las Casas, García de Villalta, Estébanez Calderón, Espronceda, Núñez Arenas, Fermín Caballero, Reinoso, Oliván, Pacheco, Pérez Hernández, Borrego, González Bravo, Donoso Cortés, Rancés, Lafuente (*Fray Gerundio*), Pedrosa, Ayala, Selgas, Nocedal, Aparisi y Guijarro, Rubio, and others. The Revolution of 1868 marks a new impulse, and spread journalism throughout the Peninsula, tending to convert the journal into an organ of political propaganda and culture, combined, and multiplying the periodicals of a literary and scientific character. Notable journalists of this last period were: Lorenzana, Rivero, Castelar, Calvo Asensio, Chao, Robert, Mañé, Santa Ana, Nocedal, Pí, Tuero, Escobar, Gasset, Rodríguez Correa, Albareda, Miquel y Badía, Bremón, Moya, Fernández Florez, Mellado, Cavia, Calderón (A.), Troyano, Nakens, Vicenti, Figueroa, Morote, Burell, Oliver, Castell, etc. In this group, as in that before 1868, there were various journalists who were also great orators, a kind of literature much cultivated in the 19th century, especially in the realm of politics, and one to which the natural faculties of the race easily lent themselves. Oratory passed through two characteristic movements, the florid and impassioned, which shone especially in the acute phases of political struggles, which are, to a large extent, contemporary with literary romanticism (§ 121), and whose highest representative is Castelar; and the sober and reasoned style, more concerned with the matter than the manner, and yet of an energetic and sometimes majestic eloquence. Two men, each in his own way representative of this second period, were Salmerón and Canalejas. Many others might be added to these; among them we will cite Ríos Rosas, Pí y Margall, Moret, Martos Cánovas, Maura, and Silvela.

The newspaper represents in Spain to-day the principal organ of popular literary culture, through the encyclo-paedic, and not purely literary character it is wont to adopt, through its cheapness, and through the elementary and popularizing form of its articles, which are well adapted to the lack of knowledge of the mass of its readers.

Like the Press, but in a higher and more independent sphere, the *Ateneo* of Madrid, founded in 1820, has con-tributed to the spread of culture. It is a very singular in-stitution in our intellectual history, and without its interven-tion many things in our intellectual development would be impossible to explain. The principal function of the *Ateneo* lay in presenting, even in times of reaction (except from 1825-1835, when it was closed), and in periods of the most vital political struggle, a centre of absolute tolerance, to which men of every kind of ideas were admitted on an equal footing, and in which these ideas enjoyed complete freedom of expression. The lectures and discussions of the *Ateneo* were in many cases the channel by which those ideas, which in other places would have been repressed, were made public and promulgated. In its tribune almost all the great orators of the century distinguished themselves: Pacheco, Pidal (Pedro José), Alcalá Galiano, Donoso, Ríos Rosas, Castelar, Moreno Nieto, Revilla, Cánovas, Martos, Pí, Azcárate, Moret, Pedregal, Labra, Canalejas, etc.

In another sphere, and for another audience than that of the *Ateneo*, a similar service was performed for many years by the association called *Fomento de las Artes*, whose origin was the *Velada de Artistas y Artesanos*, founded in 1849 by the priest Inocencio Riesco, with the help of the printers Repullés y Pita, and others.

123. *The Fine Arts.* The neo-classicism of the 18th century continued to dominate the architecture of the beginning of the 19th century. However, a reaction soon set in against it, parallel to the romantic reaction in literature, whose characteristic note was the imitation of mediæval styles (§§ 58, 59, 60, and 90), and that of the early renaissance (§ 78), and in its enthusiasm for preserving and restoring buildings of these periods, which frequent wars, and still more of the lack of historic and patriotic sense in Spain for a long period, had destroyed or kept in the most deplorable disrepair. Examples of this new tendency are the churches of San Jerónimo (pseudo-Gothic on a real Gothic basis of the 15th century), del Buen Suceso and de las Calatravas, in Madrid ; the Palace of Museums and Libraries; some private houses, such as the pseudo-Arab house of Xifre (Madrid); others, mediæval in type, in Barcelona, and the restorations of San Juan de los Reyes, the cathedrals of Seville, Barcelona, and Burgos, and especially of that of León. The most notable architects who worked in this way are Alvarez, Colomer, Gándara, Enríquez, Mendívil, Coello, and Juan Madrazo, who was the

leading spirit in the work on the Cathedral of León, Velázquez, and Lampérez.   The two last were not only restorers,
but also the historians of our architecture, a task in which
Beruete (the son) collaborated in the history of painting.
In the last years of the century, architecture, though in
general continuing to copy, studied and combined all the
foregoing styles, without creating an original type.   Yet it
came to be transformed through the predominant use of
new materials, such as iron, reinforced concrete, etc., which
obliged it to seek suitable forms.   Constructions of this sort
are, for example, the railway station of the Southern Lines
(Madrid), the so-called Palacio de Cristal in the gardens of
the Retiro, the market of the Plaza Cebada, etc.   Finally
there came about a marked restoration, in private buildings,
of our architectural styles of the 16th and 17th centuries,
and of certain characteristic types of regional styles.

Painting also underwent the various influences which
characterized the different periods, all of which had more
important effects on painting than on architecture.   Goya
went on painting in the first years of the century; so did
López, who did not die until 1850.   The neo-classic reaction came about through the influence of the French
painter David, and was represented in Spain by Aparicio,
Juan Ribera and Jose Madrazo, especially by the two latter,
who were professors at the *Academia de San Fernando* in the
middle of the century.   Madrazo was also the organizer of
the *Museo del Prado* (which was opened in 1819), and founder
of the Prix de Rome, which produced a renaissance of art.
At the same time the following declared themselves as
imitators of Murillo: Esquivel, Bécquer (the father),
Gutiérrez de la Vega and Tejeo.   Romanticism, brought in
through German influences (Overbeck), and French influences (Proudhon, Gericault, and later Delacroix, Ary
Schoeffer, etc.), was first seen here in the work of Federico
de Madrazo and Carlos Luis Ribera, followed, in various
different manners, by Pérez Villaamil, Eugenio Lucas, and
Valeriano Domínguez Bécquer, and developed and modified later by the stimulus of new influences and by a greater

progress in the conception and technique of painting. The first official exhibition, held in 1856, revealed various new artists, among them Carlos Haes, whose realism had great importance in the later history of our landscape painting. Later, other painters appeared, all inspired by romanticism (almost exclusively expressed in paintings of historical scenes), such as Gisbert, Casado, Manzano, Llanos, Fierros, Palmaroli, Mercadé, Sans, Alvarez, and above all, Rosales, whose *Testamento de Isabel la Católica* (1864), is the best romantic picture of the epoch. Descendants of this school, with innovations brought about by changes of the times, were Pradilla, Plasencia, Villegas Casanova, Muñoz Degrain, and others who are still alive. Fortuny (1838-1874), has special characteristics, the results of special conditions made fruitful by his travels and by French influences, especially that of Meissonier, which are characterized by the brilliance of his colouring and the strength of his lighting effects.

Realism, which in a way came as a reaction against romanticism and modified it (bringing with it indifference to the subject and a striving to express nature sincerely), was followed by impressionism, *pointillisme*, symbolism, etc., which produced, at the end of the century, a great number of styles, individualizing them, and giving rise to notable works of art. Of all these movements, which were very complex and rich in manners and modes of expression, we can only record here certain names, such as those of Sorolla, Pinazo, Beruete, Plá, Urgell, Regoyos, Sáinz [Zuloaga, Picasso, Vázquez Díaz].

Sculpture was less important until the last third of the century, in which there were men whose work brought about a Renaissance of this art. Amongst the earlier names we find Piquer (professor at the Academy), Ponciano, San Martín, the Bellvers, Pérez, Medina, Susillo, Grajera, Oms, Mélida, Querol, Inurria, Julio Antonio.

Music was, in the early years, dominated by the Italian opera, which had an enormous vogue in the theatres of Madrid, Barcelona, and other towns. With it are associated

the names of Carnicer, a Catalan composer, certain of
whose works were introduced into those of Rossini (sym-
phony and serenade of the " Barbier de Seville "), and of
García, who also influenced Rossini in the same opera.
The following were also notable: Gómiz (*d.* 1836), Saldoni,
the Basque Arriaga, who died prematurely in 1825, and is
notable for his string quartets. Religious music, though
decadent, continued to be cultivated by certain choir-
masters, among whom these were outstanding: Eslava,
Arriolas, Cuellar, Ledesma, Gómez, Pérez y Gascón, Crevea,
and others. In 1849-1850 there reappeared the mixed
genre (operatic and dramatic) called *Zarzuela* (§ 91), which
took root rapidly, being at that time the national form of
musical expression. Barbieri, Gaztambide, Oudrid, Hernando, Inzenga, Salas, Olona, Arrieta, and many others,
stimulated this genre with works which are still sung, and
some of which have real artistic merit. Later, an attempt
was made to create a Spanish school of opera, an enterprise in which almost all modern musicians have striven.
Meanwhile the *Zarzuela* after giving rise to a new period,
in which writers such as Chapí and Usandizaga—each in
his own way and direction—managed to incorporate novelties of dramatic music, more often degenerated into minor
works of little importance, usually in what is known as the
Genero chico. Yet certain composers stand out from the
bulk of these by means of their technique and their assimilation of popular music. Of these the first rank is undoubtedly held by the " La Verbena de la Paloma " of Tomás
Bretón. " La Revoltosa " of Chapi also deserves mention.

Spain has also contributed to the progress of music with
notable executants, such as the singers la Malibrán and
Viardot, sopranos who have already been mentioned
(§ 103), Salas, the tenor, Gayarre, and many others.

As for non-operatic music, cultivated in private circles
until well into the 19th century, with performances of the
classics (Haydn, Beethoven, etc.), it began to influence the
public taste from 1863 onwards, thanks to the quartets of
the *Conservatorio*, instituted by Monasterio, which were fol-

lowed by orchestral concerts, first organized by Barbieri,
in order to increase the knowledge of, and enthusiasm for,
the great masters of the 18th and 19th centuries, especially
the Germans. This aim was also furthered by great
pianists, such as Pedro Albéniz, Guelbenzu, Mendizábal,
Vázquez, Power, and others, and by violinists such as
Sarasate, and later by various associations formed in Valencia, Bilbao, Barcelona, and other places. To this movement (extended later by the introduction in Madrid of
concerts of contemporary music, German, Scandinavian,
French, etc.), was added recently one for the restoration of
the old Spanish religious music (Cabezón, Victoria, etc.),
a movement which was due at first to Felipe Pedrell,
Federico Olmeda, and Rafael Mitjana, and in virtue of
which the old music came again to be used in the churches,
and was appreciated by the musicians of all nations.
Ledesma, Olmeda, and Valdés Goicoechea stand out as
composers in this genre.

The popular cultivation of music received great stimulus
by the formation of Catalan choral societies or *orfeones*,
directed by the master Clavé, a keen musician and prolific
composer. The example of Clavé, followed by other
Catalan musicians, was imitated later in various regions.
This coincided with a tendency to seek in our popular
music motives which should regenerate cultivated music
and give a firm basis to the national opera. This tendency
[which found a redoubtable exponent in Pedrell], soon set
on foot again the history of this genre, and secured the
preservation (by means of collections and adequate tran-
scriptions) of the remains of this treasure of our lyric soul.
Its highest expression in the higher forms of modern musical
technique lies in the pianoforte works of the great executants
Albéniz and Granados [and in the orchestral works, operas,
and ballets of Manuel de Falla]. Apart from their respective compositions, Spanish music owes to them the prestige,
and the serious interest that it has awakened in the whole
world. Another notable musician, Garreta, who died
prematurely, made his name in Catalonia, and was also

inspired by popular themes. He began as a writer of
Sardanas. The same movement was represented in Valen-
cia by Giner, composer of symphonic works [and by López
Chavarrí].

124. *The Pessimism of* 1898, *and the National Reaction.* The
Cuban war of 1897-1898, and especially the war against
the United States with its inevitable conclusion, resulted,
amongst other things, in stressing in the public mind the
gravity of those political and national defects to which the
disaster of 1898 was attributed. Public opinion considered
this as significant of our inferiority, in the face of the enormous advance made by North America and by many
European States. In accordance with the natural
vehemence of our character, made more acute at this time
by the bitterness of defeat and by the circumstances under
which it happened, this opinion changed rapidly into
pessimism—not such a logical outcome of the former feeling as was then thought. This pessimism embraced not
only the situation of the moment, but the whole history of
Spain, that is to say, the work of the Spanish spirit throughout the ages, and the fitness of its qualities for modern
civilization. Among the various writers who then expressed
this exaggerated attitude, Costa and Macías Picavea stand
out as the most marked, and, later on, as the most influential.

The result was to produce immediately in the public
mind a complete disbelief in its powers of reaction. Along
with this there continued that scepticism about the Spanish
body politic which had been felt and expressed by men so
representative of our 19th century political history as
Cánovas and Silvela. In this common feeling of hopeless-
ness which lasted for some years, there were only isolated
voices which dared to disagree and proclaim optimism.
It is clear that they based it upon an energetic advance in
all spheres of national activity, specially in teaching, and
on their recognition that the faculties shown by the Spanish
people in past centuries, were a proof of natural capabilities.
Thus, that re-vindication of Spain, which Menéndez y

Pelayo had set vibrating twenty years before (§ 120), was renewed in another spirit, which looked mainly towards the future and set itself in line with modern ideas and needs.

Little by little this thought gathered force and, with it, among the less optimistic, there arose the conviction that it was their duty to strive to conquer the obstacles, to leave the road followed in latter years, and finally (if, as the most pessimistic supposed, there exists some sublime impediment to the human will), not to give way until they had made every effort to remove it. One spoke then of an " active pessimism," which included both this moderate attitude of the unhopeful and the concession made by some of the optimists to the unshakable passivity or negation of the masses. Thus, year by year, opinion changed, carried forward by the success which attended those who worked with faith in their respective professional spheres, so that, by the end of the period, towards 1914, a renewal of collective confidence in its own powers was perceptible, and the recognition of the positive value of what the history of Spain has contributed to the universal work of human civilization, as conceived by the European spirit in past centuries. Embodiments of this change were: the return to classical national types in architecture, pottery, furniture, and other arts; the growing appreciation of our early writers; the renewed honour done to our men of science, who, in other ages, had conceived doctrines and sown ideas which in modern times have served as constructive elements; the desire to cultivate the natural wealth of the country, and to redeem from the hands of foreigners what they had acquired through our own lack of enterprise; finally, the strengthening of a people which believes in itself and desires to show what it is capable of in every sphere of life.

With this sane national orientation, from which have arisen many of the facts mentioned in foregoing paragraphs, we come to the end of this period, and also of this book. Although this was not much more than the orientation of an intellectual minority, at grips with the indifference of a great part of the population, and with many of the obstacles which had given rise to the pessimism of 1898, it reveals, nevertheless, a change in the most vital elements of the country, the only factor from which one may expect great results in the future. But the future is outside the field of History.

APPENDIX

THE following bibliography makes no attempt at being complete. It includes only such books as may be useful to the two groups of readers whom I have had in mind in writing this book: the larger public which does not pretend to specialize in historical studies, and students of Spanish history in schools and colleges.

For other classes of readers I may perhaps be permitted to point out, with reference only to my own works, the bibliographies printed at the end of vol. iv of my *Historia de España y de la Civilización Española* (Barcelona, 1913-14), in *Psicología del Pueblo Español*, 2nd ed. (Barcelona, 1910), and in the chapters on Spanish history written by me for the *Cambridge Modern History* and the *Cambridge Mediæval History*.

SUBJECTS

1. Prehistoric Period

The bibliography of prehistoric Spain is difficult to compress into a few references. The fragmentary state of these studies, which are increased daily by new discoveries, does not give the necessary stability in the general outlines; and there is also considerable confusion between the later prehistoric periods and the earlier Iberian and Celtiberian epochs.

For these reasons I shall only mention the standard work of Hugo Obermaier, *El hombre fósil* (2nd ed., Madrid, 1925), and his discourse read before the Academy of History, entitled *La vida de nuestros antepasados cuaternios en Europa* (1926). There is also the excellent introduction by Pierre Paris, *Essai sur l'art et l'industrie de l'Espagne primitive* (Paris, 1903-4), and its sequels (*Promenades archéologiques en Espagne*, etc.). As summaries the following may be useful: L. Pericot, *La prehistoria de la Peninsula ibérica* (Barcelona, 1923), and J. Pérez de Barrada, *Prehistoria: cartilla de divulgación* (Madrid, 1925). For the Cave of Altamira, the culminating monument in the prehistoric art of northern Spain, may be recommended the guide book signed H.O. (Hugo Obermaier), *La cueva de Altamira y la villa de Santillana del Mar* (Madrid, 1926), a pamphlet of 46 pages with illustrations and maps. A general introduction, better adapted to elementary studies than the above-mentioned works of Obermaier and Paris, is to be found in two monographs by Hernández Pacheco (*La Exposición de Arte prehistórico español*), and Tormo (*Catálogo de la Exposición de Arte prehistórico español*), both illustrated, and published by the Sociedad Española de Amigos del Arte.

Partly referring to this section, although it also includes the Roman period, is Schulten's *Hispania* (Spanish translation, 1920).

2. Muslim and Jewish Culture

An excellent summary of the first is: A. González Palencia, *Historia de la España musulmana*, Colección Labor, No. 69 (Barcelona), and *Historia de la Literatura arábigo-española* (Nos. 164 and 165 in the same series), which condense the previous studies of orientalists in Spain and other countries. [A work of fundamental importance is J. Ribera, *Disertaciones y opúsculos*, 2 vols. (Madrid, 1928).] [In English, R. Dozy, *Spanish Islam*, translated by R. A. Stokes; R. A. Nicholson, *A Literary History of the Arabs* (2nd ed., Cambridge 1930); the *Encyclopaedia of Islam* and the Oxford *Legacy of Arabia*, both in course of publication.]

For Jewish influences, there are the introductory works of Menéndez y Pelayo [and Gayangos], and the *Historia de la Filosofía* of Bonilla. [The most complete account available in English is that given in *The Legacy of Israel* (Oxford, 1928).]

3. Spanish Art in General

Finely illustrated works are now available in English and other European languages; those published by the *Hispanic Society of America* are especially noteworthy. [An admirable, illustrated introduction, with a good bibliography, is *Spanish Art*, a monograph published by the *Burlington Magazine*, 1927.] The Spanish *Comisaría Regia del Turismo* has edited a number of excellent studies which may sometimes be obtained gratis [by teachers or serious students],

*El Arte en España, Propaganda y defensa de la España monu-
mental, Museos, Viajes por España, Arte monumental hispano,
Itinerarios de arte, Hospederías rurales,* etc. [A useful series,
controlled by the same body, consists of a number of small
books of excellent illustrations, with introductions in
Spanish and English, entitled *El Arte en España* (Editorial
Thomas, Barcelona).] There are also the publications of
the *Sociedad Española de Amigos del Arte*, the collection of the
Boletín de la Sociedad Española de Excursiones [and the *Junta
para ampliación de Estudios.* A good Spanish art quarterly is
the *Archivo Español de Arte y Arqueología*].

An illustrated *Catálogo monumental y artístico de España* is
being published by the Ministry of Education and Fine
Arts. Among the volumes which have already appeared,
those relating to *Cáceres* (José R. Mélida) and *León* (M.
Gómez Moreno, 2 vols.), are specially noteworthy.

The history of the ideas and theories which have been
held on Spanish art can be seen in the collection of texts
undertaken by Sánchez Cantón, *Fuentes literarias para la
historia del Arte español,* vol. i, 16th century (Madrid, 1923),
and in Prof. Murillo's *Documentos para la historia del Arte en
Andalucía.* See also the data and appreciations contained
in the *Historia de las ideas estéticas* of Menéndez y Pelayo, and
in his academic discourse *Tratadistas de bellas artes en el
renacimiento español* (included in *Estudios de crítica literaria,*
4th series (Madrid, 1922).

Photographs: the firm of Arxiu Mas, Barcelona, has
upwards of 60,000 on sale. (See their catalogues.) Lacoste
[and Moreno] of Madrid also have large numbers. In
Saragossa, J. Mora Insa has founded an *Archivo fotográfico
de arte aragonés.*

4. PAINTING

The best modern account of Spanish painting is that to be
found in the *History of Art,* by A. Pijoán (English Edition,
Barcelona, 1925). There is no smaller work which does not
leave wide gaps in dealing with the subject as a whole. The
manual by A. L. Mayer, *Pintura Española,* in the " Colección Labor " (Barcelona, 1926), is a useful introduction to
the larger work by the same author. Referring specially to
the middle ages, is the work of Gertrude Richert, *La pintura*

medieval en España, translated from the German by José Ontañon (Barcelona, 1927). For the 19th century, A. de Beruete, *Historia de la pintura española en el siglo XIX* (Madrid, 1926), and D. H. Vegué, *Catálogo de la Exposición de Pinturas españoles de la primera mitad del siglo XIX* (Madrid, 1913). Among regional monographs, there is the notable work of Sanpere i Miquel on the Catalan painters of the Middle Ages and the 15th century, *Estudis sobre la pintura mig-eval catalana*, 6 vols. (Barcelona, 1906-1928). For Toledo, the indispensable book is *El Greco*, by Manuel B. Cossío (Madrid, 1908), and his admirable guide to the city, published by the *Comisaría Regia de Turismo*. [Selections from his writings on art and education will be found in *Manuel B. Cossío: de su Jornada* (Madrid, 1929). For other works on El Greco, Velázquez, and Goya, see the *Burlington Magazine* monograph mentioned in § 3. An interesting study is Lord Derwent's *Goya* (1930). See also C. R. Past, *A History of Spanish Painting* (Harvard, 1930; in progress), and *Spanish Illumination*, by J. Dominguez Bordona, translated by Bernard Bevan, 2 vols. (Paris, 1930).]

5. SCULPTURE

Elías Tormo has published two parts of an inclusive work on Spanish sculpture, *La Escultura Española en la antigüedad* (1926), and *Edad media* (1926). [A complete account is given by G. Weise, *Spanische Plastik aus sieben Jahrhunderten* (Reutlingen, 1925-7); see also A. Kingsley Porter, *Spanish Romanesque Sculpture*, 2 vols. (Paris, 1928), and, particularly for Santiago, the same author's *Romanesque Sculpture of the Pilgrimage Roads*, 10 vols. (Boston, 1923), of which only vols. i (text), v and vi refer to Spain.] Sculpture in Andalucía is dealt with in the monumental work by Prof. Murillo, *La Escultura en Andalucía*, vol. i (Seville, 1927). [For Renaissance sculpture and works imported from Italy, see *Sculpture of the Renaissance in Spain*, by M. Gómez Moreno.]

Orueta's work, *La Escultura funeraria en España* (Madrid, 1919), is valuable [also his study of *Berruguete*. The carving on mediæval capitals is admirably described and illustrated by M. S. and A. Byne, *La Escultura en los capiteles españoles* (Madrid, 1920)].

6. ARCHITECTURE

The two fundamental works are those by Lampérez: *Historia de la arquitectura cristiana española en la Edad Media* (Madrid, 1903), and *Historia de la arquitectura civil en España* (Madrid, 1922). A. L. Mayer, author of the *Historia de la pintura Española* (§ 4), has a work on Spanish architecture which has been translated into English: *Architecture and Applied Arts in Spain* (New York, 1921). [An inclusive work on Spanish architecture is in preparation by Bernard Bevan.]

The following deal with special periods: J. R. Mélida, *Monumentos romanos en España* (Madrid, 1925); M. Gómez Moreno, *Iglesias Mozárabes*, 2 vols. (Madrid, 1919); [G. G. King, *Pre-Romanesque, Mudéjar, The Way of St. James* (Hisp. Soc. of America)]; Puig y Cadafalch, Falguera and Goday, *L'Arquitectura romànica a Catalunya*, 3 vols. (Barcelona); [G. E. Street, *Some Account of Gothic Architecture in Spain* (1865), new edition by G. G. King, 1914]. The 17th century has been dealt with in the sumptuous work by M. S. and A. Byne (New York, 1917); the Baroque period by Otto Schubert (Erlangen, 1908: Spanish translation, 1924).

The development of the Spanish house, which has begun to be studied both in the Peninsula and in America, is shown by Luis M. Cabello (monograph published by the *Sociedad de Amigos de Arte* (1920), by the Catalogue (with explanatory notes) of the exhibition of *La Casa antigua española* (1914), and by the Spanish Houses Monographs, published by the *Hispanic Society of America*. Spanish houses of the colonial epoch are illustrated in the albums published in some of the South American republics, especially Mexico.

[Gardens: M. S. and A. Byne, *Spanish Gardens and Patios* (Philadelphia, 1924); R. S. Nichols, *Spanish and Portuguese Gardens* (New York, 1924); G. Gromort, *Jardins d'Espagne*, 2 vols. (Paris, 1926); C. M. Villiers-Stuart, *Spanish Gardens* (London, 1927).]

7. INDUSTRIAL ARTS

The book which first attracted attention to this subject in Spain was the study by Francisco Giner (1892), reprinted as vol. xv of his complete works (1926). His brother,

D. Hermenegildo, included much information about Spain in his *Artes industriales desde el cristianismo hasta nuestros días* (Barcelona, n.d.). [Notable also is *The Industrial Arts in Spain*, written in English by Juan F. Riaño, and published by the Victoria and Albert Museum (1879).] Other works are: P. de Azola, *El arte industrial en España* (Bilbao, 1892); M. Pérez Villamil, *La tradición indígena en la historia de nuestras industrias artísticas* (Madrid, 1907). Referring more particularly to the decorative arts: C. Davillier, *Les Arts décoratifs en Espagne* (Paris, 1879); [see also Royale Tyler, *Spain: A Study of her Life and Arts* (1913)]. For certain industrial arts there exist manuals or historical studies, some of which are mentioned below.

8. CEILINGS

There is a small explanatory work and a sumptuous album of illustrations by M. S. and A. Byne (Hisp. Soc. of America, 1920). The manual by J. F. Rafóls, *Techumbres y artesonados españoles* (Colección Labor, No. 86), is useful, but incomplete, as it omits all reference to certain parts of Spain in which the art of "coffered ceilings" (*artesonados*), had an important development.

9. IRONWORK

E. Orduña Viguera, *Rejeros españoles* (Madrid), M. S. and A. Byne, *Rejería of the Spanish Renaissance* (New York, 1924), a luxurious monograph with photographs and drawings; see also the same authors' *Spanish Ironwork* (New York, 1925). A. Rico y Sinobas, *Trabajos de metales* (Madrid, 1900), P. M. de Artíñano, *Catálogo de la Exposición de hierros antiguos españoles* (Madrid, 1919), E. de Leguina, *Obras de bronze* (Madrid, 1907). For ironwork in the Basque Provinces, see the chapter on *Las Ferrerías Vascongadas* [by M. Zuaznavar], in *La tradición del pueblo vasco* (San Sebastian, 1906).

Swords, etc.: Two monographs by E. de Leguina; Conde de Valencia de Don Juan, *Armas y tapices de la Corona de España* (Madrid, 1902), *Catálogo histórico descriptivo de la Real Armería* (Madrid, 1898). [See also the fine illustrated catalogue of the arms in the Museo de Valencia de Don Juan (Madrid).]

The history of tools in Spain was traced by Rico y Sinobas, *Historia de las herramientas de artes y oficios mecánicos en España,* in the review "Historia y Arte" (Madrid, 1896).

10. FURNITURE

Catálogo de la Exposición de mobiliario español de los siglos XV, XVI y primera mitad del XVII (Sociedad Española de Amigos de Arte, 1912); R. Doménech and L. Pérez Bueno, *Muebles antiguos Españoles* (Madrid and Barcelona, 1921); P. Quintero, *Sillas de Coro,* 2nd ed. (Cadiz, 1928); J. Lázaro, *Mobiliario artistico español* (Madrid, 1917); Gudiol, *El mobiliari liturgic* (Vich, 1920) ; *Exposicío internacional del moble y decoracío d'interiors* (Barcelona, 1923). [For Furniture, as for other Spanish Arts, the English reader should consult the *Burlington Magazine* monograph, referred to in §3.]

11. LACE, EMBROIDERY, ETC.

Marqués de Valverde, *Catálogo de la Exposición de lencería y encajes españoles del siglo XVI el XIX* (Amigos de Arte, 1915), P. de M. Artíñano, *Cat. de la Exp. de tejidos españoles . . . (id.* 1917), M. S. and A. Byne, *Tejidos y bordados populares españoles* (Madrid, 1924), C. Alfaya, *Notes sobre un cursillo de bordados populares para maestras* (Revista de Pedagogía, Sept., 1924), J. Sanchís Sivera, *El arte del bordado en Valencia en los siglos XIV y XV* (Madrid, 1917), J. Ventalló, *Historia de la industria lanera catalana* (Tarrasa, 1904), F. Fiter, *Consideraciones relativas a los encajes . . .* (Barcelona, 1896), *Exposición retrospectiva de Arte* (Saragossa, 1908). This well-illustrated catalogue includes various arts besides embroidery, *e.g.,* tapestry, goldsmiths' work, etc. L. Pérez Bueno, *La industria del tejido en España, siglo XVIII* (announced by the Comisaría Regia de Turismo).

12. COSTUME

See, amongst other works, Juan de la Cruz Cano, *Colección de trajes de España obtenidos del natural* (1777); Th. Hampe, *Das Trachtenbuch* (Berlin, 1927), treating of Spanish costume as shown in the book of Cristóbal Weidlitz (early 16th century); Conde de Clouard, *Discurso histórico sobre el traje de los españoles hasta el reinado de los Reyes Católicos* (Mem.

de la R. Acad. de la Historia, IX; F. Danvila, *Trajes y armas de los españoles desde los tiempos prehistóricos hasta los primeros años del siglo XIX* (Madrid, 1878); J. Puiggari, *Monografía del traje* (Barcelona, 1886); Isabel de Palencia, *El traje regional de España* (Madrid, 1926); Asociación Artístico-Arqueológica de Barcelona: *Monografía histórica e iconográfica del traje* and *Album de indumentaria española*.

13. COLONIAL ART IN SPANISH AMERICA

Spanish art in America has now begun to be studied seriously, together with the influences which affected it and the forms it took in different regions, and there is already a copious literature on the subject. Without pretending to know it all, I will mention a few general works leaving aside those exclusively devoted to the pre-Columbian period [*i.e.*, the period before the arrival of the Spaniards, for which see the works of T. A. Joyce, and other authorities on American archaeology].

Mexico: Manuel G. Revilla, *El Arte en Mexico*, 2nd ed. (Mexico, 1923); Francisco Diez Barroso, *El Arte en la Nueva España* (Mexico, 1921); J. J. Tablada, *Historia del Arte en Mexico* (Mexico, 1927); M. Toussaint, J. R. Benítez, and Dr. Alt, *Iglesias de Mexico*, 6 vols. (Secretaría de Hacienda, Mexico). Among the special subjects treated are *El ultra-barroco en el Valle de Mexico*, and studies of Mexican church architecture in various centuries. There is also a series of *Monografías Mexicanas*, published through Venustiano Carranza: vol. i, *Catedral y Sagrario de Mexico* (1927). Add the study by Lucas de Palacio, on old Mexican inns: *Mesones y ventas de la Nueva España* (1927). Of a more general, but very considerable importance, is the monumental work of Dr. Alt, *Las artes populares en Mexico*, 2 vols. (1922), which, in spite of referring to the present, contains numerous indications (music is also included), regarding the Spanish origins of many of the subjects with which it deals. [See also *L'art vivant*, No. 122 (16th Jan. 1930) devoted to Mexican art.]

Argentina: Martin S. Noel, *Contribución a la historia de la arquitectura Hispano-Americana* (Buenos Aires, 1928), dealing with the character and influence in South America of the Andalucían Baroque style; J. Kronfuss, *Arquitectura colonial de la Argentina*; J. B. Ambrosetti, *La influencia morisca en la ornamentación de las artes industriales del periodo colonial americano*; Miguel Solá, *Arquitectura colonial de Salta* (Buenos Aires, 1926); Angel Guidi, *Fusión hispano-indígena en la arquitectura colonial* (Buenos Aires, 1927); Fausto Burgos y María Elena Catullo, *Tejidos incaicos y criollos* (Buenos Aires, 1928).

Other Republics: R. Pizano, *Gregorio Vazquez de Arce y Ceballos* (Paris, 1926), a study of this Spanish-American painter; J. G. Navarro, *La escultura en el Salvador en los siglos XVI y XVII*.

14. Gold and Silver Work

P. M. de Artiñano, *Catálogo de la Exposición de Orfebrería civil española* (Amigos del Arte, 1925); N. Sentenach, *Bosquejo histórico sobre la orfebrería española* (Madrid, 1909); A. Gascón de Gotor, *El Corpus Christi y las custodias procesionales de España* (Barcelona, 1916); E. de Leguina, *La plata española* (Madrid, 1891); *La espada: apuntes para su historia* (Sevilla, 1885); *La espada española* (Madrid, 1914); *Arquetas hispano-árabes* (Madrid, 1911); Ch. Davillier, *Recherches sur l'orfevrerie en Espagne au Moyen âge et à la Renaissance* (Paris, 1879).

15. Ceramics—Leather

See P. M. de Artiñano, *Historia comparada de la cerámica en España* (in " Coleccionismo," 1916), and the important series of monographs by Guillermo J. de Osma, which include Hispano-Moresque pottery from Valencia and Seville. Also, *Catálogo de la Exposición de antigua cerámica española* (Amigos de Arte, 1910), and the various studies by [A. van der Put (especially on the heraldic designs)], and by E. A. Barber, on the pieces in the collection of the Hispanic Society of America.

For Córdoba leather (*guadamacilería*), see Davillier, *Notes sur les cuirs de Cordove* (Paris, 1878), and *Guía de Excursión a Córdoba* (comisaría Regia del Turismo).

16. Tapestry

On the Royal collection, see Conde de Valencia de Don Juan, *Tapices de la Corona de España* (Madrid, 1903), and the sumptuous *Tapices del Rey N. S.*, by E. Tormo and Sánchez Cantón (Madrid, 1919). Pardo collection: *Tapestries and Carpets of the Pardo* (Hispanic Society of America, 1917). Saragossa (Flemish Tapestries) Bertaux, in the *Gazette des Beaux Arts* (1909), and also *Catálogo de la Exposición retrospectiva de Arte* (Saragossa, 1908).

17. FANS

Catálogo de la Exposición de "El abanico" en España. Datos para su historia, by J. Ezquerra (Madrid, 1920).

18. IVORY, JET, AND ENAMELS

J. Ferrandis, *Marfiles y azabaches españoles* (Colección Labor, No. 67); Guillermo J. de Osma, *Catálogo de azabaches compostelanos* (Madrid, 1916); E. de Leguina, *Esmaltes españoles* (Madrid, 1911).

19. GLASS

Rico y Sinobas, *Del vidrio y sus artífices en España* (Madrid, 1873); J. B. Lázaro, *El arte de la vidrería en España* (Resumen de Arquitectura, 1897-98) ; E. A. Barber, *Spanish Glass in the Collection of the Hispanic Society of America* (New York, 1917) [and the studies by B. Rackham, mentioned in the *Burlington Magazine* monograph on Spanish Art].

20. MUSIC

The fundamental works on Spanish music are the studies and editions of Felipe Pedrell. The most complete work, however, is the volume relating to Spain (by R. Mitjana) in the *Encyclopédie de la Musique et Dictionnaire du Conservatoire*, vol. ix (Paris, 1920). [See also the studies and editions of Higini Anglés, chiefly on Catalan music of the 16th and 17th centuries, and Padre Suñol on Gregorian chant and Catalan music of an earlier period.] For later periods, José Subirá on the *tonadillas* of the 18th century [and, for subsequent periods, Adolfo Salazar]. The following are subsequent to Mitjana : [Grove's *Dictionary of Music and Musicians*, 3rd ed. (1926), with numerous references to Spanish composers; the *Oxford History of Music*, 2nd ed.

(1930), vol. ii ; and *Cobbett's Cyclopedia of Chamber Music* (1929), vol. ii, art. "Spain"]. J. B. Trend: *The Music of Spanish History to* 1600 (Oxford, 1926), *Luis Milán and the vihuelistas* (Oxford, 1925), [and *Manuel de Falla and Spanish Music* (1929)].

Mitjana's volume includes an appendix, by R. Laparra, on popular music and dances in Spain. Pedrell did much work on this subject, summarized in his *Cancionero popular musical español*, 4 vols. (Valls, Cataluña, 1919-21). Important [for the historical notes on Muslim Spanish music rather than for the actual musical transcriptions] is the work of Julián Ribera, *La música de las Cantigas* [English version, *Music in Ancient Arabia and Spain* (Stanford, Univ. Press), 1929], and *La Música árabe medieval*, a small book which summarizes the conclusions of the former. See also his *Disertaciones y opusculos*, 2 vols. (Madrid, 1928) [in which several important papers on Muslim Spanish musical history are reprinted]. Barbieri, *Cancionero musical de los siglos XV y XVI* (Madrid, 1890) [is a transcription and commentary of a MS. of about 1500 in the Royal Library, Madrid]. A useful book on Spanish popular music is E. López Chavarrí, *Música popular española* (Colección Labor, 1927). For collections of folk-songs [see the list in Grove's *Dictionary*, 3rd ed., art. "Song (Spain)"], and as an example of studies in popular music in Spanish America: Jesús Galindo y Villa, *El folklore y la música mexicana* (Mexico, 1927), E. Sánchez de Fuentes, *El folklore en la música cubana* (Habana, 1923), *Cantos españoles de California*, ed. Chas. F. Lummis, and *Cantos populares de Hispano-America*, by E. Hague (Memorias de la Sociedad Americana de Folklore, 1917).

[For musical instruments in Spain, see Pedrell, *Organografía*, Curt Sachs, *Reallexikon der Musikinstrumente*, and the works of Mitjana and Ribera mentioned above.]

21. POPULAR POETRY AND THE THEATRE

Respecting the Spanish epic, see the different works of R. Menéndez Pidal, particularly *L'epopée castillane à travers de la littérature espagnole* (Paris, 1910), *El Romancero español* (Hispanic Society of America, 1910) [these are summarized together with much new information, in *Flor nueva de romances viejos* (Madrid, 1928)], and *Poesía juglaresca y juglares*

(Madrid, 1924). Add the two editions of the *Poema de Mio Cid*, originally in 3 vols.; the smaller, with an extensive introduction, is in the series of *Clásicos castellanos*, vol. xxiv. For elementary reading, vols. xxv (*Romancero*), and xxx (*Cantares de gesta y leyendas heroicas*), in the *Biblioteca literaria del estudiante*, published by the Instituto Escuela. Excellent, also, is the modernized version of the Poem of the Cid [by Pedro Salinas], *Poema de Mio Cid puesto en romance vulgar y lenguaje moderno* (Madrid, 1926). [See also *Spanish Ballads*, by Guy le Strange (Cambridge, 1920), a selection of *romances* in historical sequence, with commentary.]

For the theatre, a good guide is the introduction to the *Obras* of Tirso de Molina, *Clásicos Castellanos*, vol. ii, 2nd ed. (Madrid, 1922), by Américo Castro. [In English, H. Rennert, *The Spanish Stage in the time of Lope de Vega* (Hispanic Society of America), and see the bibliography of the Spanish theatre in Fitzmaurice Kelly, *A New History of Spanish Literature* (Oxford, 1927).]

Influences : J. Fitzmaurice Kelly, *The Relations between Spanish and English Literature* (Liverpool, 1910), and P. P. Rogers, *Spanish Influence on the Literature of France* (in " Hispania," Stanford University, Oct. 1926), which condenses previous works, especially those of Farinelli, mentioned below. Of the human themes which characterize our theatre, I have treated in my articles on *El alcalde de Zalamea* and *Las mocedades del Cid*, the former incorporated in *Arte y realidad* (Barcelona, 1921); also in my lecture at the Sorbonne (Jan. 1926), *El teatro de tesis en la literatura española*, and in the lecture to the Royal Society of Literature in 1924: *The Spanish Drama as an Element of Moral Education*. The great spiritual value of our theatre is recognized by almost all modern critics. See, as noteworthy examples, Huizka, *Molière et l'Espagne* (Paris, 1908), and A. Farinelli on Calderón and *La Vida es sueño* [" Life's a Dream "].

Apart from Castilian, the Peninsular literatures were without early epic poems, except for short and sporadic examples. It has been debated whether there were early epics in Catalonia, and whether, or no, vestiges are to be met with in the prose chronicles [as in Castille]; the supposition is doubtful. But in other orders of popular literature, Catalonia is rich, and the printed collections numerous.

22. NATURAL SCIENCE

M. Colmeiro, *La botánica y los botánicos de la Península ibérica*. S. Calderón, *Los naturalistas españoles en América* (Sevilla, 1892). Odón de Buen, *Historia natural*, edición popular, tomo 1, introducción (Barcelona, s.a., 1896?). E. Reyes Prosper, *Dos noticias históricas del . . . D. José Antonio Cavanilles* (Madrid, 1917). Quintin Chiarbone y C. Mallaina, *Ensayo sobre la Historia de la Farmacia* (Madrid, 1847, 2nd ed., 1862). E. Maffei y R. Rua Figueroa, *Apuntes para una biblioteca española de libros, . . . relativos al conocimiento y explotación de las riquezas minerales*, 2 vols. (Madrid, 1871-72).

On the geographical studies of the time of Philip II, see A. Merino, Papers read before the *Real Sociedad Geográfica* (March, 1927), and the chapters on *La Ciencia Española en el siglo XVI* (by Padre Barreiro), and *Felipe II y la alquimía* (by F. Rodríguez Marín), in the book entitled *Reivindicación histórica del siglo XVI* (Madrid, 1928); also the academic discourse of P. Barreiro, *Caracteres de la fauna y la flora filipinas y labor española en el estudio de las mismas* (Acad. de Ciencias, 1928), and the *Diario de la expedición de D. Márcos Jiménez de la Espada*, published by Barreiro in *Bol. de la R. Soc. de Geografía* (Madrid, 1928).

Medicine: Dr. M. Dussolier, *Aperçu historique sur la Médecine en Espagne, particulierèment au XVI⁰ siècle* (Paris, 1906); Dr. Luis Comenge, *La Medicina en el siglo XIX. Apuntes para la historia de la cultura médica en España* (Barcelona, 1914); Roca, *La Medicina catalana en temps del rey Martí; Apuntes para la historia de los Colegios de Médicos, Cirujanos y Boticarios*, by Dr. Peset Cervera (Valencia, 1896); and Nicasio Mariscal, *Relaciones históricas de la Medicina Española con la italiana* (Madrid, 1924).

For the achievements of Spanish men of science in America, see the preface to the *Relaciones geográficas de Indias*, by Jiménez de Espada. A summary of this will be found in Barreiro, *Historia de la Comisión española del Pacífico de 1862 a 1865* (Junta para Ampliación de Estudios, 1926).

The book by S. Calderón referred to above, deserves particular consideration. It contains more than its title promises, and is a very full exposition of the work done in

America by Spanish naturalists and men of science. It also considers the question I have examined in the text of this book, as to the nature of the productions of Spanish men of science. Calderón gives interesting information on the diffusion of the works of these men, expressed in the number of languages into which they were translated, and rectifies the general belief, that since the 17th century Spain has made no contribution to the history of science, by reminding us of the names and achievements of Azara, Mutis, Ruiz, Pavón, Jorge Juan, Ulloa, etc. See J. Rodríguez Carracido, *Estudios históricocriticos de la ciencia española*, 2nd ed. (Madrid, 1917), and the same author's sketch of *El P. José de Acosta y su importancia en la literatura científica española* (R. Acad. Española); *cf.* my *Psicología del pueblo español*, pp. 302-14, and 319-23, where amongst other works reference is made to the article by Menéndez y Pelayo, *Esplendor y Decadencia de la cultura científica española* (reprinted in *Estudios de crítica literaria*, 4th series, Madrid, 1927).

23. NAVAL HISTORY

See the fundamental bibliography in my *Psicología del pueblo español*, and the general summary of the Spanish contribution to these subjects in my *Historia de España*, vols. iii and iv. Add the important work of Gervasio de Artíñano, *La Arquitectura naval española en madera* (Madrid, 1920), which, apart from the text, presents a series of plates and figures of the greatest value in the history of civilization. [See also *A Bibliography of British Naval History*, by G. E. Manwaring, 1930.]

24. GEOGRAPHICAL DISCOVERIES IN AMERICA

The earliest book dealing systematically with Spanish geographical discoveries was that of Seixar y Lovera (1690), continued by Navarete: *Colección de los viajes y descubrimientos que hicieron por mar los españoles desde fines del siglo XV*, etc. (Madrid, 1829-59). Next in importance, although it includes other matters, is the *Historia de la Armada española desde la unión de los reinos de Castilla y Aragón* (Madrid, 1895-1903), by C. Fernández Duro. The documents completing these works are printed in the collection of *Relaciones geo-*

gráficas de Indias, published by Jiménez de Espada and continued by Beltrán y Rózpide. Short expositions are to be
found in the lectures given in 1891-92 in the *Ateneo*, Madrid,
and subsequently collected in *El continente americano* (Madrid,
1892). *Cf.* also the notable discourse delivered in 1922 at
the University of Valencia: *Intereses españoles derivados de la
oceanografía* (Anales de la Universidad de Valencià, No. 17),
and my own lecture at San Francisco (1915). The most
recent work on the subject is: S. de Ispizúa, *La primera
vuelta al mundo: Historia de la geografía y cosmografía de las
Edades Antigua y Media*, 2 vols. (Madrid, 1922-26). It is the
history of the maritime discoveries made by the Spanish
and Portuguese in the 15th and 16th centuries.

25. PHILOSOPHY AND MATHEMATICS

The only general history of Spanish philosophy, that by
Bonilla (Madrid, 1908-11), does not reach beyond the 12th
century, and was partly anticipated by Menéndez y Pelayo
in his *Heterodoxos* and his *Historia de las ideas estéticas*. The
monographs of Asín Palacios on Muslim Spanish philosophers and their influence on the Christians, have corrected
statements contained in certain parts of the above works.
On the interesting thesis of Asín, *La Escatología musulmana en
la divina comedia* [English version, *Islam and the Divine
Comedy* by Harold Sutherland, see the notice by Sir Thomas
Arnold, *Mod. Lang. Review* (Oct. 1919), and more recently],
by Prof. S. Merkle, at the International Congress of Historical Science at Oslo (1928).

For the age of the Renaissance there is no fundamental
work on Spanish philosophy apart from the studies by
Menéndez y Pelayo. Bonilla wrote on Luis Vives (1903)
[as also Foster Watson, in English]. See also Bonilla's
*Fernando de Córdoba: orígenes del Renacimiento filosófico en
España* (1911), and further notes in my *Psicología del pueblo
Español*, 2nd ed.

For mediaeval philosophy in Catalonia, Carreras Candi,
Evolució històrica dels jueus i juehisants a Catalunya (*Estudis uni-
versitaris*, 1909); Xiberta, *La metafísica i la psicología del
mestre Guiu de Terrena*; Pijoán, *Els educadors de la gent catalana.
Oliva* (*Empori*, 1909); numerous references to Lulio, see my
Psicología del pueblo español, and *La Historia del lulisme*, by

Avinyó, Rubió y Lluch in *Estudis Universitaris Catalans*, 1912. Rubió, *La cultura catalana en el regnat de Pere III* (*Estudis*, 1914), *Documents per l'historia de la cultura mig-eval catalana* (2 vols., Instituto d'Estudis Catalans); Corominas, *Estudi sobre 'l pensament filosòfic dels jueus espanyols a l'Edat mitja*; Nicolau, *Gerbert* (*Silvestre II*), *i la cultura catalana del segle X* (*Estudis*, 1910).

The contribution of Spanish mathematicians is described in the following books: E. Fernández y Echevarría, *El Metro* (Oviedo, 1908); J. Rey Pastor, *Los matemáticos españoles del siglo XVI*, 2nd ed. (Buenos Aires, 1926); C. Jiménez de Rueda, *El genio español a través de la Historia desde el punto de vista matemático* (Acad. de ciencias Exactas, 1926).

26. LAW

For general data, see my *Psicología del pueblo español*, and for penal law, P. Montes, *Precursores de la ciencia penal en España*, and the lectures by F. Cadalso on *Iniciativas penitenciarias en España*, 2 parts (Madrid, 1926), and his chapter, *Instituciones jurídicas y penitenciarias en el siglo XVI* in the book entitled *Reivindicación histórica del siglo XVI* (Madrid, 1928).

The tercentenary of Hugo Grotius, *De jure belli ac pacis*, in 1925, has revived the study of his predecessors and affirmed the influence of Spanish jurists. A general indication of this will be found in my *Hugo Grocio y España* in the *Revista de ciencias Jurídicas y Sociales* (Madrid, 1926). See C. Barcia, *Francisco de Vitoria fundador del derecho internacional moderno* (Madrid, 1928), and J. Brown Scott, *El orígen español del derecho internacional* (Madrid, 1928). A series of publications is still to be desired to bring out the social and " corporativist " attitude of Spanish jurists of the Renaissance which, as regards property in land, was so much emphasized by Costa in opposition to the individualist attitude of Roman law, so noticeable in non-Spanish jurists of the time.

Among the institutional innovations due to Spanish juridical thought, should be cited that of the doctrine of *compraventa mercantil*, which had its origins in the Middle Ages, and which, in the 19th century we were the first to naturalize in our legislation (*Ordenanzas de Bilbao, Código de Comercio*, 1829). The law of *tasa del interés* (income tax), bears in Spain the date 1856.

S

The study of Spanish *derecho consuetudinario* is due principally to Joaquín Costa, especially in his *Derecho consuetudinario y economía popular de España* (Barcelona, 1902).   Con-
siderations and general data on the significance of this in
our history may be found in my book, *Cuestiones de historia
del Derecho y de Legislación comparada* (Madrid, 1914), pp.
199-201, and 214-29.

27. EDUCATION

See Altamira, *Epítome de historia de España* (Madrid, 1927),
pp. 149-52. The general impression derived from this
should not lead to the neglect of pedagogic initiatives and
influences to be found in Spanish history, *e.g.*, the men who
worked for the deaf and dumb (Ponce de León, Ramírez
de Carrión, J. P. Bonet), and the co-operation of many
Spanish professors in the creation of South American systems of education. See my *Huella de España en América* (ch. v,
§ 11), and an article in the *Boletín de la Institución Libre de
Enseñanza* on José María Torres (1926, No. 800). [See also
Manuel B. Cossío, *De su jornada*, 1929.]

28. THE CONQUEST AND EXPLORATION OF AMERICA

For a general orientation in the modern directions of
American historiography, see Lummis, *Los exploradores españoles del siglo XVI* (Barcelona, 1916), and my own work,
La Huella de España en America (Madrid, 1924), where detailed bibliographical information will be found, including
the more elementary books such as: J. Dantín Cereceda,
Exploradores y conquistadores de Indias, vol. xvii of the "Biblioteca literaria del estudiante," published by the Junta para
Ampliación de Estudios. See also the series of *Las grandes
viajes clásicos*. [The English reader will not forget the
volumes of the Hakluyt Society, which has published the
original accounts of all the great voyages, in translations
with introductions and notes; or the studies by Cunning-
hame Graham on individual explorers.]

For American institutions, see *Nota bibliográfica de orien-
tación para el estudio de la historia de las instituciones políticas y
civiles de América* (Madrid, 1926). For the history of Spanish
influences in the districts to the north of Mexico (now part

of the United States), see A. Torres Campos, *España en California y en el Noroeste de América* (Madrid, 1892), in the collection " El continente Americano " : Ateneo de Madrid; Alice H. Bushee, *Spanish Influences in the South-West* (in " Hispania," vol. vi, No. 3, May 1923), and *A History of California: the Spanish Period* (New York, 1921).

29. PHILOLOGICAL AND SOCIOLOGICAL INVESTIGATIONS IN AMERICA

Philological works are catalogued by the Conde de Viñaza, *Biblioteca histórica de la Filología castellana* (R. Acad. Española), and in the *Catálogo del Museo Mitre*, mentioned above. The sociological contribution, although used fragmentarily by many modern " Americanists " still awaits its compiler.

The new historiographical sense expressed in the writings of the old Spanish historians of the Indies has not yet been appreciated at its full value; I have called attention to it on various occasions. Notable also is the comparative method employed by these historians; it is, indeed, one of their great characteristics. For the tradition of this method in history and jurisprudence, see my monograph, *Los estudios de Derecho comparado en España* (in the annual of the *Academie internationale de Droit comparé*, and, in Spanish, with additions, in *Universidad* (Saragossa, 1927).

Regarding the geographical accounts and the scientific plan upon which they were based, see the above-mentioned collection of Jiménez de Espada, and his introduction. This collection, in spite of its importance, does not exhaust the material. Certain *Relaciones* have been published since, *e.g.*, *Relaciones históricas y geográficas de América Central* (Madrid, 1908), vol. vii of the " Colección de libros y documentos referentes a la Historia de América."

30. RENAISSANCE HUMANISM

Menéndez y Pelayo, *Humanistas españoles del siglo XVI* (Rev. de Madrid, 1883), *Horacio en España* (1877), *Traductores españoles de la Eneida* (1879), *Traductores de las Eglogas y Geórgicas de Virgilio* (1879), and *Bibliografía hispanolatina clásica*, tomo I (único, 1902). See also the works of Bonilla,

Luis Vives y Fernando de Córdoba y los orígenes del Renacimiento filosófico en España.

The last deals with Bishop Pedro García, the adversary of Pico della Mirandola, of the celebrated " Chariteo " (the Catalan Bernat Gareth), of Juan Ginés de Sepúlveda, and other humanists. A. F. G. Bell has published a series of small books in English, on Spanish humanists: Arias Montano, el Brocense, Juan Ginés de Sepúlveda, etc. [and a standard work on *Luis de León*, which goes thoroughly into all questions of Spanish humanism].

It is worth pointing out that among the Spanish humanists there was a marked tendency towards Hellenism in opposition to the Romanism of most European countries; and this has interesting consequences in juridical and sociological matters. See also the monographs on Francisco Cascales, Ambrosio de Morales, and other writers of the epoch published by the Spanish Academy. Of wider range though it refers only to a single author, and of greater penetration as regards certain aspects of the Renaissance and its influence on Spanish thought, is Américo Castro's study of the mind of Cervantes, *El Pensamiento de Cervantes* (Madrid, 1927).

31. Economic History

This is one of the elements in the history of Spanish civilization which has been very little studied. There are a few works upon the legislation relating to special branches of economic life, agriculture, cattle-breeding [*e.g.*, Klein's work on the *Mesta*]. There is no work dealing with the whole subject in which entire faith can be placed, though possible exceptions are Goury de Roslan, *Essai sur l'histoire économique de l'Espagne* (Paris, 1887); P. Boissonnade, *Les études relatives à l'histoire économique de l'Espagne et leurs résultats dès origines à* 1453 (Paris, 1914).

For bibliographical details see my *Historia de España*, vol. iv, and the *Plan referente a las investigaciones de Historia económica española que deberían ser emprendidas*, by Eduardo Ibarra (Sociedad de Economía Nacional, Madrid, 1919).

The original documents will be found reprinted in the *Colección de documentos de asunto económico correspondentes al reinado de los Reyes Católicos* (1475-1516), part i, (Madrid,

1917). Regarding ancient works on the subject see:
Historia de la economía política en Aragón, by Asso (Saragossa,
1798), the *Biblioteca Española económico-político*, of Sempere y
Guarinos, 4 vols. (Madrid, 1806-32), and the *Historia de la
Economía política de España*, by H. Colmeiro, 2 vols. (Madrid,
1863).

32. MODERN ECONOMIC LIFE AND THE CO-OPERATION OF SPANISH " INDIANOS "

On the present economic revival in Spain, see the book
(richly documented), containing the papers read at the
eighth international course for commercial expansion,
held at Barcelona in 1914: *España Económica, social y artística*
(Barcelona, 1914). Also Alberto I. Gache, *España pro-
gresiva: producción y cambio* (Barcelona, 1914).

With reference to the " Indianos " (returned emigrants),
and their achievements, see my books, *España en America* and
Mi viaje a América. During 1926 a series of interesting
articles was published in *La Prensa* (Buenos Aires) on the
subject of *El aporte de los indianos al progreso general de España*.

33. SPANISH HISTORICAL PORTRAITS

Refer to the following works: *Retratos de personajes
españoles*, 4 parts (Madrid, 1904-6), Ignacio Calvo y Sánchez; *Retratos de personajes españoles del siglo XVI, relacionados
con la historia militar de España* (Madrid, Junta de Icono-
grafía Nacional, 1912); *Retratos de grandes españoles. Cartilla
popular* (*idem*, 1921); *Catálogo y catálogo-guía de la Exposición de
retratos de mujeres españoles anteriores a* 1850, Prólogo de A. de
Beruete (Sociedad Española de Amigos del Arte, 1918); *Exposición de retratos de niño en España*. Catálogo general ilustrado (*idem*, 1925); J. Sánchez Cantón, *Retratos del Museo del
Prado* (Madrid, 1919); *Exposició de retrats* (Barcelona, 1910).
Edición de la *Ilustració Catalana*, 4 parts; *Catálogo de la
Exposición de la miniatura-retrato en España*. Notas por D. J.
Ezquerra (Madrid, 1916); *Exposición de pinturas españolas de la
primera mitad del siglo XIX. Catálogo ilustrado* (Madrid, 1913:
Soc. esp. de Amigos del Arte).

The above contain a fair number of historical portraits.

The initiator of this study was V. Carderera, with his *Icono-grafía Española* (Madrid, 1855-64).

34. Geology and Geography

Among general works the following may be cited: L. Fernández Navarro, *Paleogeografía. Historia geológica de la Península ibérica* (Biblioteca Corona, Madrid, 1916). Completed by *Las Costas de la Península ibérica* (Asociación Española para el Progreso de las Ciencias. Congreso de Saragossa de 1908); J. Dantín Cereceda, *Resumen fisiográfico de la Península ibérica* (Madrid, 1912); *Ensayo acerca de las regiones naturales de España* (Madrid, 1922, vol. i only); R. Torres Campos, *Estudios geográficos* (Madrid, 1895); A. Carbonell, *Nuevas ideas sobre la tectónica ibérica*, a work written on the basis of a study by Dr. Staub, *Ideas sobre la tectónica de España*, and published in the proceedings of the " Asociación Española para el progreso de las ciencias " Cadiz meeting: vol. vi (Madrid, 1928). Also Reyes Prósper, *Las Estepas de España* (Madrid); Gómez de Arteche, *Geografía histórica militar de España y Portugal* (Madrid, 1866); and E. Hernández Pacheco, *Los cinco ríos principales de España y sus terrazas* (Madrid, 1928).

Among general geographies of Spain may be mentioned vol. iii (España y Portugal) of the *Curso de Geografía*, by V. la Blache, C. d'Almeida y A. Blázquez (Barcelona, 1914), and the little book entitled *España*, by Sánchez Cantón (Comisaría Regia de Turismo).

Spanish landscape and its relation to history is a subject which has not yet been sufficiently studied. Some indications are given in my *Arte y realidad* (Barcelona, 1921), in the part entitled *Los paisajes y las urbes*; and, above all, in the chapter *El paisaje, monumento nacional*.

Hernández Pacheco has begun a systematic study of Spanish landscape from the point of view of geology, in lectures given at the Residencia de Estudiantes at Madrid, *La Geología y el paisaje. Ensayo de un estudio científico de los paisajes españoles*. See also Marcel Chevalier, *El paisatge de Catalunya*, in vol. vi of the *Enciclopedia Catalunya* (Barcelona, 1926-8).

Illustrations will be found especially in the publications of the " Mountain Section " (*Sección de Montaña*) of the

Comisaría del Turismo (especially, *Gredos, Pedriza de Manzanares, Sierra Nevada, Picos de Europa*), and many published in Catalonia by *Sociedades excursionistas*, and by the *Club Alpino de Madrid*.

35. GENERAL WORKS ON SPANISH INFLUENCE ON CIVILIZATION

A general account of the contribution of Spain to modern civilization will be found in two works of Martin A. S. Hume: *The Spanish People* and *Europe's Debt to Medieval Spain*. In Spanish: Menéndez y Pelayo, *La Ciencia española*; Altamira, *Psicalogía del pueblo español* and *Historia de España y de la civilización española*; A. Farinelli, *España y su literatura en el extranjero a través de los siglos*, published in " La Lectura," 1901, vol. ii, pp. 523 and 834, and included with several other Hispanic studies by the same author in *Ensayos y discursos de critica literaria hispano-europea* (Rome, 1925). See also Maurice Legendre, *Portrait d'Espagne* (Paris, 1925).

36. GENERAL BIBLIOGRAPHY OF SPANISH HISTORY

I have thought it necessary to add this paragraph, not only for its utility, but also for the ignorance of Spanish historical bibliography, which I have noticed almost without exception in non-Spanish publications, including those recently issued by the League of Nations.

The modern works most to be recommended are: B. Sánchez Alonso, *Fuentes de la Historia española. Ensayo de bibliografía sistemática de las monografías impresas que ilustran la historia política nacional de España, excluídas sus relaciones con América*, 2nd Edition, 2 vols. Centro de Estudios Históricos (Madrid, 1927). Rafael Ballester, *Bibliografía de la Historia de España. Catálogo metódico y cronológico de las fuentes y obras principales relativas a la Historia de España desde los orígenes hasta nuestros dias*, 1 vol. (Gerona, 1921). This includes not only political history, but also the history of civilization. Id., *Las fuentes narrativas de la Historia de España durante la Edad Media* (417-1474), 1 vol. (Palma de Mallorca, 1903). Id., *Las fuentes narrativas de la Historia de España durante la Edad Moderna* (1474-1808). Fascículo 1: Los Reyes Católicos, Carlos I, Felipe II (Valladolid, 1927).

A second part is announced dealing with the discovery of America.

[In this, and all the preceding sections, the student of Spanish civilization will be well-advised to consult the *Subject-index of the London Library*, vol. i, 1909, vol. ii, 1923.]

INDEX

A BAD, —, 174.
    Abdu'llāh, 53.
Abdu'r-Rahmān I, 47.
Abenamar (Ibn Ahmār), 79.
Abenarabi (Ibn 'Arabī), 75.
Abencuzmán, Song-book of, 50.
Abenhazam (Ibn Hazm), 72.
Aben Said (Ibn Sa'id), 72.
Abentofail (Ibn Tufayl), 71, 75.
Absolutism, 135, 160, 188-190.
Acuña, Bishop, 135.
Agriculture, 15, 51, 64, 70, 123, 130, 165.
Ahrens, —, 221, 222.
Alamiria, palace of, 51.
Alani, 39.
Alaric, laws of, 41, 43.
Albacete, 18, 19.
Albornoz, B. de, 122.
Albornoz, Cardinal Don Gil de, 86.
Alcalá de Henares, university of, 124.
Alcántara, bridge of, 33.
Alexander VI, Pope, 118.
Alfonso II, 82.
Alfonso V of Aragon, 82, 84.
Alfonso VI, 53, 73, 77.
Alfonso VII, 74.
Alfonso X, 74, 104; literary works of, 84, 85, 87, 96.
Alfonso XII, 191.
Alfonso, Maestro, 97.
Alfonso el Sabio, 50. See Alfonso X.
Algazel, 72.
Alicante, 18.
Aliseda, 14.
Almanzor, 49, 54.
Almedinilla, necropolis of, 19.
Almohades, 57, 69.
Almorávides, 57, 69.
Alonai, 14.

Altamira, cave of, rock paintings, 10.
Alvarez, Manuel, 182.
Alvaro, Don, 105.
Alvaro (San Alvaro de Córdoba), 55, 56.
Amadis de Gaula, 124.
American colonies—the discovery, conquest, and organization of, 117-122, 130, 141; protection of trade routes to, 139; administrative, economic, and commercial reforms, 166-168; art, 155; end of the Spanish dominion in, 197 *et seq.*
Andalucía, 16, 17, 69; Phœnicians in, 13; archaeological remains, 18, 19; silver mines, 25; Romanization of, 27; occupied by the Byzantines, 39; music of, 50; painting of, 98.
Annobón, 159.
Antilles, the, 117, 120, 121, 134, 199-205.
Aparicio, —, 234.
Arabic, 50, 54-56, 71, 74, 75, 87, 124.
Aragon, 63, 69, 70; the Celts in, 16; the Cortes of, 106; government and administration, 107, 113-116, 160, 193, 194; united to Castille, 110; social classes in, 101, 102, 115; political agitation during reign of Philip II, 135; law, 107; the Inquisition 109, 112; literature, 82-87; industry and commerce, 89, 123.
Aragonese, 18.
Arango, —, 202.
Arcas, Pérez, 218.
Archaeological remains, 18-20.
Archaeologists, Spanish, 226.

T

Valladolid, *Audiencia,* 107.
Vallfogona, Pedro Juan de, 99.
Vandals, 39.
Vascones, 21.
Velazquez, —, 152, 153, 183, 234.
Venezuela, 167, 198, 199.
Ventones, 21.
Verdaguer, —, 230.
Vespasian, Emperor, 28, 29.
Viana, Prince of, 104.
Vicente, Gil, 125.
Vich, Bishop of, 65.
Vihuela, 156.
Vilanova, Arnaldo de, 87.
Villaneuva, Juan de, 181.
Villaricos, 25.
Villaverde, —, 226.
Villegas, Pedro de, 152.
Villena, Don Enrique de, 81.
Visigoths, the dominion of the, 39
  et seq.; their civilization, 40; atti-
  tude towards the Spaniards, 41;
  conversion to Catholicism, 42;

juridical unity, 43; social in-
  equality, 44; culture, 45.
Vitoria, Francisco de, 147.
Vives, Luis, 144, 147.

Weyler, General, 204.
William II of Germany, 206.
Witiza, 77.
Women, their work in renewing
  Spanish culture, 172.
Women's Education, Association
  for, 222.

Zaida, daughter of King of Seville,
  54.
Zamora, —, 184.
Zamora, siege of, 78.
Zamorano, Navarro, 221.
Zanjón, Peace of, 202, 203.
Zaragoza, Lorenzo, 97.
Zárate, Gil de, 212.
Zorrilla, —, 229.

GLOSSARY

ADELANTADO, 107, 154.
adprisión, 64.
adventores, 29.
aediles, 29.
alcabala, 91.
alcalde, 107, 118, 135, 143; *alcalde mayor*, 116.
alfoz, pl. *alfoces*, 62.
alguacil, 107.
aljamía, 56.
allodiales, 60.
audiencia, 107.
auto de fe, 112.
ayuntamiento, 136.

bayle, 107.
beneficiarii, 60.
buccellarii, 44.

cajas reales, 168.
Cámara de comptos, 107.
Capitulaciones de Santa Fe, 117.
carta puebla, 63.
cassatas, 59.
Cien jurados, Los, 108.
cofradías, 64.
coloni, 44; *colonia*, 28.
comarca, 108.
concelleres, 108.
concilium, 30.
condado, 58; *conde*, 63.
consejo, 62; *Consejo de ciento*, 118; *Consejo real*, 107; *Consejo supremo de Indias*, 118.
corregidor, 116.
cort, 106.
cortes, 105; *cortes constituyentes*, 225.
criationes, 59.
criollos, 142.
cristianos algaraviados, 54.
curia, 29.

curiales, 31.

decurio, 31.
desamortización, 194.
desnaturarse, 62.
diputación (Catalan, *diputació*), 106.
duelo judicial, 68.
duumviri, 29.

emparats, 101.
encomendados, 120.
encomienda, 59, 120.
enjuiciamiento, 202.

fieles, 62.
foederati, 28.
fuero, 63; *fuero judicial*, 101; *fuero juzgo*, 61; *fuero real*, 193; *fuero viejo*, 86; *fueros generales*, 108.

generalidad (Catalan, *generalitat*), 106.
gentiles, *gentilitas*, 22.
gremios, 88.

hacienda pública, 110.
homes de paratge, 101.
hospites, 29.

immunes, 28.
incolae, 29.
insaculación, 115.
intendencias, *intendentes*, 167.

juez, pl. *jueces*, 62.
juniores, 60; *juniores de cabeza*, 60; *juniores de hereditate*, 100.
juntas provinciales, 186.
jurados, 62.
jurisconsultos, 113.
justicia, 107.

CHISWICK PRESS : CHARLES WHITTINGHAM AND GRIGGS (PRINTERS), LTD.
TOOKS COURT, CHANCERY LANE, LONDON.

BAY OF BISCAY

ATLANTIC OCEAN

MEDITERRANEAN SEA

FRANCE

AFRICA

Gulf of Lions

BALEARIC ISLES

PITHYUSÆ ISLES

Minorca
Majorca

ASTURIAS
GALICIA
BASQUE PROV.
NAVARRA
CATALONIA
OLD CASTILE
LEON
ARAGON
ENTRE MINHO E DOURO
TRAZ OS MONTES
BEIRA
SPAIN
NEW CASTILE
VALENCIA
ESTREMADURA
ESTREMADURA
ALEMTEJO
MURCIA
ANDALUSIA
ALGARVE
SEVILLE
GRANADA

Cantabrian Mountains
Pyrenees Mountains
Sa. de Guadarrama
Sierra Morena
Sª Nevada

Corunna
Santander
S. Sebastian
Oviedo
Bilbao
Santiago
Lugo
Vitoria
Pamplona
Leon
Burgos
Logroño
Huesca
Gerona
Valladolid
Soria
Saragossa
Lerida
Barcelona
Salamanca
Segovia
Avila
MADRID
Guadalajara
Teruel
Tarragona
Coimbra
Toledo
Cuenca
Castellon de la Plana
Valencia
Lisbon
Badajoz
Merida
Caceres
Ciudad Real
Albacete
Alicante
Cartagena
Cordoba
Jaen
Murcia
Seville
Granada
Malaga
Cadiz
Gibraltar (British)
Faro
Oporto
Ceuta

Gulf of Valencia
Gulf of Cadiz
Strait of Gibraltar
Cape Nao
C. St. Vincent
C. Finisterre
C. da Roca
C. Trafalgar

Scale 1:5,000,000
English Miles
0 20 40 60 80 100
Kilometres
0 20 40 60 80 100 120 140 160
Boundaries
Principal Railways

NOTE TO COLOURING	
9000 Feet	
6000 "	
3000 "	
1500 "	
1000 "	
600 "	
SEA LEVEL	
600 Feet	

Longitude West of Greenwich

Secant Conic Projection

John Bartholomew & Son, Ltd, Edinburgh

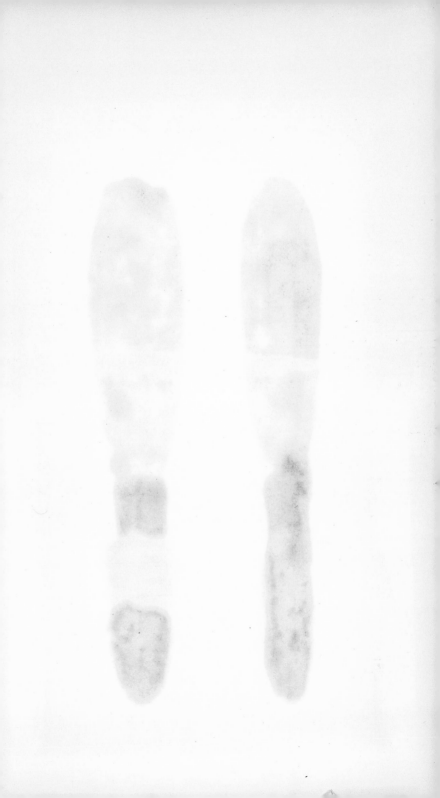